PRAISE FOR *B2B SOCIAL*

'Social selling' is nothing new. People have been doing it for years over breakfast, lunch, dinner and invites to events. But the numbers are generally small, and it takes time. Social selling today is on a different scale and to manage a strategy at this scale needs some guardrails. Julie has written a much needed 'how to' guide which brings everything up to date for us.
Tony Spong, Lead Consultant, AAR Group and Chair of DMA Creative Committee

Building trusting relationships – as Julie rightly points out in the opening pages – is central to any successful business and *B2B Social Selling Strategy* offers the complete 'go to' guide to making this a reality. It covers all the bases from why social selling works, what an effective plan looks like, and how to deliver results and embed best practice.
Susan Walkley, Managing Director, Public Relations & Creative Comms, Havas Health & You

B2B marketing and sales has long been recognized as relationship-led. Relationships are increasingly online, social media continues to grow and traditional media and sales landscapes are upended, so new strategies are needed – and this book offers just that. Practical, accessible and evidence-based solutions for today's and tomorrow's B2B issues, relevant to novice and professional alike, helping businesses and individuals navigate and succeed in this VOCA environment. A great and timely achievement.
Donald Lancaster, University of Exeter Business School, Director of MBA; Assoc Professor, FHEA, CMBE, Fellow, Worshipful Company of Marketors

As an experienced marketing practitioner and tutor, Julie doesn't just give you the theory but demonstrates the practice of how you can truly put the customer at the heart of B2B social media to build authentic relationships and deliver results.
Rachel Aldighieri, Managing Director, Data & Marketing Association

B2B Social Selling has seen significant growth in recent years. However, many seem to miss the point that success comes from building trusted relationships rather than from a continuous sales pitch. Julie draws on her wide and deep experience, explaining how to use social selling as a key relationship and business-building technique. I thoroughly recommend this book to anyone serious about social selling.

Mike Berry, strategic marketing lecturer, trainer, consultant and co-author of *Digital Marketing Fundamentals*

B2B Social Selling Strategy is a great addition to the literature. Insight-driven, it provides a guide to best practice in social selling that will help improve business and personal performance. It is ideal both for those running businesses or studying this often-overlooked aspect of marketing.

Matt Housden Principal Lecturer, University of Greenwich and Chair of the Marketing Skills Trust

A Julie Atherton book is always essential reading. This one doesn't disappoint. Clear, constructive but practical insights and advice adorn every page! The text represents a manual for B2B selling that few students and practitioners will want to miss out on.

Rob Angell, Associate Professor in Marketing, University of Southampton, and co-author of *The State of Martech* **survey**

Julie is one of the most respected professionals in the social media sector. Her experience gives her a unique perspective on the challenges facing marketers trying to get to grips with the complexities of social media selling. This book explains how to target and convert prospects with optimal efficiency and effect in a channel that is increasingly important.

James Sutton, Strategy and Commercial Director, Chartered Institute of Marketing

Packed full of actionable and impactful tactics that I'll certainly be implementing with my own clients.

Jenna Yhearm, MD at Gumption Agency and Founder of The Social Media Union

Social engagement is well recognized as a valuable way of building engagement and – more importantly – trust, with clients. In my experience, far too few companies truly embrace this cultural approach across their client facing teams. With this book, Julie provides a great overview with excellent insights that will help to truly drive social client-facing and trusted engagement.

Chris Boorman, independent business adviser

B2B Social Selling Strategy

Connect with customers,
build relationships and drive sales

Julie Atherton

KoganPage

Publisher's note

Every possible effort has been made to ensure that the information contained in this book is accurate at the time of going to press, and the publishers and authors cannot accept responsibility for any errors or omissions, however caused. No responsibility for loss or damage occasioned to any person acting, or refraining from action, as a result of the material in this publication can be accepted by the editor, the publisher or the author.

First published in Great Britain and the United States in 2023 by Kogan Page Limited

2nd Floor, 45 Gee Street
London
EC1V 3RS
United Kingdom
www.koganpage.com

8 W 38th Street, Suite 902
New York, NY 10018
USA

4737/23 Ansari Road
Daryaganj
New Delhi 110002
India

Kogan Page books are printed on paper from sustainable forests.

ISBNs

Hardback   978 1 3986 0461 2
Paperback   978 1 3986 0449 0
Ebook   978 1 3986 0460 5

British Library Cataloguing-in-Publication Data

A CIP record for this book is available from the British Library.

Library of Congress Control Number
2022947272

Typeset by Integra Software Services, Pondicherry
Print production managed by Jellyfish
Printed and bound by CPI Group (UK) Ltd, Croydon, CR0 4YY

This book is dedicated to my husband and sons who will always be my heroes. The last few years have been a struggle for so many people as Covid stole loved ones, jobs and savings, but I hope your family like mine has come out strong, close and more appreciative of what we have. Thank you, my Baker boys.

I also want to thank Mandy, for once again coming to the rescue with her invaluable PR knowledge, and my lovely clients for all the great work we have done together. Finally, a huge thank you to the wonderful, talented, super-clever people who made the time to share their experience, wisdom, research and case studies which you will find inside.

And Fi, still here and with us all.

Finally, a huge thank you to the wonderful, talented, super-clever people who made the time to share their experience, wisdom, research and case studies which you will find inside.

Anita Veszeli, Malin Liden, Steve Kemish, Richard Robinson, Kim Watts, Nathan Shilton, Raven Wheatley-Hawkins, Danny Bermant, Nigel Church, Jack Stevens, Katy Howell, Laura Hannan, Ryan O'Keeffe, Erica Neal, Sarah Stephenson, Kathryn Strachan, Kinga Kusak, Sean Gallagher, Amanda Wood, Paul Armstong, Joe Mowles, Miles Bradley, thank you!

CONTENTS

LIST OF FIGURES

LIST OF TABLES

CASE STUDIES

Direct Line for Business – B2B branding – Chapter 4

Copy House – using personal brands for social selling - Chapter 4

Copy House – using relevant content for social selling – Chapter 4

The Marketing Practice – a sustainability-focused social selling programme for a major telecommunications company – Chapter 5

Immediate Future Facebook live –Using Facebook for social selling with a global technology brand – Chapter 5

SAP – proving social selling works at SAP – Chapter 5

Copy House – taking a hyper-personalized approach to social selling – Chapter 6

The Marketing Practice – using LinkedIn groups to support lead generation in the manufacturing sector – Chapter 6

Pitch121 – maximizing lead generation with automation – Chapter 7

Leadfamly – global enterprise technology firm – using Leadfamly's gamification to drive engagement, increase knowledge, and generate leads – Chapter 7

SEEN Connects – using archetypes to match influencers to brands – Chapter 8

WDADTW (what did Amazon do this week?) – creating a compelling narrative as an influencer – Chapter 8

Ericsson – implementing a social selling programme – Chapter 10

Global technology company research – social selling: the supports and challenges to personal branding – Chapter 10

DOWNLOADABLE TOOLS AND TEMPLATES

DOWNLOADABLE CHECKLISTS

Rules of personal branding checklist – Chapter 4
LinkedIn usage best practice checklist – Chapter 7

INTERVIEWS

Malin Liden, Vice President, Head of EMEA Marketing Transformation
   Office, SAP – Chapter 1
Steve Kemish, Chief Marketing Mixologist, Intermedia Global – Chapter 1
Richard Robinson, Director, Coplow – Chapter 2
Kim Watts, Senior Lecturer, University of Bath,
   B2B Consultant – Chapter 3
Nathan Shilton, Digital Director, and Raven Wheatley-Hawkins, Digital
   Marketing Manager, Adroit – Chapter 3
Danny Bermant, Director, CaptainJV – Chapter 5
Nigel Church, CEO, Emerge Digital – Chapter 6
Katy Howell, CEO, Immediate Future – Chapter 6
Laura Hannan, Co-Founder, Pitch121 – Chapter 7
Ryan O'Keeffe, Founder, Jago – Chapter 8
Erica Neal, Head of Outbound, and Sarah Stephenson, Associate Director,
   Social Media, The Marketing Practice – Chapter 9
Kathryn Strachan, MD and Owner, Copy House – Chapter 10

ORIGINAL RESEARCH

Social selling: the supports and challenges to personal branding

Background

This original research was conducted in 2021 by Sean Gallagher. It focused on the sales team of a global technology business. The majority of the sales team were actively using social selling and the research was conducted to see how they could improve its performance specifically in the area of personal branding.

Methodology

A two-step approach was taken:

1 Interviews: seven semi-structured interviews with managers enabled an in-depth exploration of the topic and indicated the most useful topics for the survey.

2 Survey: 34 sales professionals from across the business completed an online survey. The group included a range of ages, genders, sales experience, and social and technology confidence and expertise.

ABOUT THE AUTHOR

Julie Atherton is the founder of the social transformation advisory Small Wonder. A business leader, public speaker, consultant and strategist, she specializes in advising organizations (B2B, B2C and third sector) on embedding social media in their strategic development and growth.

Her social media strategy books are built on her 30 years' experience gained advising and training global brands, small independents and innovative start-ups, including Deloitte Digital, Mott MacDonald, Nissan, St John Ambulance, Parcelforce Worldwide, Emerge Digital, Arnolfini, SmartViz and Send Me A Sample.

FOREWORD

Let's do a thought experiment. Bring to mind someone in your life you deeply trust. Someone you can confide in, count on, feel committed to. Now ask yourself: how did they earn that trust? Of the thousands of people in your network of human connections, why is this relationship so highly prized by you? When I ask that question of myself, I see recurring patterns of qualities in the people I trust the most. They have high levels of empathy – they try to see things from other people's perspective. They listen carefully and withhold judgement. They are not pursuing an agenda, they have my interests at heart – but they're not afraid to ask challenging questions to encourage positive change. They are constantly available, and consistent in the quality of the conversation. And of course, it's a two-way relationship. The more they help me, the more I want to help them.

Can we hope to build relationships like this with our prospects and clients, as sales professionals on social networks? It's not easy. It may not even feel normal to bring ourselves into the conversation like that. We have targets, and we have to prospect and win on scale. We don't have time to build deep relationships. We often find ourselves operating in the semi-dark on social networks, with relatively few insights on the prospects and leads we have uncovered or been presented with. And of course we are competing with others for that coveted trust position. It would be a lot easier to be less personal and just broadcast reasons why our prospects should buy our products and services, and hope that someone says yes. But if you've picked up this book, you already have an inkling that that approach doesn't work and you want to try something different.

Developing a trust-centred, human approach to selling on social networks is not straightforward. But as this book shows us, it's essential. Developing mastery of social selling delivers results. To get there, we must be open to change and willing to learn. There's so much to learn in this book about how to bring about a change in mindset, and to enact that change through tools and techniques that will build a new set of habits for your social selling practice.

The best sales professionals I have had the privilege to work with are first and foremost great learners. They are hungry for insights. They stay on top of developments in their sector, and they're passionate about helping people by sharing those insights. They curate insights (sourcing content from the web and social networks) and create their own. This is the currency for developing trust: having something helpful to share. But effective social sellers spend it carefully: they are not just broadcasters. They consider the tone of the conversations on social networks before contributing. They listen before speaking. They identify who in their prospects' wider network they could also build relationships with: decision makers, influencers, stakeholders and so on. They are skilled in the tools and techniques that facilitate prospecting, social listening and personal brand building – many of which are covered in detail in this book. But most of all, they believe in the value of building trusted relationships.

LinkedIn defines social selling as 'Leveraging your social network to find the right prospects, *build trusted relationships*, and ultimately, achieve your sales goals'. It's those three words in the middle that are so often skipped over in the rush to achieve sales goals. Building trust requires patience and humility. It can only be earned at the pace our prospects will allow. We have all been on the receiving end of a seemingly helpful outreach on a social network that quickly turned into a sales pitch. No trust is earned, no relationship is built, no sales goal is achieved. What Julie shows us in this considered and practical addition to the field is how to put trust at the centre of our social selling endeavours.

There's no shortcut to social selling success. But there are methods to accelerate the steps of prospecting, creating insights and having meaningful conversations. This book is full of practical guidance on the tools and techniques of effective social selling, and it's rooted in doing it from a place of authenticity. As someone put it, social media gives us an opportunity to show the world who we are at scale. Use these tools and techniques to show that you are someone who's here to help. Sales must come second to that goal.

As Julie rightly points out, selling is about storytelling. The heroes in the social selling story are not us as sales professionals. They are the prospects we will seek out and build relationships with, through trusted insights. They want your help. They're out there listening and waiting. This book will show you how to find them and become part of their story. If you can do that in a genuine way, there's a great ending ahead.

Stephen Walsh
Co-founder, Anders Pink and author of Selling Is Sharing.
Find me on LinkedIn: https://www.linkedin.com/in/stephentwalsh/

Introduction: how to use this book

Who this book is for

This book is an essential read for everyone involved in B2B marketing and sales who wants to embrace social media transformation and improve their B2B results. It provides a simple and structured approach for all practitioners in the industry or anyone studying for digital marketing or sales qualifications. Aiming to both inspire and educate about the benefits of a strategic approach to social selling, it will guide you in generating and nurturing relationships to create strong leads and sales, whatever field your business operates within.

Why I wrote this book

Social media is embedded in global culture. We use it every day for work, with friends, with family and even with strangers. No organization can function without it, we cannot imagine conducting a relationship, organizing a meeting or party, or sharing information without it. And it continues to be even more important year on year as we use it more widely and for longer, the number and variety of channels continues to grow, and their functionality increases as we demand more nuanced ways to experience social behaviour. This means that every business needs to build social media into every level of its organizational strategy. It isn't optional or an add-on, it is a fundamental pillar of success, and those businesses that embrace social transformation and use it to enhance and grow their customer and employee relationships will be more competitive, more customer focused and more successful.

In B2B, whether you are an entrepreneur, work in an SME or the sales team for a large organization, in PR or business development, or are a director of sales and marketing for a global organization, your world has been transformed by the introduction of social selling. Social media, when deployed strategically and effectively, offers a uniquely personal long-term networking opportunity for sales teams and business professionals. For many, this has supercharged their sales performance, with empowered teams, faster results and higher revenues. For others, the challenges of navigating social channels for business can be daunting. Concerns over social media confidence, personal and professional conflicts of interest, and a loss of management control can lead to a lack of action or just plain dull and ineffective modes of engagement.

Social selling includes four areas of activity – personal branding, information exchange, networking and social listening – all needing to be conducted confidently and consistently. During the Covid pandemic many organizations and individuals realized they had neglected social media as a sales channel, whereas others saw unprecedented growth as they capitalized on strong networks and personal brands.

I wrote this book to provide a simple but effective strategic approach to social selling which can give everyone the confidence to use social media to support and drive their sales process. Building on my ABC approach to social strategy (Atherton, 2020), developed in my previous book, *Social Media Strategy: A practical guide to social media marketing and customer engagement*, I have explored how, when the three core elements of networked audiences (A), mature interdependent brand relationships (B) and continuous integrated campaigns (C) are applied to the sales process, a clear and powerful social selling strategy can not only be created but also implemented and measured to ensure success.

Now is the time to embrace the opportunity, and this book will enable you to consider every element of transformation, integrating traditional and social channels, closer collaboration between marketing and sales, building a value-based content plan, and embedding a social selling culture with consistent social selling activities.

What the book contains

B2B Social Selling Strategy takes a practical approach to using social media to connect with customers, build relationships, and ultimately drive leads and sales. The book explains how to create and apply a strategy that not only improves business performance but also improves the confidence and skills of your sales and business development professionals, whether you are an individual looking to improve your own performance or lead a team.

Supported by original research, case studies and interviews with leading experts demonstrate real-world applications. The book provides a toolkit to enable you to successfully apply the templates, frameworks and approach to your own business.

The book aims to help you:

- learn how to create a B2B social selling strategy
- identify and connect with your core target networked audience
- build strong relationships in social media with customers and prospects
- create a differentiated positioning for your business and your personal brand
- identify the best social channels for your business and use them effectively
- integrate social selling with your other sales and marketing activity
- utilize automation and insight tools to maximize efficiencies
- harness the power of influencers
- create a confident social selling culture in your organization
- measure and continually improve performance
- deliver increased sales revenues and customer loyalty.

How the book is structured

Chapter 1 – The modern B2B sales challenge: who sells, how they do it and why it works

What is social selling and why does it work? This chapter outlines the impact B2B social selling has had on sales and marketing performance. It explains the key terms, roles and actions involved in social selling, and includes original research and insights to help you understand the changes in mindset, culture and behaviour required to make it work.

Chapter 2 – Getting started: creating your own B2B social selling strategy with achievable objectives and KPIs

This chapter introduces the social selling strategy framework and explains the B2B application of the ABC approach to social selling strategy. You will understand the importance of taking an integrated strategic approach and how to create your own objectives and KPIs.

Chapter 3 – The networked audience: finding your networked audience on social media, what they look like and how you can understand them

What does a networked audience look like and how is it connected to other audiences? This chapter shows you how to visualize a networked audience. It explains how social listening and other tools can be used to create networked personas and how you can use this approach to build valuable and engaged relationships on social media.

Chapter 4 – The Interdependent brand: differentiating your business through mature relationships and effective content marketing

Developing your personal brand alongside your company brand is an essential component of a social selling strategy. Learn about how interdependent brand relationships help you to differentiate yourself and your business in a competitive environment with compelling thought leadership, engaging content and a consistent approach.

Chapter 5 – Campaigns: how to take an integrated approach to B2B social selling channel selection

What are the best channels for B2B social selling? Use the channel characteristics comparison table to identify the most important channels for your business goals. This chapter will enable you to confidently decide where and how you need to invest your social selling time and resources.

Chapter 6 – Campaigns: building and implementing a B2B social selling plan

Every strategy needs a delivery plan. This chapter shows you how to organize and deliver your strategy with example plans and templates to ensure an effective customer journey from lead generation to nurturing and sales conversion, through to enduring relationship building. Plus, you will find useful tactics that can enhance the effectiveness of your plan.

Chapter 7 – B2B social selling tools: how to select the best tools to improve efficiencies, increase insight and transform results

There are lots of tools on the market which can save time and resources, but how can you make sure you are spending your money wisely? This chapter considers some solutions, provides checklists to aid decision making, and explains the benefits of integrated CRM, in addition to discussing the pros and cons of using LinkedIn Sales Navigator.

Chapter 8 – Using B2B social media influencers: making the most of influencer relationships

Influence is in the DNA of social media and this chapter unpicks the wide range of opportunities available to you. Learn how to find B2B influencers and gain tips on how to both work with influencers and become more influential yourself.

Chapter 9 – Monitoring and measurement: measuring the effectiveness of your B2B social selling strategy

Delivering results is essential for success. Make sure your tracking and analysis provide meaningful monitoring and measurement. Use the ROI calculator to ensure you keep on track and learn how and what to measure in the short, medium and long term.

Chapter 10 – Social transformation: creating a B2B social selling culture in your business

Social selling is all about confidence and attitude. This chapter looks at the dynamics of an effective social selling team. Supported by original research into personal branding, it explores the behaviours that are essential to success, and the importance of leadership and role modelling in creating a rewarding and supportive social selling culture in your business. A useful personal action plan for LinkedIn can help get you started.

Bibliography

J Atherton (2020) *Social Media Strategy: A practical guide to social media marketing and customer engagement*, 1st ed. Kogan Page, London

01

The modern B2B sales challenge

Who sells, how they do it and why it works

> What is social selling and why does it work? This chapter outlines the impact that business-to-business (B2B) social selling has had on sales and marketing performance. It explains the key terms, roles and actions involved in social selling, and includes original research and insights to help you understand the changes in mindset, culture and behaviour required to make it work.

What is B2B social selling?

Social selling is a highly personalized and effective sales activity. Individual sales and business development professionals build relationships with customers, prospects and influencers via social channels to build trust, create reputations, generate leads, nurture engagement, deliver sales and continue to add value.

As Howell notes:

'Growth and sales are everything. Social selling is a spectrum. It uses social to align brands with the sales process and includes everything that drives memorability and persuasion from branding, to trust and credibility. It also includes the individual connections the organization has with their potential customers. Not just driven by the sales teams but all employees advocating for the brand from the top down. By using social insight, creativity, and positioning to help the business make connections across the purchase funnel, and being extraordinary to gain cut through, social selling can help you perform better and drive growth. In fact, about 40% of our business comes directly from LinkedIn, Facebook, Twitter, and TikTok.' (Howell, 2021)

FIGURE 1.1 Comparing the social selling and traditional selling approaches

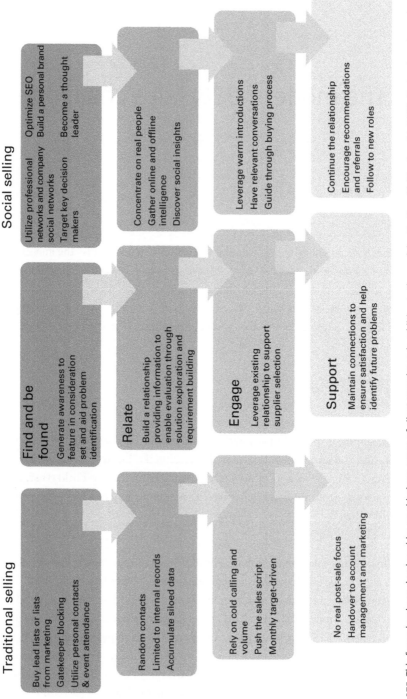

Traditional selling

Find and be found

Buy lead lists or lists from marketing

Gatekeeper blocking

Utilize personal contacts & event attendance

Relate

Random contacts

Limited to internal records

Accumulate siloed data

Engage

Rely on cold calling and volume

Push the sales script

Monthly target-driven

Support

No real post-sale focus

Handover to account management and marketing

Social selling

Find and be found

Utilize professional networks and company social networks

Target key decision makers

Optimize SEO

Build a personal brand

Become a thought leader

Relate

Concentrate on real people

Gather online and offline intelligence

Discover social insights

Engage

Leverage warm introductions

Have relevant conversations

Guide through buying process

Support

Continue the relationship

Encourage recommendations and referrals

Follow to new roles

NOTE This figure has been developed by considering a range of client experience in addition to the work by MacDonald (MacDonald, 2021), Gartner's customer buying journey (Gartner, 2020) and the McKinsey customer decision journey (Atherton, 2020).

A social selling approach differs from a traditional approach as it extends the role of the sales relationship, has access to useful shared insights and adopts a personalized approach, as shown in Figure 1.1.

Traditional selling can often be a baton-handing connection, with marketing driving awareness and providing leads to sales teams focused on short-term sales targets and an over-reliance on their personal contacts and event attendance, or cold calling lists. Social selling focuses on the longer term, building relationships as part of a team within your organization and benefiting from a synergy between individual and corporate social media activity. There are four key stages in the social selling pathway:

- **Find and be found** – The goal here is to be able to find potential buyers on social media, and crucially to also be found by buyers looking for new partners. In traditional selling this stage is often focused too much on the find element rather than being found. You may be over-reliant on attending events or limited by your current network of contacts. And even if your business buys in lead lists, you may find it difficult to overcome the decision makers' gatekeepers. Social selling balances both the finding and being found elements by recognizing the importance of creating useful and informative content that can be accessed via both personal and corporate social media channels. By taking a strategic approach to thought leadership and personal branding, SEO improves for both you and your business, and potential buyers start to seek you out. In addition, social targeting and network sharing across your organization enables everyone to widen their network and identify new contacts to approach with your proposition.

- **Relate** – This stage is about building relationships and providing information to enable your potential buyers to evaluate their options and ensure they have consensus on the requirements and specifications of any new solution. In a traditional selling approach, information can be limited and is often held with individuals in an unstructured way. Social selling focuses on identifying the people who are ready to interact. Social insights and listening can be used to inform the content they would like to consume, identify their connections and fellow decision makers, generate triggers for next-step activity from buying signals, and ensure outreach calls are timely and relevant to the buyer's challenges.

- **Engage** – Here you are trying to ensure the potential buyer picks you and your solution. You may be under pressure to meet sales targets and deliver results. In traditional selling, a volume, one-size-fits-all approach can sometimes be taken, or you may use cold calling to increase the potential buyer pool size. Social selling focuses on leveraging the existing relationships you have built to support you being chosen as the new supplier. Your reputation as a thought leader and informed adviser is important here, enabling you to leverage a warm relationship and help guide the buying process with highly relevant and insightful conversations.

- **Support** – This final stage considers the post-sale relationship. Often in traditional selling sales professionals may have a very limited role, with responsibility handed to onboarding teams, account management or marketing. Social selling means you retain the connection to ensure customer satisfaction and are ready to help identify possible future problems or needs. By continuing the relationship, you can also encourage recommendations and referrals and follow your contacts when they move to new roles or new companies. Having built up trust with your network, this is a great way to continue your thought leadership reputation with them and be front of mind for the next opportunity.

Importantly, social selling focuses on the long-term relationship between individuals rather than a fast sale from one business to another. Showing your personality and challenges and investing in those relationships is a key factor for success, and your personal brand and its interaction with your business profile will be important. Social selling increases the number of touchpoints and interactions in the customer journey and integrates seamlessly with traditional sales channels such as events, telephone and email. Crucially, with direct access to their network of potential customers via social media, professionals who use social selling bypass traditional gatekeepers and are more successful and efficient.

However, introducing social selling to your business isn't as simple as just starting to use social media. You need to take a strategic approach, bring teams with you and support new skills and behaviour, and make decisions about which channels and tools will be right for you and your buyers. In the interview here, Liden, who spearheaded the introduction of social selling at SAP (SAP, 2022), shares her thoughts on why it worked so well for them.

INTERVIEW
Malin Liden, Vice President, Head of EMEA Marketing Transformation Office, SAP (Liden, 2022)

SAP is the market leader in ERP software and enables businesses of all sizes to become more agile, improve operational efficiency, raise productivity, increase profits and enhance customer experiences. After a long career in marketing, sales enablement and innovation, Liden heads up SAP's EMEA marketing transformation office and works with the head of marketing to shape the strategy for the organization. An expert in creating and running pilot innovation programmes that can be scaled across SAP, she is committed to embedding innovation with training, enablement and peer-to-peer learning, as success comes not just from knowledge but knowing where to go to ask questions and gain support. The successful social selling programme at SAP began as an innovation pilot programme.

How do you define social selling?

Social selling is actually the same as selling because we are social human beings. And if your customers are on social media, then that's where you should be when you're selling, utilizing the social media platforms, techniques and mindset of being part of a conversation.

It is dangerous to limit the definition to the tools and a platform. If you do, then you are more likely to see people using LinkedIn Sales Navigator to spam people (like a Yellow Pages on steroids). Social selling isn't finding more people to spam and hard sell to. The definition is more about the mindset, being part of a conversation, meeting the customer where they are, not just on the platform but in their thought processes around their business.

Join in, see what they are talking about, what they are interested in, and tag onto that discussion. Try to add value and be a good conversationalist, not sell, because the selling comes later. The more we move from push to pull, the more we also practise patience. We need to enter the discussions much earlier when the customer doesn't yet know that they want to buy something. If you're not there, before they know that they want to buy something, someone else will be there before you, and then you've missed out.

How important is the relationship between marketing and sales in social selling?

The SAP social selling programme generated a $1.4 billion pipeline value within two years and the reason we were so successful was due to the tight collaboration between marketing and sales.

Each community has different strengths. It was absolutely critical to have the buy-in from sales leadership, making this new way of selling a priority that is supported with a top-down commitment and reflected in a regular sales cadence. We couldn't have done it without that. But social selling begins much further up the sales cycle where marketing started using social practices earlier. We already knew the techniques around how to find people, how to put an opinion out there that could start a conversation, how to make yourself interesting enough so that people see you as an expert on a certain topic, come to you for information and then, all of a sudden, they discover that they can also buy from you.

We trained salespeople in how to use the social platforms to sell and gave them the content to get started. Collaboration was key.

How did you motivate the salespeople to give it a try?

Salespeople have a competitive spirit and we used that to make it a bit of a competition when we implemented the social selling strategy. The hardest people to convince were the really successful salespeople, many of them with a long track record and years of experience. So, we started with the social savvy ones, often early talents, the people who wanted to stay ahead of the game and who were hungry and eager and open to start something new. They created the success stories and shared how, by improving their social selling index (SSI), they improved their sales performance.

Success was a combination of highlighting and supporting the ones that were keen to adopt the training and celebrating their achievements. But also creating this notion of the champion, this narrative that, as buyer behaviours change and digital research becomes more important, the boat that you're sitting on is getting slower and slower, you can still jump ship to the fast one, but if you wait, eventually you will be too late to jump and will get left behind.

How has the changing buyer journey affected social selling?

The big selling point for introducing the social selling programme was that 70 per cent of the buyer's journey is over before someone talks to a vendor and

90 per cent of the decision is already made by the time they want to talk to a vendor, so you need to be talking to buyers long before they are ready to buy. Unless you find a way to engage with them that is not perceived as selling, you are going to lose the game before it gets started. And that's how we try to visualize it.

You need to be part of conversations, you need to put your expertise out there, you need to make sure that they know about you or that they can find you on their research journey, so that by the time they are ready to talk to someone about buying, it is going to be you.

What channels do you use for social selling?

LinkedIn is still our biggest corporate investment in social selling. However, the right platform is always where your customers are. For example, in some countries people use Facebook for corporate business and B2B. So, then Facebook is the right platform for them. We made the central investment in LinkedIn because, for us, it is the most important globally.

Are there differences in social selling in different parts of the world?

It is different from culture to culture, and it depends on the audience there and how digitally savvy they are. That is why we started with one of the first pilots in Southeast Asia because they're very digital savvy, both the employees and the customers.

However, although there are different cultures around the world, I haven't seen a market where social selling is not successful or where customers don't react well to it. The difference is adjusting the style of how you do it. If you apply an American style of selling in Germany, people will be annoyed and vice versa. Just as for other channels, you need to make sure you find the right tool and the right message, the right way to engage with the customer, and that will vary by market and culture.

What do you think drove the success of SAP's social selling programme?

One of the bigger success factors for us, especially as a large organization, was a 'train the trainer' programme. We immediately realized that if you're an early mover and you're doing something that is ahead of the curve, you will, by definition, have a limited amount of people who really know how to do it well. And we realized that if we relied on that small group of people to help everyone through social selling, it wouldn't scale.

So, every time we trained a team, the sales manager agreed to two things:

- to be trained themselves and to personally champion social selling
- to help us identify someone who will be a trainer in their team.

We trained the entire team, but we stayed in touch with this trainer, so that they could always be there to remind the team of their goals in social selling, support people, and keep them updated on the tools and techniques as they continued to develop.

We continued to build this community of trainers that were trained to support and train the wider organization. This was a major game changer for us. We have so many people out there in the organization, but we didn't just send them to a workshop and then leave. We left them with their own trainer that we stayed in touch with.

Why does B2B social selling work?

As Liden champions in the interview, social selling works. It generates leads at a lower cost than other channels, social sellers outperform their peers (Figure 1.2) and social media supports C-suite decision making.

To understand why you need social selling and why it works you need to consider the current business environment and the effect the pandemic has had on future networking and business communications. The factors are compelling and cannot be ignored.

FIGURE 1.2 Measuring the success and efficiency of social selling

75%
Lead generation costs less in social
(75% less than any other channel)

78%
Social sellers perform better
(78% of those using social selling outperform their peers)

84%
Social supports purchase decisions
(84% of C-level executives consult social media before a decision)

Data from Hubspot (Alfred, 2021).

1 *Professional networking and relationship building have moved irreversibly online*

During the Covid-19 pandemic business and networking events were cancelled or moved online. For some, this move may be permanent, and for many, the option of hybrid, virtual and in-person attendance is an attractive way to increase participation and reach.

Sales professionals have always found in-person events important opportunities, with 47 per cent ranking them as a top channel to drive demand (Anderson, 2019). Increasingly, however, with three in four B2B events planned as hybrid (Marketing Charts, 2021), they will need to justify the time and expense of attending in person and find new ways to make virtual events successful networking occasions as well.

Social selling can help you to combat these challenges in the following ways:

- Relationships are important to both buyers and sellers. Eighty-four per cent of buyers would buy from a supplier that they had a great relationship with, even if the terms were less preferable (Sana Commerce, 2021). Social selling supports building and strengthening remote relationships for long-term value creation on both sides.

- Buyers place a lot of trust in their professional networks and social media networks are a valuable and time-saving way to access these. '[Social media offers] a way to correlate information and cross-reference opinions from a wide range of colleagues and fellow industry professionals' (Schaub, 2014) and 84 per cent of C-level executives consult their social media network before making purchasing decisions (Alfred, 2021).

2 *Buyers increasingly control the speed and nature of the customer journey*

The way in which buyers approach a new B2B purchasing decision has changed and is a factor of the increasingly digital basis for organizational operations. In a study by Gartner (Gartner, 2020), buyers reported spending only 17 per cent of their time meeting with sales professionals during the process and this time was by far outstripped by independent research and internal stakeholder meetings (Figure 1.3).

FIGURE 1.3 The distribution of buying groups' time by key buying activities

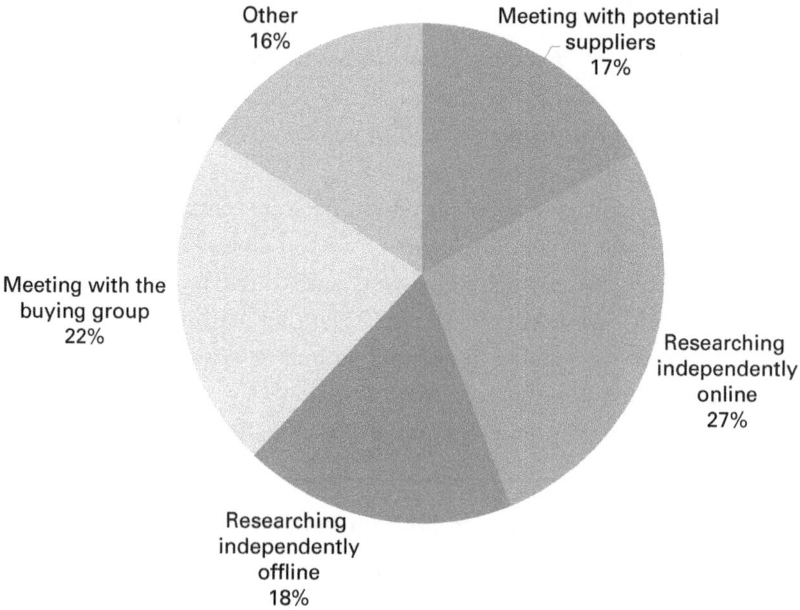

Based on information from the 2017 Gartner digital B2B survey (Gartner, 2020)

Social selling can help you to combat these challenges in the following ways:

- Involving multiple stakeholders in the process on social media, from both the vendor and the buyer, ensures that buying groups can be identified and supported with relevant information before they meet. In fact, many sales professionals increasingly take an account-based selling (ABS) or account-based marketing (ABM) approach to their social selling strategy. Chapter 3 looks at how to understand not only your key buyer but also the networked audience around them, which is essential when taking an account-based approach.

- With limited face-to-face time available with buyers, personalized social interactions can be a useful way to stay front of mind and maintain a conversation.

3 Communication channels are more diverse and online is increasingly important

Pure cold calling has been on the wane for many years, with 90 per cent of decision makers saying they 'never respond to cold calls' (MacDonald,

2021), and online channels and vendor websites have become increasingly important, with 70 per cent of B2B buyers doing their research online (Kinnear, 2019).

Gartner reports that millennial decision makers are 2.2 times more sceptical about sales rep claims than baby boomers are (Gartner, 2020), and as the number of millennial decision makers increases, so will their impact on purchasing decisions. In some sectors, the impact is already pivotal in decision outcomes. For example, 60 per cent of all B2B technology buyers are millennials (TrustRadius, 2021) and they are much more likely to find out about a product or service by searching online than older buyers are.

Social selling can help you to combat these challenges in the following ways:

- Social media channels, such as LinkedIn, and lead management tools, such as Cognism, enable sales professionals to connect and interact with potential buyers prior to a call. In addition, by using social listening and social search insights to understand the prospect's challenges and interests, calls are not only more warmly received, they are also more likely to result in a positive outcome. In a recent Forrester report, the most important aspect of vendor selection for B2B buyers was the sales rep's knowledge of the buyer's business (80 per cent) and industry (78 per cent) (Alfred, 2021).

- Social media has a direct impact on SEO performance. A strategic social selling approach aims to deliver more positive brand engagements, web mentions, third party links, and keyword content occasions, all of which drive higher SEO rankings.

4 People still buy from people they know and trust

B2B purchases are generally expensive, and the decisions buyers make can impact their professional reputation for many years. The risks are therefore high, and buyers want to trust and respect the individuals and organizations they partner with.

Social selling can help you to combat these challenges in the following ways:

- Customer reviews and case studies provide important information when making B2B buying decisions and can significantly help to build trust in sales reps and their organizations. Social media is a great tool for generating and distributing this type of content by encouraging and facilitating recommendations and referrals. In the tech sector, free trials, product demos and user reviews were seen to be the most trustworthy and influential information sources (TrustRadius, 2021).

- Business professionals use a variety of social channels to build and develop relationships. Although LinkedIn is generally viewed as the most important, B2B businesses increasingly use Facebook, Twitter, Quora, Slack and other channels which offer a variety of tools for community and individual engagement, and knowledge sharing (Trier, 2021; Alfred, 2021).

- Building your personal brand and a reputation for thought leadership in an area of expertise enables you to gain the trust of your network and influence their decisions as they move through the buyer's journey.

5 Technology leaps have streamlined the process and increased efficiencies

Technology, and the internet in particular, empowers B2B buyers with vast amounts of information and support available 24/7. As a result, competition is increased and vendors who fail to deliver great customer experiences, high-quality products and value for money are easily exposed.

However, technology also empowers social selling. Although social selling is possible without technology plugins and tools, the advantages of using even a few of these options can significantly increase your commercial outcomes. Chapter 7 talks about these tools in more detail, but it is important to note that there are many options, and they cover every aspect of the social selling infrastructure. Just remember not to be seduced by shiny toys – it is vital for you to assess your needs and select tools that really do add value to the process. Example areas where technology can help include:

- social listening and insights into companies and individuals
- social CRM
- lead management
- account-based selling tools
- content management
- measurement and optimization.

Who is involved in B2B social selling?

Although the core responsibility for social selling sits with marketing, sales and business development teams, the wider organization has a role to play in ensuring success. Social selling uses the combined impact of personal and corporate social channels and networks to amplify engagement and reach, personalize and contextualize conversations, and build consistent momentum to support the brand proposition and improve SEO. Therefore, when building a social selling strategy for your business you should consider the opportunity and practicality of including your colleagues in its deployment.

Often this will be vital to success. For example, creative marketing agencies are often appointed using a very consultative sales process. The potential client will want to assure themselves that the agency can deliver the services required, is able to flex those services to suit changing client needs, and that the team (on both sides, and at every level, from strategic to operational) will have a good working relationship (chemistry). Including the agency leadership and potential agency team in the social selling strategy delivery can significantly improve the likelihood of a positive result from the consultation.

Many organizations implement this by adopting a sales enablement approach where sales-focused leadership, content management, training and coaching, and analytics are underpinned by a technology solution. A structured approach to sales enablement has resulted in 15% higher win rates (Miller Heiman Group, 2019). Therefore, when considering who should be involved in your social selling activities, ensure you include senior leadership, marketing, client-facing and pitch teams as well as sales. This integrated approach is synonymous with social media transformation, the embedding of a social approach to your strategic development.

How B2B social selling integrates with the wider sales and marketing mix

Although social selling focuses on making the most from corporate and professional social media relationships, it doesn't work in isolation. To be successful, you will integrate your social media interactions with all the other touchpoints you have, such as email, phone, website. In addition, it is important to maintain a continuous dialogue with marketing, sharing insights and data, and refining content to ensure it meets the customer needs and is easily editable for social selling personalization.

In the interview, Steve Kemish recognizes the importance of a joined-up approach that considers the wider teams across the business and the culture change required for the integration of your personal brand with the wider business activity.

INTERVIEW
Steve Kemish, Chief Marketing Mixologist, Intermedia Global (Kemish, 2021)

Kemish heads up the team at Intermedia Global (Intermedia Global, 2022), a UK-based, market-leading full-service provider of B2B data, digital, direct marketing and database solutions on a global scale. Clients include Capita, Regus, SAP and EDF. A leading marketer and social selling expert, Kemish has worked with B2B brands for more than 20 years.

What does the term social selling mean to you?

Social selling means much more than selling. It isn't just about sending out a few tweets or LinkedIn posts and expecting orders to come flooding in. In reality, it is a longer game. It's social engagement, social relationship building, and social selling. The onus isn't just on the salesperson. A good social selling strategy works with sales, business development, marketing and across the organization. For example, marketing can help with the creation and curation of the content, and data and insight can help target the people sales professionals should be connecting with on the right platforms.

Do you use social selling as a marketing service provider?

Yes, it's all referral and recommendation for lead generation in our space and therefore social selling is really important. Social selling is a different way to reach a decision maker. At one level, the classic gatekeeper protection is not there. It is a subtler and more human approach. Rather than a cold calling replacement, the savvy salesperson uses it as a chance to build relevance, reputation and credibility with that prospect, and their customers.

How should marketing and sales work together?

I think that sales start and lead the journey, and although marketing might be more involved in some stages, at the very least marketing should be supporting behind the scenes. At the front is me, a salesperson. But the marketer is feeding me with helpful content and insights and even doing some of the legwork that says that prospect X has just done ABC. Whether it's done manually or using technology to help with notifications, a salesperson shouldn't be expected to day-to-day manage, and marketers need to be careful they don't abdicate communication to people who aren't typically communications experts.

How do you encourage the wider team to get involved with social selling?

My mantra internally is:

- Get comfortable with the platform by just being present and absorbing how people behave and what type of content is there.

- You have two eyes, two ears, one mouth, use the former more than the latter. You don't need to go and broadcast at first, just go and listen in to see what people are doing.

- Remember the simple joy of liking something. If you posted something and somebody liked it, how would you feel? That's how other people will feel if you engage with their content.

- Aim to create and curate. Curating non-competitive third-party content makes us look informed and in good company. It is valuable and a good mix with your own content. Just share interesting stuff that's relevant to you and it will be relevant to your audience.

- Create your own unique content that can talk at a different level.

- Give it a go.

How do you use content in social selling?

The most beneficial social content is help content or educational content. People come back to it over and over again, always revisiting, and because it tends to be a bit more long form, it's great for SEO. At Intermedia Global (Intermedia Global, 2022) we've got 20 years of being smart and knowledgeable on data. We use social media to remind people we exist and share relevant and new information. We're not selling but helping. Social selling supports our inbound strategy by people following us and seeing us active in social media, so when they have a problem, they think of us when looking for the answer.

What factors should you consider when running social selling activity?

It's important to set the right expectations. You might be lucky and somebody sees your content who has just come into the market, but it is more likely to be longer-term commitment. So, if you do shift budget from traditional marketing and sales activity into social selling, make sure you keep the short-term lead-generation tap running.

Social selling means that you need to spend more time building relationships online and that's a cultural shift for sales. It's a leadership culture change as well. Leaders need to be bought into considering different metrics and KPIs and not just demanding short-term leads and sales for social selling to stick. This is a quality not quantity exercise.

Which channels do you think are the most important for social selling?

For me personally, LinkedIn is 90 per cent of the energy because of the space our business operates in. We rarely use personal Twitter accounts. Even for our corporate accounts, LinkedIn is the most important. We use Facebook more for recruitment.

How do you use your own strong personal brand?

I've been involved in social networking for many years because I come from a digital background. I've been given a platform, through speaking, whether that's tutoring or keynote speaking, that I recognize is a good way to raise awareness. It's not about me, it's about how my personal brand can help the organization I represent. Then I don't have to sell, I can just inform, and that sells.

How sales team culture has changed to meet the social selling challenge

Social media has transformed the world of B2B sales and marketing. Previously very separate functions, the lines are blurring as sales professionals need to consider their personal brand and employ marketing techniques in their activity, and marketers recognize the importance of integrating with sales and adopting an ABM approach. It is therefore essential for both professions to understand the complementary effects of an integrated and strategic approach.

The modern sales professional is open to change, continually learning from their experience, peers, and ongoing training and coaching. An active listener, they gather insights and share them across the business, recognizing that social selling is most successful when it is implemented and supported company wide. Chapter 10 explores the cultural changes needed to embed social selling in your business as part of a wider process of social transformation, but research shows that leadership and active role modelling can have a dramatic impact on improving social selling and personal branding practice and success. Gallagher's personal branding research, covered in detail in Chapter 10, identified both challenges and supports within organizations, with a key support being leadership and modelled behaviour:

> 'I guess, just be more proactive and encourage it on a more regular basis. Provide some guidelines around what good looks like by putting a framework around the rollout of social selling. If somebody is particularly passionate about building a personal brand, then provide a framework of what good looks like, where to find all the content and the right format to use, and understand how we can help them to ensure that they are getting traction on their posts and comments on LinkedIn and other channels.' Sales manager interviewed in *Social Selling: The supports and challenges to personal branding* (Gallagher, 2021)

So, social selling works, it delivers results, but it does require an investment in time and a strategic approach. You need to recognize that cultural change is likely to be needed both in the sales and marketing teams and across the wider business, but that this process of social transformation will increase your competitive advantage, build reputation, authority and trust, and generate leads, revenue and increased lifetime value.

In the next chapter you will explore the social selling framework and understand how the ABC approach to social strategy can provide the stepping stones to social selling success.

Bibliography

L Alfred (2021) 37 LinkedIn social selling stats you need to know, blog.hubspot.com/sales/social-selling-stats (archived at https://perma.cc/K9P5-SGV7)

B Anderson (2019) 2019 Demand Generation Benchmark Survey, view.ceros.com/g3-communications/dg093-surv/p/1 (archived at https://perma.cc/72H3-VLG5)

J Atherton (2020) The digital marketing customer journey. In: *Social Media Strategy: A practical guide to social media marketing and customer engagement*, Kogan Page, London, pp 17–23

S Gallagher (2021) *Social Selling: The supports and challenges to personal branding*, DMI, Dublin

Gartner (2020) 5 ways the future of B2B buying will rewrite the rules of effective selling, www.gartner.com/en/sales/insights/b2b-buying-journey (archived at https://perma.cc/J7PY-YQ57)

K Howell (2021) CEO, Immediate Future [interview] (13 November 2021)

Intermedia Global, Beyond boundaries, www.intermedia-global.co.uk (archived at https://perma.cc/YJ34-7V5J)

Intermedia Global (2022) Home page, www.intermedia-global.co.uk (archived at https://perma.cc/PV6G-Q77C)

S Kemish (2021) Chief Marketing Mixologist [interview] (30 November 2021)

C Kinnear (2019) B2B buyers do 70% of their research online, blog.passle.net/post/102fqjl/b2b-buyers-do-70-of-their-research-online (archived at https://perma.cc/FPP3-TCZA)

K Kusak (2022) Marketing Manager [interview] (12 January 2022)

M Liden (2022) Vice President, Head of EMEA Marketing Transformation Office, SAP [interview] (18 February 2022)

S MacDonald (2021) 38 Social selling statistics: How to master the art of social selling, www.superoffice.com/blog/social-selling-statistics/ (archived at https://perma.cc/SR4Z-8VMK)

Marketing Charts (2021) 3 in 4 B2B marketers are planning hybrid events – here are their perceived challenges, www.marketingcharts.com/industries/business-to-business-117826 (archived at https://perma.cc/KEL5-ZH43)

Miller Heiman Group (2019) CSO Insights: Fifth Annual Sales Enablement Study, www.brainshark.com/sites/default/files/CSO-Insights-5th-Annual-Sales-Enablement-Study-Brainshark-2019.pdf?ref=thankyou (archived at https://perma.cc/9HXJ-W89K)

Sana Commerce (2021) B2B Buyer Report: The power of buying relationships in the evolving B2B online world, info.sana-commerce.com/rs/908-SKZ-106/images/2022-B2B-Buyer-Report-ENG.pdf?mkt_tok=OTA4LVNLWi0xMDYAAA GARwc8SiOKkzCGPhq-dFMDO7krMRdPsGvGmJF22h0ND2BwsVJkrxchqQ Ca0lRpW73i_rwJdtbERiF3QjNFk4NMP0pxgPVeXgaFaO3Jv2Tce6YNxg (archived at https://perma.cc/6VKY-JAQR)

SAP (2022) SAP homepage, www.sap.com (archived at https://perma.cc/HTZ6-SDU4)

K Schaub (2014) IDC report. Social buying meets social selling: How trusted networks improve the purchase experience, business.linkedin.com/content/dam/business/sales-solutions/global/en_US/c/pdfs/idc-wp-247829.pdf (archived at https://perma.cc/YNW3-L49L)

R Trier (2021) 6 professional networking sites: LinkedIn alternatives, www.weidert.com/blog/professional-networking-sites-platforms-b2b (archived at https://perma.cc/K48L-V364)

TrustRadius (2021) B2B buying disconnect, https://www.trustradius.com/wp-content/uploads/b2b-buying-disconnect-2021.pdf (archived at https://perma.cc/YZ7C-BQE7)

02

Getting started

*Creating your own B2B social selling strategy
and setting achievable objectives and KPIs*

> This chapter introduces the social selling strategy framework and explains the
> B2B application of the ABC approach to social selling strategy. You will
> understand the importance of taking an integrated strategic approach and how
> to create your own objectives and key performance indicators (KPIs).

Introduction to the B2B social selling framework

Perhaps the biggest challenge when creating and implementing a social selling strategy is how to cut through the complexity to keep it simple, practical and therefore achievable. This chapter will help you get started and create the backbone for your plan using a simple but effective framework.

Because social selling is about building long-term, mutually valuable relationships, the framework considers both the buyer and the seller as equal partners. Figure 2.1 maps the buyer's goals at each stage of their decision journey to the social seller's partnership pathway. Let's explore each element and how they work together.

The buyer's journey

The first six elements of the buyer's journey are inspired by Gartner in their B2B research (Gartner, 2020) and a seventh (future problem solving) has

FIGURE 2.1 The B2B social selling framework

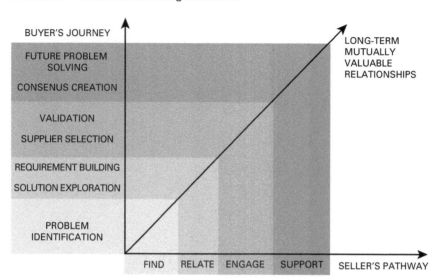

been added which focuses on the additional long-term benefits available with a social selling approach. The elements are as follows:

1 Problem identification – This is the trigger to find out more, an initial catalyst that a new supplier/product/service is required. It can be sparked in many different ways, including a new problem being identified, dissatisfaction with a current supplier, reading about new technologies or innovations, or shared ideas via networking. It is important to remember that problem identification can also be a result of some of the later stages, for example as requirements are built and options investigated, new problems might be identified. In addition, problems may be identified up to several months or years before any action is taken by the buyer to identify a new supplier or partner. White papers, thought leadership content and relevant industry or sector problem-solving examples are highly relevant here.

2 Solution exploration – At this stage the buyer has recognized that they have a problem and is ready to review how that problem might be solved. They will start to research what is available to help, asking their network for recommendations, visiting websites and events, downloading white papers, and considering levels of budget and resources that might be available and whether a buying group or committee needs to be assembled. More time will be spent here on specific supplier websites, reviewing

relevant trends and developments, in relevant social media groups and conversations, and in initial exploratory meetings.

3   Requirement building – As the buyer builds a request for proposal (RFP), either formally or informally, they will start to establish the organization's specific needs and priorities. Scope will be limited by budget and resources, and internal compromises may have to be made, but at this stage decisions on the priorities and timings for the solution are crucial. Although website and other self-serve content is used at this stage, buyers may actively reach out to potential suppliers to ensure their requirements are realistic and future focused, and those suppliers could influence the hierarchy of requirements. In addition, the balance of needs between internal stakeholders and across the buying group will be an important factor. There is a high level of movement back and forth between this stage and the solution exploration stage.

4   Supplier selection – At this stage the responses to the buyer are highly personalized and targeted at the specific problem(s) identified in the RFP. As the buyer decides what to buy and who from, they will compare proposals and explore additional information such as case studies, and perhaps trial some solutions. Individuals in a buyer group may prefer different options and new problems or ideas may be sparked from a variety of proposals. Selecting a new supplier is often a high-risk decision, so content that helps reach a consensus and reduces risk with positive return on investment (ROI) and onboarding examples is useful here.

5   Validation – An important partner to the supplier selection stage, here the buyer is keen to ensure they are making the right decision and will seek reassurance from their network, and from references and case studies. At this stage the reputation of the seller and their organization in terms of thought leadership, relevant award wins or market positioning can be an important decision factor.

6   Consensus creation – As contracts are negotiated and transitions and onboarding agreed, it is important that everyone feels part of the same team to make the decision a success. Reiterating the shared values and culture of the buyer and supplier can be very powerful.

7   Future problem solving – Social selling is about creating long-term partnership synergies. Much time and effort has been deployed to deliver a sale and a strong and trusting relationship has been created. Do not waste this. Stay close to your buyer with inspiring and useful content, respond to their activity, and congratulate them on achievements and events. Importantly, look out for signs that there is a new problem ahead.

So, we know that buyers have different decision points which move them into a new stage, but what do we know about the way buyers make those decisions? As sellers, we want to ensure that we correctly respond to and anticipate buyer signals. Understanding what drives buyer decision making helps us to do this more intuitively and empathetically. Although decision making will change from business to business, sector to sector and group to group, there is some consensus that most B2B buyers exhibit the following attributes:

- **Iterative** – A buyer may initially have identified a problem that they want to solve. Perhaps the business is growing, opening a new branch, going through digital transformation or has a new leader, any of which could initiate a need for new services or products to support the change. However, whatever the problem initiator is, it is unlikely that this will be the exact problem that finally gets solved. As the buyer moves through the process they will shape and refine the challenge, both using their own research and through interaction with potential partners. This iterative process is useful and important – it enables the buyer to be certain of what they need and allows the seller to build a deeper understanding of both the requirements and the standards for success. Gartner have mapped an illustrative buyer's journey showing the complexity and circularity. The journey shows the initial four stages outlined above: problem identification, solution exploration, requirement building and supplier selection. In the Gartner example, social media is highlighted around conversion, but in this book I will explain how social media can support your involvement with the buyer at every stage, including validation and future problem solving, as in social selling you will have a role to play beyond the sale.

- **Consensual** – Although some purchasing decisions will come down to an individual making a choice, it is much more usual for the decision to be made by a group of people from the buyer's organization. Gartner report that on average between six and ten individuals will be involved in a B2B purchasing decision (Gartner, 2020) and research in the tech sector specifically indicates that the average is as high as 15 (B2B Marketing, 2019). This could be a formal purchasing committee or a looser team of relevant stakeholders. In some instances, the decision-making group may also include external consultants or other partners. For example, if a business was appointing a new database agency, they may ask their creative agency for input into the process.

- **Remote** – The pandemic forced businesses to change the way they worked both internally and with partner organizations. Consequently, many interactions became remote rather than in person. Research by McKinsey

FIGURE 2.2 B2B buyer interaction preferences for interacting with suppliers' sales reps during different stages

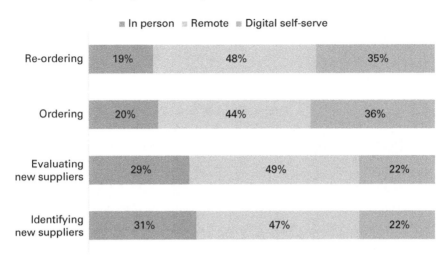

■ In person ■ Remote ■ Digital self-serve

	In person	Remote	Digital self-serve
Re-ordering	19%	48%	35%
Ordering	20%	44%	36%
Evaluating new suppliers	29%	49%	22%
Identifying new suppliers	31%	47%	22%

Based on research included in McKinsey October 2020 report (Bages-Amat, 2020).

indicates that we won't go back, with 70–80 per cent of B2B decision makers preferring remote or digital self-serve solutions (Bages-Amat, 2020). Although in-person meetings are likely to increase, most buyers prefer remote interactions and there are strong commercial and practical reasons on both sides for this preference, such as meeting scheduling ease, travel cost savings and safety. When you are building your social selling strategy, you will need to be considerate of this preference and how your content will need to change to support a much more self-serve and remote experience.

- **Slow and buyer-led** – When building your strategy, you should consider the length of your buyers' typical sales cycle. You may have targets that you need to meet, but setting unrealistic expectations can drive unhelpful behaviours which may prevent rather than encourage a sale. On average, 75 per cent of B2B companies take at least four months to win a new customer (Marketing Charts, 2019) (Figure 2.3). For software-as-a-service (SaaS) sales, the value of the end sale has a big impact on the sales cycle. HubSpot reports that the average SaaS sales cycle is 84 days, rising to 170 days (five and a half months) for average contract values of over $100,000 and reducing to 40 days for average contract values of less than $5,000 (Prater, 2020).

FIGURE 2.3 Typical B2B sales cycle length

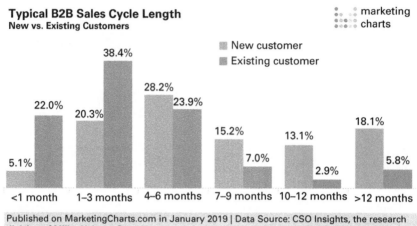

Published on MarketingCharts.com in January 2019 | Data Source: CSO Insights, the research division of Miller Heiman Group

Based on a survey of 886 sales leaders around the world conducted in summer 2018

TEMPLATE 2.1 Average sales cycle calculator

Calculate your average sales cycles using the template to understand and set expectations.

Average sales cycle calculator				
	Sales	Initial contact date	Date of final sale	Number of days taken to complete sale	Average sales cycle (days)
	Sale 1	3-25-2022	3-25-2023	365	
	Sale 2	10-24-2022	3-25-2023	152	
	Sale 3			0	
	Sale 4			0	
	Sale 5			0	
	Sale 6			0	
	Sale 7			0	
	Sale 8			0	
Total	2			517	258.5

Download the average sales cycle calculator and use it to understand your average sales cycle. Add up the total number of days taken by each sale and then divide that number by the number of sales. The cycle length is likely to be longer for larger and more complex sales and shorter for existing customers. Remember that because a large proportion of the buyer journey is self-serving, you will need to decide at what point you believe the sales cycle starts. Is it when they first connect with you on LinkedIn, when they ask for some information or when they accept the first call? For ease you may want to break the sales cycle into stages, perhaps mapping the buyer's journey, and decide on how you will know they have moved from one stage to the next. We will discuss some of these signals in Chapter 9.

The social seller's partnership pathway

As a seller you want to match your behaviours, content and interactions as closely as possible to your prospects' needs and priorities. For this reason, I call the seller's journey the partnership pathway. The pathway features four types of activity:

1 Find and be found – This is about creating awareness to feature in a buyer's consideration set and thereby help problem identification and seeking out potential buyers who have problems you could help solve.

2 Relate – Ensure you build a relationship to provide information to enable evaluation through solution exploration and requirement building.

3 Engage – Now you can leverage the existing relationship to support supplier selection and validation.

4 Support – Maintain connections to ensure purchase satisfaction through consensus creation and help identify and solve future problems.

This book guides you through the process to create a social selling strategy that will enable you to improve how you approach each stage of the buyer's journey and build long-term, mutually valuable relationships. The result will be an effective plan with clear objectives and KPIs, co-ordinated tasks and activities, meaningful personalized content and great results.

As discussed in Chapter 1, the social selling pathway differs from a traditional sales approach. The emphasis is on building and nurturing sustained relationships with identified individuals and businesses. Crucially, your relationship doesn't end with a sale, rather a sale opens new possibilities both within and beyond the new customer's organization.

In his blog, Steven MacDonald articulates the difference between social selling and traditional selling (MacDonald, 2021) by referring to the different way sales professionals find, relate to and engage with potential buyers.

FIGURE 2.4 Comparing the social selling pathway to traditional selling

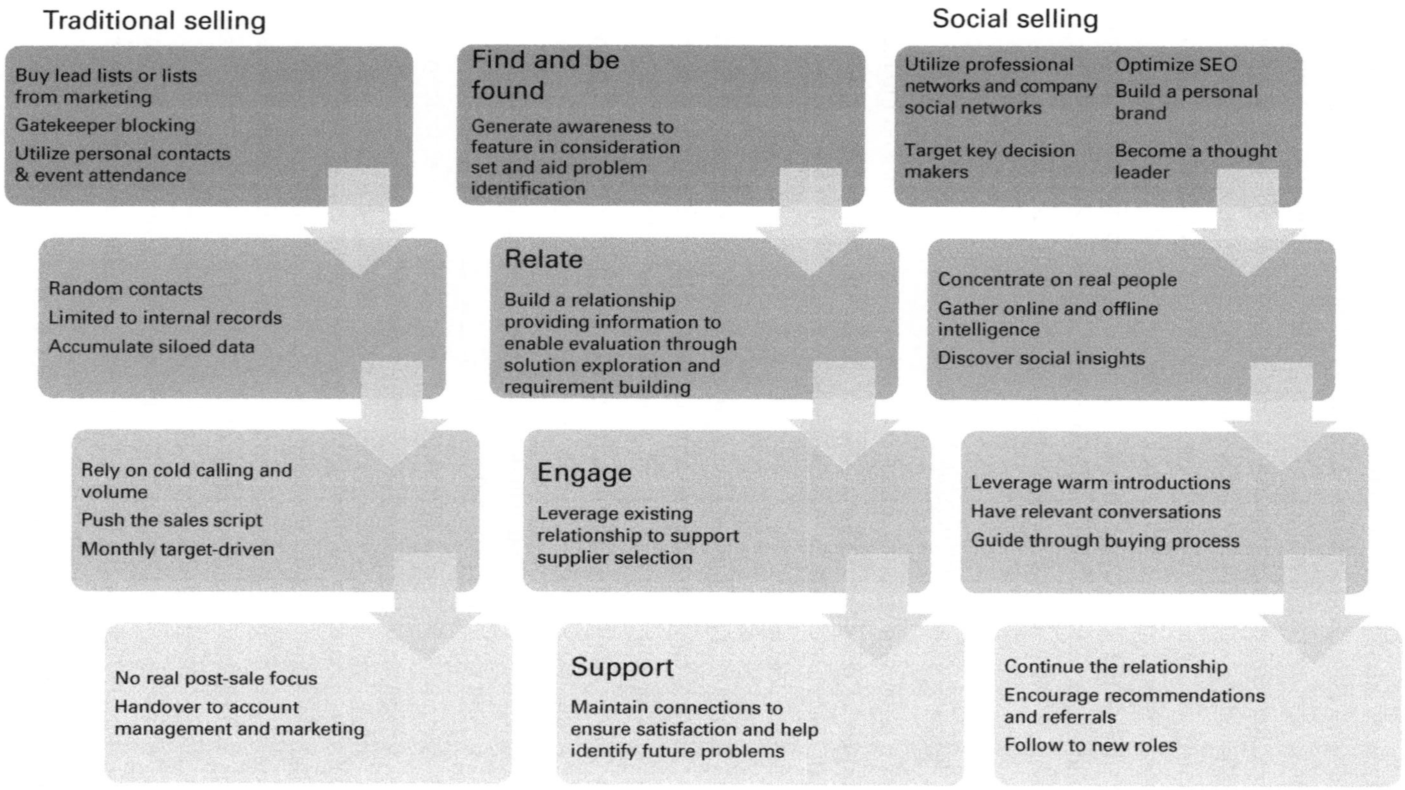

Traditional selling

Buy lead lists or lists
from marketing
Gatekeeper blocking
Utilize personal contacts
& event attendance

Random contacts
Limited to internal records
Accumulate siloed data

Rely on cold calling and
volume
Push the sales script
Monthly target-driven

No real post-sale focus
Handover to account
management and marketing

Find and be found

Generate awareness to
feature in consideration
set and aid problem
identification

Relate

Build a relationship
providing information to
enable evaluation through
solution exploration and
requirement building

Engage

Leverage existing
relationship to support
supplier selection

Support

Maintain connections to
ensure satisfaction and help
identify future problems

Social selling

Utilize professional
networks and company
social networks
Target key decision
makers

Optimize SEO
Build a personal
brand
Become a thought
leader

Concentrate on real people
Gather online and offline
intelligence
Discover social insights

Leverage warm introductions
Have relevant conversations
Guide through buying process

Continue the relationship
Encourage recommendations
and referrals
Follow to new roles

In Figure 2.4 I have considered these new behaviours and developed them into the social selling pathway. The support stage extends the relationship beyond the sale to build a long-term valuable connection.

In the interview here, Richard Robinson shares his experiences of the changed nature of the buyer's journey and the resulting need for a new social selling approach.

INTERVIEW

Richard Robinson, Director, Coplow (Robinson, 2021)

Coplow is a boutique consultancy that helps marketers develop highly effective go-to-market strategies through the effective use of digital, data and technology. Its clients are drawn from B2B and B2C brands, marketing technology vendors and investment firms. Richard leads the business and has more than 20 years' experience transforming brands by using the latest digital technology and implementing innovative go-to-market strategies.

How would you define social selling?

It's about using my brand, my company and my own profile, as a personal representative of the brand. It's using my social media presence to connect with prospects and develop connections, and nurture them through the whole sales process.

It's more important now than ever, and particularly in the context of the last couple of years because there just hasn't been that in-person, face-to-face contact.

When is social selling relevant in the customer journey?

In B2B, we've known for many years that the point at which a buyer starts to engage with a brand or an individual within the brand is moving later and later in that buying process. We did some work, when I was at Google, that highlighted that B2B buyers are typically 50–70 per cent of the way through the journey prior to them reaching out to a brand.

Since then, so much more has moved online, it's so important for salespeople, marketing and content marketing together to build those relationships far earlier via a digital context. That is what the heart of social selling is about.

It's important to make connections as early in the process as possible to be found by potential buyers when they are in the discovery phase. Buyers will be conducting a high proportion of the research, justification, problem identification without you being involved, or without you knowingly being involved, so you've got to be out there so that they are able to find you.

A recent example of this was when I received an inbound call from a potential buyer. On the initial call they very quickly deep dived into our product. I didn't know them or the context of what they required. And that's because they had done all the self-prospecting themselves, they had deep dived into what they're looking for, their business challenges, the types of technologies that could work for them. And it's almost as if they skipped the merry dance that we'd usually have – 'Hi, I'm Richard, and I do this, and I do that, and what do you do?' – and they just went straight to 'Right Richard, this is what we want, can you do it?' They had researched our business and me before the call.

It feels like social selling emphasizes not just your company brand but also your personal brand. Would you agree?

Yes, with social selling your buyer has not only come across the company, they've also come across you. So, they've got a view on whether they think you're the right sort of person who might fit with them as well as the right sort of organization. That's why in social selling it's not just your company brand but also your personal brand that is important.

For example, in my organization we spend time building our personal brands aligned to the company brand and using different tools and techniques that we weren't using 12, 18, 24 months ago. Video is becoming more important. Individually, we're creating snippets of video content that is seeded out through our own social media accounts, either personally or the brand's. Using both channels means that we can distribute more content and make it more relevant. Our buyers are searching for interesting content, especially if it is episodic or has a regular cadence to it.

This regular content helps our buyers think, 'Oh this person really knows what they're talking about, or they've got something interesting to say.' It's not just pitching your product, you're actually talking more widely about the business issues that it can solve, which means people are starting to identify individuals to go and talk to, not just the brands that they work for.

What are your next steps in your social selling approach?

We are starting to take a more holistic approach by recognizing what we want the business to be famous for, and then as individuals within the business, what our stances are on that. So, we're pulling that together with specific areas of expertise across the business. Ideally, we will have a number of people that produce content completely in line with the business values, but they are putting their own personality on it. This content becomes popular and those individuals become the stars in their network. But of course, from the brand's perspective, the individuals' content needs to align with the values of the business.

How important is a strong social network when hiring senior leaders in your business?

Ten years ago, when recruiting somebody, I might check their social media to verify their CV and check if their social posts fit comfortably with our company values. Today, we're starting to look at candidates' social media presence to find the additional value that person can bring to us via their social networks.

Someone who has a lot of followers on a particular channel or has built up thought leadership around a particular area is more valuable to me and the business, especially if their expertise is in an area that our company doesn't have any heritage with. For example, if a business was boosting its data offering but didn't have a strong data heritage, they could bring somebody in that has that data heritage and reputation in a social context.

How are you measuring the effectiveness of social selling?

We measure it individually and at a company level but, as for most businesses, there are so many touchpoints for any customer on that buyer's journey that it can be quite difficult.

At an individual level, the team monitor their content and make improvements based on engagement and reach. For example, one team member has been creating video clip content. She has seen a rising number of people viewing the videos over time and can identify the strongest videos and content in terms of reach and engagement. By incorporating this learning she's able to make further improvements.

At a business level, we look at our pipeline using our customer relationship management (CRM) system and identify where a lead comes from. For example, was it some particular personal activity on social media that generated the initial engagement? The next step is to monitor those through the process to see the true impact. We try to tie the classic metrics of engagement, clicks, shares and likes back into the sales process.

Where is social selling most effective?

Social selling is important at every stage of the sales funnel. At a company level, we're using it mostly at the top end of the funnel, as the acquisition piece. It's awareness raising, it drives the initial contact. At an individual level, we're trying to use it across the whole sales relationship, it covers the whole of that cycle.

Understanding and using the ABC of social selling

The framework gives us a structure for planning and deploying our activity. However, alongside this there are some strategic principles and building blocks that need to be in place.

Many businesses and brands, whether using digital or traditional sales channels, focus on themselves as the most important actor when deciding how they will communicate with their potential customers. In this traditional hierarchy, you start with your brand and the objectives you want to achieve. You set a budget of how much you want to spend to deliver leads and/or sales and then determine the channels you want to use based on viability, cost, resource requirements and even personal preference. Finally, you consider how you will communicate with your potential businesses and customers in each of those channels or experiences. This old hierarchy could be described as BAC – brand, advertiser, customer. It uses marketing or buys in leads lists to identify groups of customers who look like your best customers. For example:

- **Brand** – A software company based in New York State will initially decide the objectives and KPIs they want to achieve. Perhaps launching a new service, delivering a set number of new leads for next month's programme, or achieving a 20 per cent conversion rate for upgrading existing customers to a premium option. They will be clear about what their brand stands for, the core differentiators and the way they will represent themselves to potential customers.

- **Advertising** – Then they will decide how they will reach new clients. Perhaps they have a strong local presence and their sales team may attend and/or present at local networking events and conferences. They may advertise in local, state-wide or national business magazines, both in print and online. Perhaps the owner supports a local sports team and the business uses sponsorship benefits to entertain high-value customers or high-potential leads. Alongside this the business is likely to have a useful, SEO-optimized website and may spend money on social, digital and traditional advertising. These channels all may have potential, but often the results are hard to measure and can be clouded by personal biases. 'We always sponsor...' or 'Our competitors attend xxx' are common refrains.

- **Customers** – Finally the business looks at the customers they can reach via these channels and the specific messages or content they might want to share to encourage a meeting or deliver a sale. Who is attending the meeting? What is the readership of the magazine? What profile shall I use to target my ads? Do I have a special offer to promote? What features of the product will appeal to this business or customer? Some channels will offer access to high volumes of target customers and be especially interesting to the business.

This BAC thinking leads us to build strategies that create brands that people aspire to, tell potential customers what we want them to hear, and deliver lots of new businesses and individual customers who look like our existing customers. The strategy focuses on what the business wants to say and not necessarily on what their customers' needs are and where they are in the buyer's journey.

No bad thing, you may argue, but perhaps a missed opportunity. To create an effective social selling strategy, this hierarchy and language need to change. This is because in social media we do not, and should not, focus on a narrow definition of the customer. Yes, ultimately we want to drive revenues and sales through customers, but social media has a bigger audience with an important and wide-ranging role to play. In particular, this audience is full of connections within multiple networks and the businesses and individuals in these networks play a variety of roles at different times in the sales cycle. We therefore talk about piercing networked audiences rather than customer and this audience takes pole position in the hierarchy.

Next comes brand. We do still care about business objectives and the key messages and unique elements of our proposition. But we also care about the personal brand of our sales professionals and the relationship between our audience and our brand. How do we co-create interdependent brand experiences that embrace the community?

Finally, rather than advertising we want to consider a continuum of symbiotic continuous campaigns where interactions are amplified and

FIGURE 2.5 ABC – the new strategy hierarchy

Audience   Brand   Campaigns

dialogue is encouraged. How do we build mutually valuable interactions, deepen trust and create environments for collaboration? As we support beyond the sale and into future problem identification, our relationship with buyers is a continuum, not a beginning-to-end process.

This new hierarchy is described as ABC – audience, brand, campaigns (Figure 2.5) – and characterized by networked audiences, interdependent brand relationships and continuous, symbiotic campaigns.

Using the new hierarchy in our software example:

- **Audience** – We would initially consider the networked audience that affects the strength of our business and its ability to drive long-term customer relationships and revenues, rather than the individual customer. This could encourage us to consider, in addition to potential customers, the users of our software in existing customer businesses as key influencers on upgrades, or existing customers in the same sector as our potential customers as introducers for new clients. Importantly, we will be thinking about how we connect with, engage and influence our audience, who they are also connected with, their relationship with them and the relevance of this to our business. We will also want to think about how our audience will find us. Are we on the right channels and engaging in the right conversations? What hashtags and keywords are helping us stand out?

- **Brand** – Mature brand relationships occur when we understand what our audience values about us, know how to build trust, and recognize what an interdependent relationship looks and feels like between our brand, our audience and our team of social sellers. Crucially, this relationship will evolve and develop in social media as well as in more traditional channels and developing a thought leadership dialogue can help with this.

- **Campaigns** – Once we understand the meaning and value of the brand experience we can consider how and where we will connect with them, the content and messaging required, and how we will build amplification and continuation into the strategy. To do this we will use the social selling framework (Figure 2.1), mapping our social selling pathway to the buyer's decision journey. Social media is the starting point for this type of activity, acting as an instigator, nurturer and developer for important business relationships.

Getting started: know your B2B business model

Your social selling strategy needs to be aligned with your core business objectives and work within your business model. Your business model will determine the range of channels that your buyers connect with you through, the offer, price, commitment levels and relationship you seek.

In B2B there are seven typical business models:

- Product-based
- Service-based
- Software – Product-based
- Software – Service-based
- Ecommerce – Supplier-centric
- Ecommerce – Buyer-centric
- Ecommerce – Intermediary-centric

The characteristics and customers/buyers of each model determine the relationship you seek with them. For example, SaaS sales are typified by freemium offers building to premium subscriptions whereas product-based software sales rely on a high-value initial sale. Table 2.1 demonstrates the characteristics of each business model.

Before you start to decide your objectives, take a look at Table 2.1. Which business model do you operate within?

- Are you within a 'pure' model or a 'hybrid'? Many businesses are hybrids, for example Microsoft Dynamics 365 is a product-based software business, but many small businesses buy Microsoft 365 on a SaaS basis.
- Are you looking for a high upfront sale or an ongoing subscription?
- Have you got significant overhead and production costs, are you easily scalable, are you facilitating the sale of other businesses' products?

TABLE 2.1 Examples of the different types of B2B business model

Model type	B2B business model examples						
	Product-based	Service-based	Product-focused software	SOFTWARE AS A SERVICE (SaaS)	Supplier-centric E-COMMERCE	Buyer-centric E-COMMERCE	Intermediary-centric E-COMMERCE
DESCRIPTION	The business sells physical products to other businesses. This business may not create the products themselves but act as a supplier to other businesses.	The business sells its services to other business. The range of services is large and many businesses fall into this category from translation services to marketing to employment.	The business provides software to other businesses that it buys and installs on its owned (cloud/non-cloud) servers. Also known as enterprise software.	The business provides software services to other businesses via a licensing and delivery model.	The business acts as a supplier to other businesses selling its own products via online marketplaces.	The business looks to procure products via its own online marketplace by inviting other businesses to put their products and prices there.	The business acts as an intermediary connecting buyers and sellers via its own marketplace.
CHARACTERISTICS	Online, offline or both. As the products are physical initial investment and overhead costs can be higher than some of the other B2B types.	Online, offline or both. Easy to set up and with lower overheads than product-based businesses.	Online. The software is bought for a large upfront fee and minimal ongoing costs. It is highly customizable for each business.	Online. The software is centrally hosted and licensed on a subscription basis. It is easy to scale up as deployment is fast.	Online marketplace. The business tends to have control over the pricing and inventory of products.	Online marketplace. The business uses the marketplace to compare standards and prices to make the best purchases for its own business.	Online marketplace. For this type of business model to work there needs to be lots of both buyer and seller businesses.

EXAMPLES						
Volvo Trucks – sells haulage vehicles to other businesses.	WPP – sells communications, advertising and PR services to other businesses.	Microsoft Dynamics 365 – sells customizable computer software to other businesses.	Salesforce – provides CRM tools and cloud services to other businesses.	Dell – provides PCs and high-end servers to other businesses via its marketplace.	Walmart – prefers to buy from local suppliers and invites them to apply to supply them via its own marketplace.	Tradekey – an online marketplace which helps worldwide businesses find new trade partners and opportunities.
Bradley's Juice – sells a range of premium juice drinks to hospitality businesses and delicatessens.	McKinsey & Company – sells consultancy and change management services to other businesses.	Sage – sells accountancy software to other businesses.	Google Workspace – provides a collection of cloud-based productivity and collaboration tools to other businesses.	Cisco – provides network equipment to other businesses via its own marketplace.	GE TPN Post – is an electronic bidding site. Buyers pay a nominal fee to join and suppliers bid to win the projects.	Alibaba – the Chinese e-commerce site mainly focuses on serving other businesses rather than consumers.

NOTE Businesses could be local, international or global, for-profit or not-for-profit, commercial or government

- Can your B2B sale self-serve or do you need sales professionals and other team members to consult with buyers throughout the process or at key stages?

- Do you operate an e-commerce marketplace?

Knowing what type of B2B business you operate within will help you determine the potential constraints and opportunities, and the most important stages of the buyer's journey to concentrate your social selling around. The next step is to decide on the objectives you want to achieve.

Getting started: define your core objectives

When setting out B2B social selling objectives we have two criteria we need to meet for our own business:

1 How do we build measurable long-term, mutually valuable relationships?

2 How do we demonstrate and measure our impact on the business's immediate (short-term) sales targets?

In B2B social selling the first objective is of primary importance, and even more importantly, we need to focus on the customer buyer experience and how we make that as valuable as possible across the different stages in the B2B social selling framework – find, relate, engage, support.

Therefore, set yourself three SMART objectives:

1 Focus on your customer/buyer – what do you want them to feel and experience about you and your business in every encounter?

2 How will you create a long-term, mutually valuable relationship?

3 What sales targets do you need to meet by when?

What is a SMART objective?

SMART objectives are specific, measurable, achievable (or aspirational), realistic and timebound. Setting SMART objectives enables you to be clear about what your priorities are, how you will measure success and clearly communicate what your focus is.

When setting your SMART objectives, break them into three sections as defined in Figure 2.6 – what do you want to do, how will you measure it and what is the timescale?

FIGURE 2.6 Creating SMART objectives

Specific / achievable (aspirational) / realistic	Measurable	Timebound
What do you want to do?	How will you measure it?	What is the timescale?
(Make sure it is realistic and possible)	(What tools will you use, how will you report it?)	(Does your timescale meet your corporate business targets?)

Each element of a SMART objective is important, but deciding on the measurement criteria can often be the most difficult. When you create your objectives, think not only about how you will determine success but also how you will demonstrate that success to the wider business. What KPIs will you use?

Getting started: decide your KPIs at each stage of the social selling framework

Let's be honest, most sales professionals feel under pressure. It is hard to qualify the value of an individual lead and because sales occur at the close of an often long and expensive prospect engagement journey, it is hard not to feel responsible if a sale isn't achieved.

Chapter 9 discusses monitoring and measurement in more detail, including specific social media measurements, but at this stage it is useful for you to decide some broad KPIs that are easily understood by the wider business:

- FIND – How many companies and individuals do you want to connect with each month either by requesting connections or through being found by them?

- RELATE – How many requests for further information should you expect? What signs will you look for to indicate your buyer is ready for the next stage in the journey?

- ENGAGE – How many sales should you expect to make? How will you measure customer confidence?

- SUPPORT – How will you ensure customer satisfaction remains strong and that a relationship is maintained after the sale?

FIGURE 2.7 Setting SMART objectives and KPIs – an example

BRADLEY'S
— DRINKS —

MY BUSINESS:
Bradley's Juice – a family-owned premium juice business in Somerset, England that sells B2B to restaurants, pubs and retail outlets.

MY BUSINESS MODEL:
Product-based. A manufacturer of a seasonal (food) product, it is important to sell stock at key times of the year to meet seasonal demand and reduce inventory costs.

Smart objective	What do i want to achieve?	What is the time period?	What does success look like?	How will i measure it?
FIND	Identify and connect with new international wholesalers Be found by independent retailers	By end of xx Over next xx months	Key decision makers in the wholesalers are aware of Bradley's juice	Number of new connections Number of new followers
RELATE	High levels of interest in our full range of products and our brand story	Ongoing but tracked monthly	Requests for product trials Interaction and sharing on social media Downloading specific content from website	Number of trials Taste trial feedback scores Number of social followers/mentions/shares
ENGAGE	Sign long-term contracts with new wholesalers Sell xxx units	By xxx	Obtain committed buyers for planned production units	Number of contracts signed Number of units sold Value of units sold
SUPPORT	Happy customers who spread the word Opportunities to expand the range of products they buy	Ongoing but tracked monthly	Existing customer satisfaction/sentiment stable/increasing Increased take-up of full product range	Monthly CSAT score/NPS score Ongoing sentiment analysis Number of new products taken/customer

Reproduced with permission from Bradley's Juice.

TEMPLATE 2.2 Setting your own SMART objectives and KPIs

MY BUSINESS:

MY BUSINESS MODEL:

Smart objective	What do i want to achieve?	What is the time period?	What does success look like?	How will i measure it?
FIND				
RELATE				
ENGAGE				
SUPPORT				

Download the template and use it to create your own SMART objectives and KPIs.

Figure 2.7 shows some SMART objectives and KPIs for a premium juice brand, Bradley's Juice, which sells to wholesalers and independent retailers.

Download and use the template to define your objectives and set your KPIs.

A LOST SALE DOESN'T MEAN THE END

Remember – social selling is about building long-term relationships. You may not be successful in a particular sale, but you have connected with and built personal relationships with lots of individuals in the process. In the future, those individuals may be important influencers in their current organization or may move jobs. Both offer you new opportunities to build on your existing relationship.

Understand how the social selling framework connects both the buyer and seller goals

A networked audience is an audience that is defined by its connections within multiple networks, and the businesses and individuals in these networks play a variety of different roles at different times in the sales cycle. Therefore, when we understand networked audiences, we no longer look just for a business or an individual who will buy from us, rather we look to build interdependent relationships with the networks they operate within.

Importantly we will want to understand both the buyers' and our own goals as we move through each stage of the social selling framework. What are the motivations and requirements of each and how will social media help us support them? Figure 2.8 shows how the buyer's goals can coincide with our selling goals to ensure a mutually valuable relationship. It does this by unpicking how the networked audience operates at each stage of the framework from both the buyer's and the seller's point of view.

The buyer wants to ensure they have the right inputs and individuals to enable them to make the best decision for their business. They will use both internal colleagues and external contacts to do this and both online and offline research.

As the seller, you want to ensure you are included in the selection process (and ultimately chosen). To do this you not only need to be known to the

FIGURE 2.8 Understanding buyer and seller goals within the social selling framework

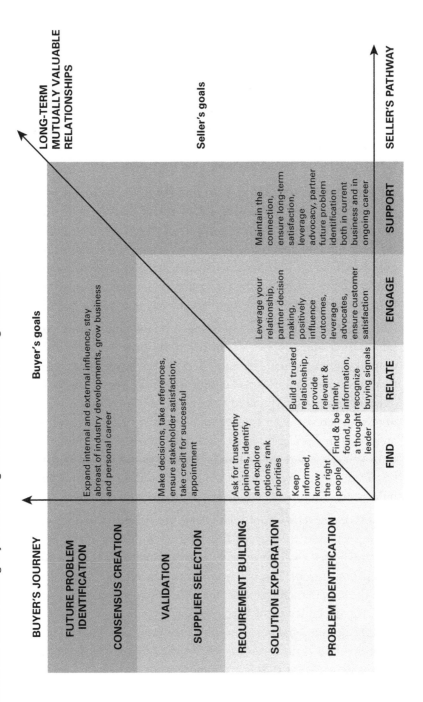

BUYER'S JOURNEY

FUTURE PROBLEM IDENTIFICATION

CONSENSUS CREATION

Expand internal and external influence, stay abreast of industry developments, grow business and personal career

VALIDATION

SUPPLIER SELECTION

Make decisions, take references, ensure stakeholder satisfaction, take credit for successful appointment

REQUIREMENT BUILDING

SOLUTION EXPLORATION

Ask for trustworthy opinions, identify and explore options, rank priorities

PROBLEM IDENTIFICATION

Keep informed, know the right people

Find & be found, be a thought leader

Build a trusted relationship, provide relevant & timely information, recognize buying signals

Leverage your relationship, partner decision making, positively influence outcomes, leverage advocates, ensure customer satisfaction

Maintain the connection, ensure long-term satisfaction, leverage advocacy, partner future problem identification both in current business and in ongoing career

Buyer's goals

LONG-TERM MUTUALLY VALUABLE RELATIONSHIPS

Seller's goals

FIND   RELATE   ENGAGE   SUPPORT

SELLER'S PATHWAY

buyer, you also need to have a great reputation, and ideally have demonstrated how suitable you and your organization are to be selected. With so much of the problem identification, solution exploration and requirement building being conducted without meeting the seller (Gartner, 2020), and with up to 80 per cent of B2B decision makers preferring remote human interactions or self-service (Bages-Amat, 2020), social media offers a way for you to use your business's, your own and your contacts' networked audiences to converse and interact one to one and personally without an in-person experience.

Using these networked audiences, you can ensure you:

- **FIND** – Identify potential buyers, find them and be found by them, to provide them with the pertinent and useful market, sector and other information to support problem identification within their business. You can seek out individuals and their networks on social platforms, joining groups, asking for introductions and engaging in relevant conversations. You can be found by building a reputation in your expertise area, being recommended and referred, and maximizing your profile for SEO.

- **RELATE** – Build trusted relationships by providing relevant and timely information and support which helps the buyer identify and explore options and rank their priorities. Because the buyer journey isn't linear, they may return to problem identification before they move on to supplier selection. As a seller, you need to be empathetic to the pace and direction of their progress and recognize their various signals to respond appropriately. By using social listening, desk research, feedback loops and other tools you can ensure you stay relevant and involved. Knowing who your buyer involves at each stage of their decision making, their influence and influencers, can provide important signals to inform your responses.

- **ENGAGE** – Leverage your relationships to become a partner in decision making. Support the buyer's consultation with their own network and your advocates and customers to enable them to make a confident decision in your favour. You will also want to ensure the buyer's satisfaction with the sale, the sales process, the onboarding and the post-sale experience. Having built a networked relationship, you can consult as a partner with the decision-making team, which may well be a different group from those involved at the earlier stages. Recognizing the development of your buyer's network at this stage is important for success.

- **SUPPORT** – Maintain the connection to ensure the buyer's long-term satisfaction with your support and your organization's solution. The buyer will want to stay abreast of current trends, new initiatives and industry developments to grow their business and their own career. By supporting them, you can partner with them in future problem identification in their current and future roles and leverage their support to act as an advocate for you when you are selling to other businesses. Over time your buyer's network will change. They may be promoted, move jobs or change company. You can use social listening and interactions to keep abreast of their progress and the changing needs of both them and their business.

This matching of the seller's pathway to your buyer's journey increases the level of empathy and understanding you exhibit and enables you to anticipate your buyer's needs. In the next chapter we will start to explore your audience. You will look at how to use social listening to understand their needs at each stage of the buyer's journey and ensure you are able to build relevant and effective relationships.

Bibliography

B2B Marketing (2019) Number of decision-makers for buying B2B tech revealed, www.b2bmarketing.net/en-gb/resources/news/number-decision-makers-buying-b2b-tech-revealed (archived at https://perma.cc/Z4QZ-HUD8)

A. H. L. S. D. S. J. Bages-Amat (2020) These eight charts show how Covid-19 has changed B2B sales forever, www.mckinsey.com/business-functions/marketing-and-sales/our-insights/these-eight-charts-show-how-covid-19-has-changed-b2b-sales-forever (archived at https://perma.cc/XBD9-FB6B)

Gartner (2020) 5 ways the future of B2B buying will rewrite the rules of effective selling, www.gartner.com/en/sales/insights/b2b-buying-journey (archived at https://perma.cc/7SWQ-M3BU)

Leadfamly (2022) Now is the time to upgrade your marketing with gamification, leadfamly.com (archived at https://perma.cc/6EHE-JUA5)

S MacDonald (2021) 38 social selling statistics: How to master the art of social selling, www.superoffice.com/blog/social-selling-statistics/ (archived at https://perma.cc/6RPB-XXP7)

Marketing Charts (2019) So what's the typical B2B sales cycle length? www.marketingcharts.com/customer-centric/lead-generation-and-anagement-107203 (archived at https://perma.cc/3QH5-8X62)

M Prater (2020) SaaS sales: 7 tips on selling software from a top SaaS company, blog.hubspot.com/sales/saas-sales-ultimate-guide?__hstc=6643565. d187eb49dc7ba78f27bf2efd3b23f478.1634985230925.1634985230925. 1634985230925.1&__hssc=6643565.1.1634985230925&__hsfp=3304104049 (archived at https://perma.cc/UVA3-NA8R)

R Robinson (2021) Director, Coplow [Interview] (3 December 2021) [Interview] (3 December 2021)

03

The networked audience

Finding your networked audience on social media, what they look like and how you can understand them

What does a networked audience look like and how is it connected to other audiences? This chapter shows you how to visualize a networked audience. It explains how social listening and other tools can be used to create networked personas and how you can use this approach to build valuable and engaged relationships on social media.

Visualizing the networked audience

Chapter 2 introduced the idea of a networked audience – an audience that is defined by its connections within multiple networks, and the recognition that the businesses and individuals in these networks play a variety of different roles at different times in the sales cycle. Understanding networked audiences means that you are no longer looking just for a business or an individual who will buy from you, rather you are looking to identify and enter their existing networks to build trusted, interdependent relationships with the members of those networks.

So how do you visualize a networked audience? Let's start by thinking about the different networks an individual operates within. In the context of B2B social selling you should focus on those networks that will impact your relationship with them and the decisions they will make when buying new products and services.

FIGURE 3.1 Visualizing the connections across a core buyer's network

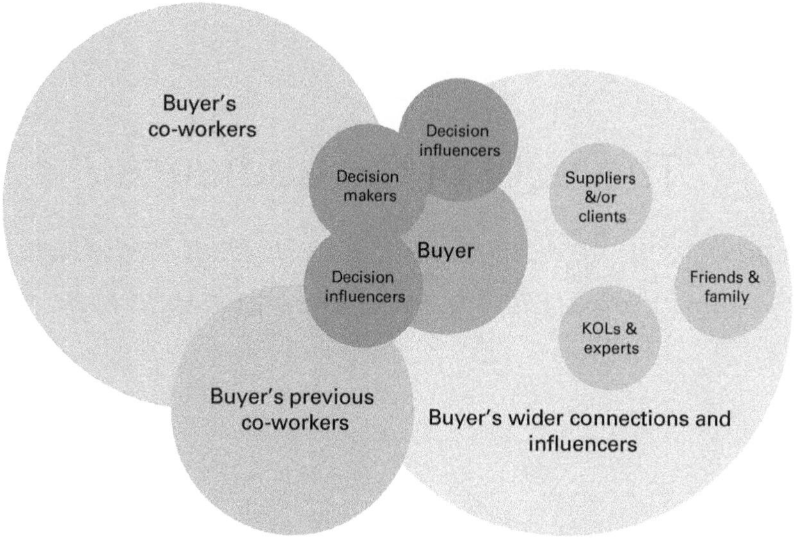

Buyer's
co-workers

Decision
influencers

Decision
makers

Suppliers
&/or
clients

Buyer

Decision
influencers

Friends &
family

KOLs &
experts

Buyer's previous
co-workers

Buyer's wider connections and
influencers

NOTE This is one way to visualize your networked audience relationships. A mind map can be another useful option.

We know that buyers rarely make decisions alone; in fact, up to 15 people on average are involved in technology purchases (B2B Marketing, 2019), but how do you know who those people will be and how do you streamline your processes to enable you to efficiently find them, understand them and build a relationship with them?

Figure 3.1 visualizes the players that might be within a networked audience. They may introduce you to your buyer or influence the decision that your core buyer makes. The networked audience includes the buyer, decision makers and decision influencers:

- **Buyer** – This is your key connection, the person who is spearheading the purchase and the lynchpin of the networked audience. They may not always have the final say or hold the budget, but the process and decision cannot exist without them.

- **Decision makers** – They may be part of a formal decision-making group (purchasing team), need sign-off from a more senior colleague such as the finance director (FD) or managing director (MD), or informally ask for others in the organization to give their opinion on the selection made.

- **Decision influencers** – These individuals could be part of your core buyer's current company, be connected from a previous role or via their wider network. Their level of influence will vary at different stages depending on their expertise and the closeness of the relationship. For example, a family member may make an initial introduction, or a key opinion leader (KOL) may highlight a problem area that needs addressing. However, if they are not using the potential supplier for the same service, then an expert, or a previous colleague who does use that service from the same supplier, is likely to have more influence at the supplier selection and validation stage. Remember, some of the decision influencers will come from outside the core buyer's network as they are members of the other decision makers' networks.

Creating a networked audience persona for your core buyer

So, our buyer does not operate alone. On the one hand, this appears to create complexity – how do we keep track of all these relationships? On the other, this networked environment opens up considerable opportunities for the organized and strategic social seller.

As a starting point it is useful to build a persona for your core buyer, decision makers and decision influencers. This is where a close relationship between sales and marketing really pays off, as your marketing team are likely to already have a lot of the information needed to populate your persona. In addition, the sales team will have vital feedback information from actual conversations to bring a more nuanced understanding. An example of this is discussed by Neal in the case study in Chapter 6, where feedback from conversations with tech buyers resulted in a better understanding of the manufacturing companies' pain points and a change in the content and approach.

Let's start with the core buyer persona. A persona is important because it enables you to articulate your ideal core buyer and understand the network that is likely to surround them. Although you may give your persona a name, preferred pronoun allocation and age, this information isn't the most useful. What is most important is understanding the information that will help you partner them in their buyer journey, information such as their goals, decision-making process, what they read, their business pain points and their level of autonomy. In particular, because this persona will be used in social media and to provide information and support at every stage of the buyer's journey, specific social media and search engine marketing (SEM) characteristics should be included, such as hashtags, keywords and group membership.

Researching your persona

It will take some time to research and collate the information for your persona, but the rewards will be invaluable as you will gain a deeper understanding of what a great customer looks like, know how to spot the different signals as they move through the buyer's journey and be able to prioritize your efforts on potential customers who are most likely to buy. To research, look widely across internal and external data sources, ask lots of questions, validate your assumptions against real examples and challenge preconceived ideas. Remember, your buyer persona is likely to have changed considerably over the last few years as the Covid pandemic super-charged the move to virtual relationships and millennials have increasingly moved into decision-making roles.

Download and use the checklist in Template 3.1 to make sure you have considered all the places you can research to build a detailed understanding of your core buyer, including your customer database, market research, social listening, internal feedback loops and data analytics.

A typical networked audience persona

So, what does a typical persona look like and what should you include in it? Remember, your persona needs to provide enough information to be useful but shouldn't be onerous to update and use. You should also share the persona across the team so that everyone knows who they are trying to attract and retain. CRM tools such as HubSpot allow you to store your target personas within the system so that they can be reviewed easily and included or excluded in different campaigns (HubSpot Knowledge Base, 2021).

Although you will have detailed customer information that you use at an individual level when you meet and talk to specific buyers, your persona should focus on an ideal buyer, not an actual customer. It represents an amalgamation of the insights and analysis you have conducted, but also should describe a pool of actual businesses and individuals who exist in your prospect pool. A persona should include four sections – the buyer, the business, the decision makers and the decision influencers.

TEMPLATE 3.1 Persona research checklist

RESEARCH SOURCES:	USEFUL FOR UNDERSTANDING:	RESEARCH INCLUDED Y/N?
Your customer database (CRM system):	Company information (firmographics) – size, turnover, sector, location Buyer demographics – job title, department, preferred pronoun, age, length of service, level of seniority Purchase information – value, frequency, number of sales, length of relationship, lifetime value (LTV), contract period, type of product or service Customer lifecycle information – customer journey, sales cycle length, touchpoint analysis (channels to market)	
Market research:	External market information – desk research, industry reports, government forecasts, event attendance, KOL social media posts could provide insight into the level of confidence in the economy or a particular sector, buyer behaviour by generation, etc Customer attitude and behaviour – polls or questionnaires on your website and at events, focus groups and interviews, provide information on demographics, attitude, needs and pain points	
Social listening:	Audience networks – forum searches, ABM analysis, page, profile, keyword and hashtag analysis provide information on how a buyer's network intersects, buyer signals Attitude – sentiment analysis tracks current feelings about your business Content and channel information – provides insight into the best channels, content and messaging at different stages in the buyer journey	
Internal feedback loops:	Audience networks – customer-facing teams provide insights and information on number of people in decision making group, how decisions are made, customer needs, buyer signals, priorities and pain points Call/interaction outcomes – feedback on response by prospect buyers to different channels, messages and content in meetings, on calls, and via social media interactions	
Data analytics:	Content and channel information – website traffic and behaviour, downloads, time on page, referrals, social media leads, conversion rates, and SEO rankings can be considered at a persona level	

FIGURE 3.2 Completing a persona – the buyer information

PERSONA SECTION 1 – THE BUYER

PERSONA NAME	Useful as a shorthand to identify the segment, could describe their behaviour or the key product they buy
JOB TITLE	Include all variants and multiple titles for SEO. For example, a buyer may typically be an FD or an MD so include: managing director (MD), chief executive (CEO), finance director (FD), chief financial officer (CFO)
SENIORITY	Entry-level, mid-level/senior-level/board-level/owner
LENGTH OF SERVICE	Number of years in current role
DEPARTMENT	For example, Executive/Finance
WORK LOCATION	You may operate nationally but your key focus could be in a specific region
DEMOGRAPHICS: AGE	Approximate age brackets can indicate behaviour – e.g. millennials are more likely to use online resources than boomers
GENDER PRONOUNS	How would they like to be addressed?
COMMUNICATION PREFERENCES	Include all channels – specify all social media and other channels and ideally how they use them. You may create a checklist here which can be ticked off for each channel they use or numbered to show channel priorities
COMMUNICATION CHALLENGES	Do they have a gatekeeper (PA reads all emails)?
CONTENT PREFERENCES	Video, longform blogs, whitepapers, checklists, case studies, email, printed materials, etc
KEYWORDS AND QUESTIONS	What keywords are associated with their typical business issues, what questions do they ask (in search) at each stage of the buyer's journey?
HASHTAGS USED/ENGAGED WITH	Are there any hashtags they follow or use themselves? These could be linked to their company or their personal interests
TYPICAL GOALS/ MOTIVATIONS	What do they want to achieve for their business? Include here their personal motivations such as looking for promotion/wanting to learn more
DECISION TRIGGERS	Are there any particular triggers that indicate where they are in the buyer's journey? Job moves or contract renewals are often hot triggers
TYPICAL CHALLENGES	What is holding them back from reaching their business goals?
EXAMPLES OF ACTUAL QUOTES	Include any quotes that bring to life the opinions and behaviour of the persona
TYPICAL OBJECTIONS	Why would they decide not to buy?
ELEVATOR PITCH	The compelling, succinct description of why your proposition is relevant for this persona

TEMPLATE 3.2 Completing a persona – the buyer information

PERSONA SECTION 1 – THE BUYER	
PERSONA NAME	
JOB TITLE	
SENIORITY	
LENGTH OF SERVICE	
DEPARTMENT	
WORK LOCATION	
DEMOGRAPHICS: AGE	
GENDER PRONOUNS	
COMMUNICATION PREFERENCES	
COMMUNICATION CHALLENGES	
CONTENT PREFERENCES	
KEYWORDS AND QUESTIONS	
HASHTAGS USED/ENGAGED WITH	
TYPICAL GOALS/ MOTIVATIONS	
DECISION TRIGGERS	
TYPICAL CHALLENGES	
EXAMPLES OF ACTUAL QUOTE	
TYPICAL OBJECTIONS	
ELEVATOR PITCH	

NOTE Download and use this template with Figure 3.2 to complete your own buyer persona.

Persona section 1: the buyer

Figure 3.2 explains how to complete your own buyer person using Template 3.2. You will see how each section is designed to provide useful insights which you will be able to use at each stage of the seller's pathway, from finding prospects through to engaging with, relating to and supporting them. Note that some fields, such as job title, content preference and channel, can be held as data tables in your CRM system. These fields can be easily monitored over time and provide useful ongoing performance analytics. Others, such as typical goals, elevator pitch and quotes, will have been gleaned from interviews, focus groups and feedback loops. They are less measurable but are no less important as they highlight the motivations and pain points of your potential buyers.

Download and use Template 3.2 to complete your own buyer persona.

Persona section 2: the business

Figure 3.3 explains how to complete the business information using Template 3.3. You will see that the persona name is the same as that used for the buyer as we want to understand the buyer in the context of their typical business environment.

There are many standard classifications for describing businesses in terms of their legal entity, size, sector, etc. By using these you will be able to apply the same analysis and targeting across social media and other channels as you are using internally. You may also want to include the business model type discussed in Chapter 2. The business section of the persona contains this important firmographic information but also more contextual information, such as the organizational structure and the mindset of the business – are they growing, transforming or well established and stable?

Download and use Template 3.3 to complete the business information for your persona.

Persona section 3: the decision makers

Figure 3.4 explains how to complete the decision makers' information using Template 3.4. Once again, the persona name is the same as that for the buyer. The buyer will be a member of the decision-making group but may not have the final say on the decision. Rather, they are the point person, their role is as

FIGURE 3.3 Completing a persona – the business information

PERSONA SECTION 2 – THE BUSINESS

PERSONA NAME	This will be the same name as that used for the buyer as the persona has four sections – the buyer, the business, the decision makers, the decision influencers
SIC CODE	Include both the high- and lower-level codes as not all lower-level codes may be relevant. For example, the higher-level manufacturing code includes lower-level codes for both furniture and tobacco products. Only one may be relevant to your business
SECTOR	This is often a useful additional field as SIC codes are not always specific enough
BUSINESS MODEL TYPE	Different models have different characteristics and some can be much more likely to use online tools than others. Is your target buyer's business product or service based, does it sell product-focused software or SaaS, or is it a supplier, buyer or intermediary-centric e-commerce business?
COMPANY SIZE	Generally determined by the number of employees and turnover value. Use the standard classifications – sole trader, SMB, SME, large enterprise
NUMBER OF EMPLOYEES	How many people work for the persona organization? These are generally classified in standard ranges
TURNOVER VALUE	Average annual turnover. These are classified in standard ranges
NUMBER OF SITES	How many offices does the persona organization have?
LOCATION	Is the persona business local, national, international? Which countries or regions do they typically operate within?
KEY INSIGHT	Are you looking for businesses in a particular stage or situation – for example, those going through digital transformation, start-ups or owner-managed SMEs?
ORGANIZATION ETHOS	Is the business traditional, hierarchical? What sort of management structure does it typically have?

NOTE Use figure with template 3.3 To complete your own business persona.

TEMPLATE 3.3   Completing a persona – the business information

PERSONA SECTION 2 - THE BUSINESS	
PERSONA NAME	
SIC CODE	
SECTOR	
BUSINESS MODEL TYPE	
COMPANY SIZE	
NUMBER OF EMPLOYEES	
TURNOVER VALUE	
NUMBER OF SITES	
LOCATION	
KEY INSIGHT	
ORGANIZATION ETHOS	

NOTE Download and use this template with Figure 3.3 to complete your own business persona.

FIGURE 3.4 Completing a persona – the decision makers' information

PERSONA SECTION 3 – THE DECISION MAKERS

PERSONA NAME	This will be the same name as that used for the buyer as the persona has four sections – the buyer, the business, the decision makers, the decision influencers
GROUP TYPE	Are decisions made by a formal or informal group – for example, a purchasing committee and strict criteria, sign-off by a senior colleague, or an ad hoc group organized for making this decision?
GROUP DYNAMIC	Is the decision typically made collectively or by a senior leader within the group? Does any role have the right of 'veto'?
GROUP MEMBERSHIP: NUMBER	How many people are typically involved in making the decision?
GROUP MEMBERSHIP: ROLES	What roles and levels of role are typically represented in the decision-making group?
GROUP PROCESS	What is the typical process for making decisions?
SALES CYCLE TIME	How long does the typical decision-making process take (from problem identification to purchase)?
CONTENT PREFERENCES	What content does the wider group require to aid decision-making?
TYPICAL OBJECTIONS	Why would they decide not to buy?
KEY INSIGHT	Are there particular points in the buyer journey where the decision-making group can have an important impact either positively or negatively?

NOTE Use figure with Template 3.3 to complete your own decision maker persona.

TEMPLATE 3.4 Completing a persona – the decision maker's information

PERSONA SECTION 3 - THE DECISION MAKERS
PERSONA NAME
GROUP TYPE
GROUP DYNAMIC
GROUP MEMBERSHIP: NUMBER
GROUP MEMBERSHIP: ROLES
GROUP PROCESS
SALES CYCLE TIME
CONTENT PREFERENCES
TYPICAL OBJECTIONS
KEY INSIGHT

NOTE Download and use this template with Figure 3.4 to complete your own deci sion maker persona.

the lynchpin of the process. They may have identified the problem, or their department may be the key beneficiary of the appointment, so they will be heavily invested and keen for the decision to coincide with their preferences.

By understanding the dynamics and members of the decision-making group you can support the buyer in supplying and sharing relevant information, build awareness and trust in you, your business and your solution, and positively encourage a decision in your favour.

You will be reliant on good feedback loop information from both customers and sales staff to populate typical decision-maker information. However, sales cycle times and content preferences can be ascertained from your CRM system and data analytics.

Download and use Template 3.4 to complete the decision makers' information for your persona.

Persona section 4: the decision influencers

Figure 3.5 explains how to complete the decision influencers' information using Template 3.5. This final section considers whether there are any important influencers you should be aware of. Influencers include someone who introduces you to the buyer, a previous customer who acts as a referee or provides a case study, and team members who may trial or use the purchase.

Remember, B2B decisions are extremely important to the buyer. Making a bad decision can have a long-term negative impact on the business and the buyer's perception and career within the organization. Influencers who support your case help your buyer justify their decision, give them the confidence to make the decision, and provide an external validation of you and your solution.

Download and use Template 3.5 to complete the decision influencers' information in your persona.

Your persona will be invaluable when you start reaching out and connecting and engaging with your prospective buyers because it not only describes what they look like and who is involved in the decision, it also digs into their motivations and helps you understand how they might behave. Kim Watts, in the interview on page 66, considers what implication these motivations might have on engagement expectations.

FIGURE 3.5 Completing a persona – the decision influencer's information

PERSONA SECTION 4 – THE DECISION INFLUENCERS	
PERSONA NAME	This will be the same name as that used for the buyer as the persona has four sections – the buyer, the business, the decision makers, the decision influencers
INTERNAL INFLUENCERS	Consider people **within** the buyer's organization who are not part of the decision-making group. They could be people who can act as introducers or the decision maker's team members. For each stage of the buyer journey highlight the internal key influencers by type: • Problem identification • Solution exploration and requirement building • Validation and supplier selection • Consensus creation and future problem solving
EXTERNAL INFLUENCERS	Consider people **outside** the buyer's organization who might influence the decision. They could be members of a LinkedIn or Facebook group, an expert, or recognized thought leader. For each stage of the buyer journey highlight the external key influencers by type: • Problem identification • Solution exploration and requirement building • Validation and supplier selection • Consensus creation and future problem solving
INFLUENCER CHANNEL PREFERENCE	How much do these influencers use social media, via which channels and what is the opportunity for you to connect and engage with them?
INFLUENCER IMPACT	How important are the influencers in the final decision?
CONTENT	Is there an opportunity to create content with/for influencers?
KEY INSIGHT	Who are they influencing – the buyer, the decision-making group?

TEMPLATE 3.5 Completing a persona – the decision influencer's information

PERSONA SECTION 4 - THE DECISION INFLUENCERS	
PERSONA NAME	
INTERNAL INFLUENCERS	
EXTERNAL INFLUENCERS	
INFLUENCER CHANNEL PREFERENCE	
INFLUENCER IMPACT	
CONTENT	
KEY INSIGHT	

NOTE Download and use this template with Figure 3.5 to complete your own buyer persona.

INTERVIEW
Kim Watts, Senior Lecturer, University of Bath, B2B Consultant (Watts, 2022)

Kim Watts lectures at the University of Bath and also works as a B2B consultant with start-ups in the technology and engineering sector. Her clients are smaller and medium-sized enterprises in scale-up mode which have recognized the need to change their business from a product and technology orientation to a market orientation.

How does mindset affect how buyers behave on social media?

I believe people are in two modes at work: they're either in self-promotion or self-preservation mode. Those who are in the self-promotion phase tend to be people who are three to six months into their new jobs, those who want to make a change in the way their business operates, want to stamp their ownership on their product or job and their role to show they've added value. People in the self-promotion phase seek out new technologies, new solutions, new ways of doing things. They're looking to make a big splash, do things in a way that no one's done it before. They are highly visible and active in social and leave a digital footprint rich in information.

Conversely, people who are in self-preservation mode are playing safe, keeping their head under the parapet, doing enough to get by but not so much as to get put into the firing line. These are the buyers that are not as visible in social, they don't need to engage there and be seen. They may have just as much power and have decision-making authority. They could be just starting a family, be in their later career, or closer to a pension, so they operate in a self-preservation mode. These buyers are often missed digitally because it's harder to find out what makes them tick. A lot of the social and digital monitoring assumes you can research a digital footprint, but buyers in self-preservation mode may not be leaving any signals there. However, this doesn't mean they aren't buying or networking and researching. They may look at information on social media, connect with people they have met at a face-to-face event, and ask for recommendations by phone. Because they are less open to risk, they are more likely to respond to direct, private messages from people they know and rely on previous relationships. They don't necessarily need to prove themselves and therefore finding something new may be less important than making a safe decision.

When you conduct your audience analysis, ensure you understand which type of behaviour they are likely to exhibit as this will help you set realistic expectations and targets.

How does social media support B2B prospecting?

Gone are the days of cold calling. People value their time and are also hesitant to answer phone calls. So, if the person on the other end of the phone call doesn't add value, you don't want to engage with them.

To make any outbound connection work, by whatever channel, you must do your research. Are you contacting the right person? Do you understand the value that you offer to them? How will you reach them in a way that adds value to their day? Social media is invaluable in providing insights to understand and find your audience because it has made people more visible. By looking on LinkedIn you can see who the decision-making unit is, the organizational structures, who works there and understand what the company does. Others such as Glassdoor, Instagram or Facebook provide an insight into the company culture so you can establish fit before you reach out. So, although you are reaching out to fewer people, your conversion rate is higher because you've done the research and you know who they are and what they are likely to be interested in.

Why are networks so important in B2B decision making?

Your network is a brilliant way not only to save time but also to reduce risk in decision making. In general, the higher up people are in their careers, the more likely they are to be risk-averse decision makers. This means they are keener to rely on proven, tested and tried solutions and go to their networks, social or otherwise, to get recommendations.

Again, it's self-preservation or self-promotion. If you're in self-preservation mode, you actively seek out recommendations. There is a wealth of information that you could research, but time is valuable, and by going to your network you instantly have six solutions from people that you kind of know or trust, instead of having 10,000 by boiling the ocean. Social media isn't the motivator, but it's a powerful tool in time saving and efficiency.

Why is social selling so useful to sales?

Probably because it is so much more than selling. It's social networking, social supporting, it's helping people to buy rather than selling. Personally, I think sales and social selling needs to be rebranded as it's really consultation.

No one bought a train from a tweet, no one spent £2 million from a post. Salespeople should only get involved when the level of risk is high enough that the buyer can't make the decision on their own. They need to speak to someone to know more. It's when that level of discomfort comes into place where the person is out of their depth. So, they need someone to consult with, a salesperson.

Sales done well is all about how you can inform, educate and support your buyers to make their choice and social selling enables you to build strong individual relationships with your network to facilitate this.

How do you decide which channels to use for social selling?

To be successful you must go where your customer is – if your customer is active in certain Discord servers in Reddit, you've got to be there and be comfortable being there.

If you haven't understood your customer segment properly and your profiles aren't developed enough, you risk going for the obvious channels, the quick wins, the lowest common denominator. It's easy to rely on LinkedIn, get a few conversions, find those self-promoters. But you're only seeing half the story, or a quarter of the story, because there are far fewer people in self-promotion phase than self-preservation. So, you are limiting yourself if you are just on LinkedIn because you're not seeing the whole of your prospect base.

There are so many channels that people could be on when making decisions. You need to decide where we are going to get the greatest impact from a sales and marketing perspective and use social listening and other research to find out where they are and what they are talking about there.

Using social listening to understand your networked audience

As detailed in the persona research checklist at the start of this chapter, social listening is useful in several areas, particularly in understanding networked audiences, attitude and content information.

Networked audiences

Forum searches, account-based marketing (ABM) analysis, page, profile, keyword and hashtag analysis all provide information on how a buyer's network intersects and can help identify buyer signals.

In the interview on page 73, Nathan Shilton and Raven Wheatley-Hawkins discuss how to identify and engage with networked audiences using forums. Used effectively, a social listening tool can find forums where communities are highly engaged around a specific topic. It is then possible to understand

FIGURE 3.6 An example demographic output for a business analysing the topic of 'sustainability'

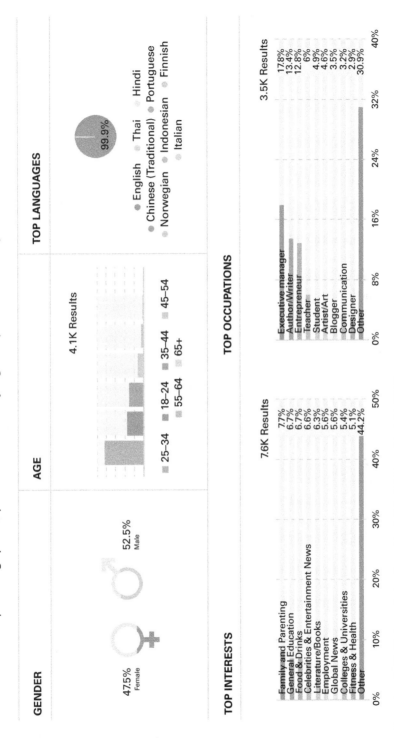

GENDER

47.5% Female

52.5% Male

AGE

4.1K Results

25–34 18–24 35–44 45–54 55–64 65+

TOP LANGUAGES

99.9%

English Thai Hindi
Chinese (Traditional) Portuguese
Norwegian Indonesian Finnish
Italian

TOP INTERESTS

7.6K Results

Family and Parenting 7.7%
General Education 6.7%
Food & Drinks 6.7%
Celebrities & Entertainment News 6.6%
Literature/Books 6.3%
Employment 5.6%
Global News 5.6%
Colleges & Universities 5.4%
Fitness & Health 5.1%
Other 44.2%

0%   10%   20%   30%   40%   50%

TOP OCCUPATIONS

3.5K Results

Executive manager 17.8%
Author/Writer 13.4%
Entrepreneur 12.8%
Teacher 6%
Student 4.9%
Artist/Art 4.6%
Blogger 3.5%
Communication 3.2%
Designer 2.9%
Other 30.9%

0%   8%   16%   24%   32%   40%

Reproduced with kind permission from Adroit (Adroit Data and Insight, 2022) the key pain points and problems, create specific valuable content for the audience and join in the conversation. In the demographic output in Figure 3.6 there is a high correlation between younger age groups and specific job roles and interest areas that could be used to develop content and conversations and identify individuals in other channels.

Attitude

Sentiment analysis tracks your audience's current feelings about your business overall or about a specific topic or content pillar.

The example output in Figure 3.7 analyses the topic of 'sustainability'. Overall, the net sentiment is positive and there are high volumes of mentions (results), engagement and potential reach. Sentiment analysis can also be used to monitor exceptional moods. In Figure 3.7 there is a spike in July. Further investigation showed that this coincided with a general increase in social media activity around the UK's 'Freedom Day' (when Covid restrictions were lifted). Many people were commenting on social media on the impact a return to commuting could have on the environment and sustainable living. A high-interest topic area with a positive net sentiment can help improve your buyers' perceptions around your business if you genuinely have value to add. However, be careful that you do not get lost in the noise.

You may wish to conduct your sentiment analysis across multiple topics to see the share of conversation for each topic and whether the sentiment varies by topic. Figure 3.8 shows how the sentiment varies by subtopic within the overall area of sustainability, with each line representing a different subtopic.

The same approach can be used to monitor share of voice for organizations, either by an organization's mentions or, if a topic is combined, by looking at how much an organization is represented in certain conversation topics.

Content information

Social listening provides useful insights into the most important content areas and potential messaging themes for different stages in the buyer journey.

The example output in Figure 3.9 analyses the topic of 'sustainability'. The key themes can be viewed as a word cloud to help pick out other potential conversations to monitor or exclude.

FIGURE 3.7 An example output for a business analysing the topic of 'sustainability', showing results (mentions), engagement, potential reach and sentiment analysis

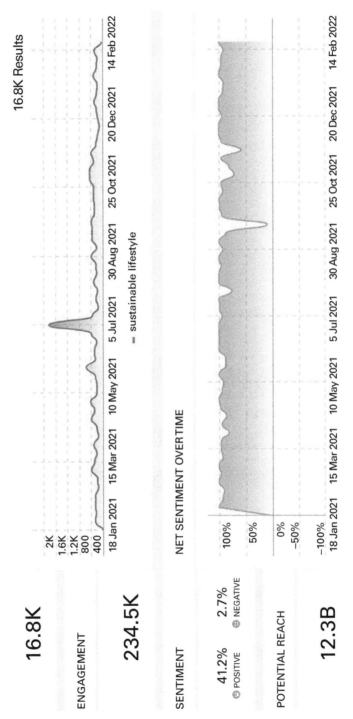

FIGURE 3.8   An example output for a business analysing the topic of 'sustainability', showing variations in sentiment for different subtopics

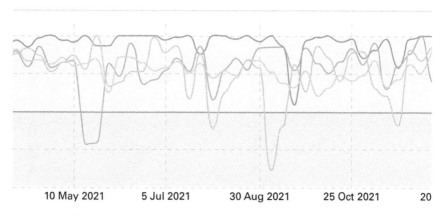

Reproduced with kind permission from Adroit (Adroit Data and Insight, 2022).

FIGURE 3.9   An example output for a business analysing the topic of 'sustainability', showing the relative importance of different themes

Reproduced with kind permission from Adroit (Adroit Data and Insight, 2022).

Reviewing the hashtags commonly used in the conversations helps to determine the key ones to use in your own campaigns to achieve best reach. The example output in Figure 3.10 analyses the topic of 'sustainability'. It includes some hashtags that you might expect, such as #COP26 and #sustainableliving, but others which you might not, e.g. #DigitalMarketing and #Onlineadvertising. Further analysis shows that there are lots of posts that use the digital marketing/ads hashtags when referring to sustainable

FIGURE 3.10   An example output for a business analysing the topic of 'sustainability', showing the most important hashtags

Reproduced with kind permission from Adroit (Adroit Data and Insight, 2022).

marketing and digital transformation. It is therefore important to confirm the context of hashtag usage to make sure you are choosing the right ones.

Social listening can also be used to identify influencers and this is discussed in more detail in Chapter 8.

INTERVIEW
Nathan Shilton, Digital Director and Raven Wheatley-Hawkins, Digital Marketing Manager, Adroit (Shilton, 2022) discuss how to identify and engage with networked audiences using forums.

Background

Adroit is an international data and insight agency that works with renowned brands such as Age UK, UNHCR, SSE, Plan International, PDSA, Baxi and the BMJ. They have a particular strength in social listening insight and analysis and use a variety of tools to help their clients differentiate themselves, identify new opportunities and respond to changing customer needs.

Nathan heads up the digital insight division and Raven is responsible for social media.

How do you use social listening for B2B?

We use social listening to find connections, to identify who people are, who they ought to be engaged with and who they should be following. It helps us understand the conversations around particular content pillars, find influencers, understand how people feel and measure the effectiveness of campaign activity.

What tools do you use for social listening and how are they useful for social selling?

We use Talkwalker (for social listening) and Audiense (for audience intelligence) as well as Google to investigate search insights, listen to and review Twitter, news articles, blogs, forums, Facebook and LinkedIn. It is harder to look at social platforms outside of Twitter because their content isn't as public.

Forums and blogs are very useful for B2B because specific niche markets will have a forum that is usually more important than any other platform. With social listening we can see what people are saying, identify specific problems and advise clients on topics and content that will really engage their audience. Listening is really valuable for B2B content development and finding out where the problems are and where the business can fix them.

Is it possible to use social listening tools to identify networked audiences?

We use Audiense (audience intelligence) to build up a view of audience networks. We group together different audience segments based on the accounts they follow, shared keywords and bio information. The data is typically Twitter-based because it is such an open channel. We can then delve into each of those individual networks to gain further insights.

We can also find networked audiences using forums. To do this we:

- use keywords, hashtags or build specific industry-clauses
- refine the keywords, hashtags and clauses to match a specific problem that is being searched for
- look at where they're searching for this problem in the forums and identify the forums where this problem is being discussed
- join the forum, which is itself a networked audience
- measure and track the amount and type of activity that's happening in that forum
- identify other forums that are also talking about this area
- create content specifically for these forums and look for linked areas of conversation to spark further content

By creating content that is really relevant to the questions/topic areas in the forum, our blogs are super-relevant. We are able to generate marketing-qualified leads when prospects request our gated content and sales-qualified leads once that content is downloaded and actioned.

How do you use social listening for competitor analysis?

We can take a sector or a list of competitors and benchmark any organization against them. A range of data can be looked at, including share of voice, engagement, mentions and sentiment. We can also look at search trends on Google in order to create a share of search, which has evidence to suggest it can be a long-term predictor of market share.

How do you use social listening for market intelligence?

We look not just at what the brand is saying, we also consider combining topics. For example, a boiler manufacturer might see that there is a whole conversation around air source heat pumps and because government legislation is affecting their ability to sell traditional gas boilers, it is important for them to be able to monitor those conversations. They can start engaging in these conversations and become an authority within an emerging topic.

Using keyword analysis to understand your audience

Hashtags and keywords are closely related. First used in 2007 on Twitter to group collections of tweets together, hashtags are now used by most social media platforms. Preceded by the # symbol, they can be brand names, words or phrases and are used by individuals and algorithms to understand areas of interest. Keywords are the words and phrases used in search queries. Google looks for content on the web that matches the keywords to decide what to serve in response to the query. Organizations try to identify the top keywords their customers use to find out about their products and services and use these in their online and social media content.

In social selling, if you know the questions your buyers are asking, and the keywords that define these, at each stage of the buyer's journey you will have some powerful information to support your company and personal social media profiles' visibility and relevant content creation.

Keyword analysis can be produced by looking at your Google Analytics, and in particular Google Search Console, to provide information on how your visitors found you and your competitors. In addition, reviewing hashtags that your buyers engage with will often reinforce the most important words and phrases. Tools such as AnswerThePublic, Semrush and BuzzSumo (BuzzSumo, 2022) can give more detailed insights. In larger organizations, liaise with your marketing and digital teams to make sure you have access to information they may already have.

What next with your networked audience understanding?

So, you now have a thorough and reliable understanding of who you are trying to find and convert to meet your long-term sales aspirations. By creating personas that can be shared with sales and marketing and input into your CRM system, you can ensure you have the right content and connect with all the relevant people in the buyer network.

In the next few chapters, we will explore how you use this insight to meet your goals and add value to these important relationships. For example, you may target specific organizations and put real names into the network for an ABM approach. In addition, as you start to deepen personal relationships with specific individuals you will gain additional knowledge that you can use to personalize and tailor the content you share and the discussion you have.

In the next chapter we will look at your personal brand and how it works in tandem with your business's brand. The work you have done to understand your typical buyer (persona) will help you identify the keywords, hashtags and groups you will want to consider using in your own branding and activity.

Bibliography

Adroit Data and Insight (2022) Social selling example output, Cirencester

B2B Marketing (2019) Number of decision-makers for buying B2B tech revealed, www.b2bmarketing.net/en-gb/resources/news/number-decision-makers-buying-b2b-tech-revealed (archived at https://perma.cc/6LAD-48MK)

BuzzSumo (2022) Find the content that performs best, buzzsumo.com (archived at https://perma.cc/WPN3-EQVV)

HubSpot Knowledge Base (2021) Create and edit personas, knowledge.hubspot. com/contacts/create-and-edit-personas (archived at https://perma.cc/ZWL4-557D)

N. W.-H. R. Shilton (2022) Digital Director, Social Media Manager, Adroit [interview] (10 January 2022)

K Watts (2022) Senior Lecturer University of Bath, B2B Consultant [interview] (5 January 2022)

04

The interdependent brand

Differentiating your business through mature relationships and effective content marketing

Developing your personal brand alongside your company brand is an essential component of a social selling strategy. Learn about how interdependent brand relationships help you to differentiate yourself and your business in a competitive environment with compelling thought leadership, engaging content and a consistent approach.

Understanding the interdependent brand

Social media has changed the relationship between consumers/buyers and brands, and in B2B it has also changed our relationship with the businesses we work for and the buyers they sell to.

FIGURE 4.1 The three-way interdependent brand relationship

FIGURE 4.2 Moving from co-dependency to interdependency

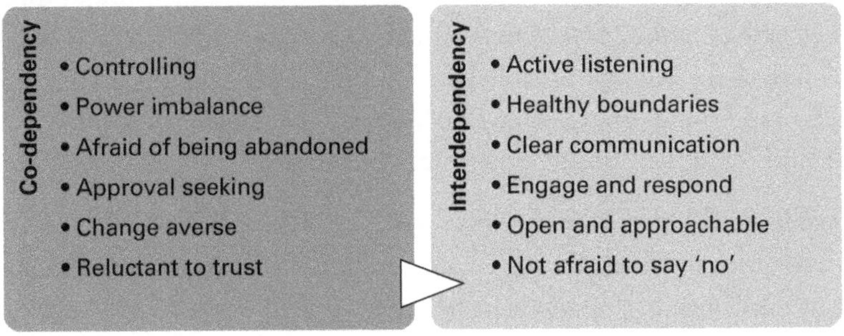

No longer is the brand-to-buyer relationship a one-way traffic of information and stories, it has become a three-way collaboration of mutual interdependency (Figure 4.1). And this change is positive – for the brand, the salesperson and the buyer. Interdependent relationships are mature, healthy and constructive and by nurturing them with your buyers and sales and marketing teams you can co-create brand experiences that embrace your community.

So, what does interdependence mean? The term derives from relationship theory. Co-dependent relationships are characterized by a power imbalance. In our personal lives this can manifest itself in many negative ways, leading to controlling behaviour, a reluctance to change and a lack of trust (The Gender & Sexual Therapy Center, 2019). When considering a brand-to-consumer relationship pre-social media (and still today for some more traditional brands), these traits prevent them from forging open and transparent interactions with their customers and followers.

Mature brands, those which have embraced social media and nurtured an interdependent relationship, are proactive in encouraging their community to be involved, to express themselves and share ideas and information (Figure 4.2). Importantly, they also are shaped by their community, changing the way they communicate, how they operate and even their views because of the community's influence, where community means not only your buyers and followers but also your staff, partners and suppliers.

Glynn and D'Esopo touch on this in their report *B2B Brands in the Human Era* (Glynn, 2018), which highlights the importance of the brand in B2B decision making. They could almost be defining social selling when they point out, 'Brand drives leads and sales, but more importantly, brand fosters lasting relationships. B2B companies establish genuine partnerships with their customers, and they infuse their internal culture with an inspiring purpose and identity. It is the B2B companies that drive their brand through their employees, and, therefore, through their customer interactions, that will thrive in the Human Era' (Glynn, 2018).

B2B brands focus on the importance of their relationships in the way they create and build their brand from their behaviour:

- **Recognize the importance of the voice of each stakeholder** – We are all brands too and the meeting of our personal brands and the business's brand is a meeting of equals. The values and beliefs of your employees, customers and wider society expectations of the behaviour of what it means to be a value-driven or ethical businesses will shape your brand values and behaviour. Your employees, customers, suppliers and followers can become partners in telling your brand story by sharing content and information they are happy to be aligned with. As almost two-thirds of consumer decisions are in part affected by the brand's position on societal or political issues (Stephens, 2019), it is increasingly important for B2B brands to be clear about their position and how they will express and defend it.

- **Demonstrate empathy and involvement** – An interdependent brand is always ready to listen, change and grow. They are confident to stand up for what they believe in and will benefit from being aligned with their community. For example, in 2021 the state of Texas passed new and very restrictive abortion laws. Wanting to support its female staff, Salesforce vowed to help *'relocate'* all employees who *had 'concerns about access to reproductive healthcare'* to outside of Texas and offered to pay relocation costs to all female staff who were concerned. When the story broke on social media, Salesforce benefited from its stance of supporting its female staff's reproduction rights with high levels of positive sentiment and wide coverage in the news (Interbrand Thinking, 2021a). Salesforce could easily have ignored this controversial issue, but they decided to demonstrate their brand values openly by taking a position on the issue.

- **Transparent and trusting** – Social selling is about empowering your business network by trusting them to share, comment on and add to the discussion around your brand. When your network can add to and enhance corporate content with their personal experience and views, it becomes more authentic, interesting and believable. Social selling encourages your team to build highly engaged social networks, create their own personal brands and add their thoughts and ideas to branded content to increase personalization and interaction. These trusted and transparent interactions encourage deeper, more loyal relationships for your business. In addition, because engagement rates on personal social profiles are much higher than those for corporate profiles, the impact and reach of your content are considerably enhanced.

So, as you develop your B2B social selling strategy, consider how you can embrace the interdependent characteristics of active listening, healthy boundaries, clear communication, ready engagement, a timely considered response, an approachable and open manner, and the commitment to stand up for what you believe in both at a brand and an individual level.

Why your company brand is so important in B2B social selling

In the three-way interdependent relationship your company brand is the backbone of your strategy. It will set the tone and parameters of your relationship with buyers and differentiate your offer in the market. The content created and used here is likely to be driven by marketing but must be connected to and collaborated on with the sales team.

There are many definitions to describe a brand. According to Interbrand, 'a brand is the sum of all expressions by which an entity (person, organization, company, business unit, city, nation, etc) intends to be recognized' (Interbrand Thinking, 2021b). Those expressions can occur in an almost endless number of ways, including personal interactions, customer experiences, and via marketing and sales content. Ultimately the expression of your brand enables you to:

- **be recognized** – your audience notices you, knows who you are and what you stand for
- **be differentiated** – you have clear, defined attributes that mean you stand out from the crowd
- **build an emotional connection** – brands tell stories about themselves triggering emotional connections which resonate at a different level than the rational motives of features and pricing
- **express your values** – your ethos is inherent in your brand and symbolizes what your audience should expect from you

- **demonstrate quality** – the brand assures your audience of the quality of the experience you deliver or product you sell
- **build trust** – by consistently behaving according to your brand values, you can build trust with your audience
- **support your pricing model** – the higher the value your audience places on your brand, the more you can use this to support your pricing, reducing the need to discount or become commoditized
- **create tribes** – communities congregate around strong brands, improving their personal branding through association with your brand and enhancing your brand's value through their support

You should strive to create a brand for your business that people (your audience) and other businesses aspire to and feel connected to at both an emotional and a rational level. Strong brands have an inherent value beyond the revenue their business generates because the reputation of the brand can carry the business through difficult times and add momentum to new opportunities. In addition, the emotional, intrinsic value of the brand is arguably even more important when making a B2B purchasing decision. When both consumer and business customers of tablets were asked about the most important factors in their decision making (Figure 4.3), the brand factor scored more highly for business customers than for consumers (Glynn, 2018).

FIGURE 4.3 How brand impacts B2B and B2C purchases: a breakdown of tablet purchases

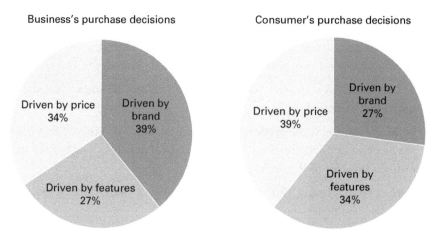

Business's purchase decisions

Driven by price
34%

Driven by brand
39%

Driven by features
27%

Consumer's purchase decisions

Driven by brand
27%

Driven by price
39%

Driven by features
34%

The case study demonstrates how important the brand is for Direct Line for Business.

CASE STUDY
Direct Line for Business: B2B branding

Direct Line is one of the UK's largest insurers. It is usually considered to be a B2C brand but with over 450,000 small business customers (B2B Marketing, 2018) and a range of products tailored to their needs, it also operates as a B2B brand (Direct Line, 2021).

Like many hybrid organizations, those that sell to both end consumers and other businesses, Direct Line for Business recognizes that B2B buyers are human too and make buying decisions both rationally and emotionally. Claire Sadler, Head of Transformation at Direct Line for Business, noted: *'B2B advertising is often rational rather than emotional but in insurance the risk to a business owner can be greater than to someone personally. We are all human beings and we do not become a different person when we go to work'* (Hemsley, 2019).

Its 2018 campaign, 'Keeping up with your world', looked to humanize the B2B relationship between the business and its customers by creating a branding campaign around SME entrepreneur Jenna. Aimed at entrepreneurs and small and micro business owners, and deployed on social media, PR, TV, radio and print, the ad (YouTube, 2018) and additional content such as the Direct Line online insurance tool, the campaign followed Jenna's ups and downs as a business owner and simplified the purchasing experience. With humour and emotion used to share her challenges and joys, Direct Line for Business showed how personal the journey is for every business owner and why it is important therefore to take a personalized approach to business insurance.

Fast paced and engaging, its compelling storytelling brought an emotional, empathetic experience into their branding, helping them stand out from their competitors and set the stage for a more personalized connection with their customers.

Watch the ad here: https://www.youtube.com/watch?v=4outMGEoOVo&t=1s

---

How to create a differentiated social selling positioning for your business

A positioning statement will hold your social selling strategy together, identifying where you and your business add value to your customers and helping you stand out, for the right reasons, from your competitors. Positioning represents a unification of communication and delivery between your business, sales and marketing, and your customers. It is the space your business occupies in the minds of your customers. For example, you cannot differentiate your company on customer service if you deliver poorly in this area. In many cases your marketing team may well have defined your business's positioning, but if not, you can use this methodology to clarify the unique position to take for your business.

Typical ways to differentiate your business

There are many ways to differentiate your business's products or services that create value for your customers, but the five most common are:

- **Price** – Competitive pricing or value is a simple and clear way to differentiate your business, however it is not without some risk. Price-sensitive buyers will be attracted to you but may not attribute much value to the other aspects of your business. If a competitor was able to beat or match your price, you may lose out to them. Businesses that do well positioning on price are those which can control their own supply chain, are highly efficient or identify a gap in the market for a product at a specific price point (for example a mid-priced option is identified in a market with only high and low prices currently). SaaS solutions to CRM such as Hootsuite and Mailchimp have been able to differentiate themselves on price against more bespoke competitors such as Microsoft Dynamics.

- **Characteristics** – Your product or service may have a particular characteristic with which it is synonymous and you can use this to differentiate yourself. Car marques do this very well, with Volvo being associated with safety, Toyota with reliability and Porsche with performance. When Kia entered the US market in 1994, they had only two models and a very poor reputation. By focusing on improving the product and offering a ten-year warranty, they began to challenge Toyota's established reliability characteristic.

- **Applications** – How to use your product can be strong positioning and can make it very clear how you meet your target audience's needs. Apple positioned itself as making products for creative people and industries, with bespoke apps and tools that designers and musicians loved. Other tech brands have created technology that more than competes and is much cheaper, but they still struggle to nudge Apple from its creative application top spot.

- **Quality/luxury** – Customers are willing to pay higher prices for quality, particularly when it is associated with luxury. The product features may be very similar, but the prestige of a luxury brand and its associations attract some consumers. In tech, IBM was always seen as a quality brand. 'You never get fired for buying IBM' is a well-known adage, but the actual quality of the service and delivery may well have been outperformed by more agile new entrants.

- **Purpose** – more recently, products have started to be differentiated by the values they embody and this has become increasingly important in B2B as more millennials are promoted to decision-making roles. Simon Sinek is perhaps most well known for encouraging businesses to focus on their purpose, their 'why'. He argues that 'people don't buy what you do… or how you do it… they buy why you exist' (Sinek, 2016). TrueStart is a family-owned challenger coffee brand whose purpose is to change people's perception of coffee and bring you 'pure coffee', a 'mind-blowing elixir' which is natural, good for you, and produced ethically and sustainably (TrueStart, 2021). Having a clear purpose attracts other businesses (and individuals) with similar values and can be a stickier, more loyalty-inducing connection than price. For TrueStart, it is ideal for them if the cafés, wholesalers and businesses that make up their B2B customers also share their values.

In reality, most businesses will use more than one element of differentiation, as the combining of two or more elements creates a more unique positioning. For example, Copy House is an independent content marketing agency which has grown exponentially since 2020 when they created a strong, unique and highly differentiated positioning for their business. Their founder's mantra is 'You cannot sell everything to everybody, if you do, you will reach no one' (Strachan, 2021). For this reason, Copy House has focused on operating in the 'double niche of content and FinTech' (Kusak, 2021). If you are a FinTech or technology business needing content marketing, then Copy House is the perfect match.

Know your competitors – their strengths and weaknesses

To differentiate your business you need to know your competitors well. Not just who they are but how they behave and their strengths and weaknesses in relation to your business. The positioning map in Template 4.4 is a good way to visualize your relative strengths and where you may be at a disadvantage. You may decide to use several maps if there are a number of different attributes you want to compare. Some example useful positioning map comparisons are:

- **Service levels and cost/price** – this allows you to tease out whether you can beat your competitors with both a high performance in customer service and a reasonable cost.

- **Specific characteristics** – these will be dependent on your industry and business but can help you focus on the most important characteristics or features you offer. For example, your highly personalized IT solution may be state of the art but take ten months to implement. If your competitor offers a less bespoke but faster solution, you could be in trouble.

- **Behaviours** – comparing how you and your competitors communicate with and gain feedback from customers can help you understand the relative stages of brand interdependence.

For example, Copy House competes against many other content-creation agencies and freelancers but because of its focus on FinTech and the technology sector it is able to carve a unique and strong positioning. Unlike broader-content agencies that work with multiple sectors or full-service agencies with a broader offering than content services, its expertise isn't diluted across multiple industries and specialisms, but it can also offer the full range of content services, unlike specialist FinTech freelancers. Therefore, as clients move from one tech business to another, Copy House's reputation and relationships endure.

TEMPLATE 4.1 Positioning map template

To use:
- Choose the attributes for each axis
- Plot the position for your business and your competitors
- Use as many maps as you need to identify your strongest differentiating attributes

FIGURE 4.4 Competitive positioning map example for Copy House

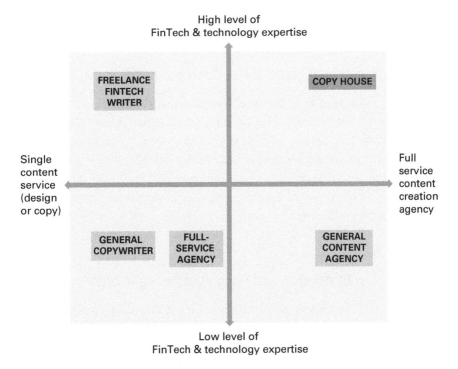

Figure 4.4 illustrates this positioning by type of competitor. In practice you should include the competitor's name or logo.

Kusak, Marketing Manager at Copy House, uses a scale not only to monitor the company's competitors on their positioning in the FinTech and technology content space, but also to benchmark Copy House's performance in terms of SEO, social following and social media impact. Kusak also monitors businesses outside of their sector which innovate in social media, making sure Copy House's social selling remains ahead of competitors.

Download and use Template 4.1 to build your own positioning maps and monitor your competitors.

When building your social selling strategy, you don't need to focus on everything your brand does but you do need to know which aspects are important to your buyers. Remember, it's important to keep on top of what is happening with your competitors. Use social listening and monitoring, sign up for their newsletters and webinars, ask your customers their opinions, compare your SEO rankings and set alerts to see when competitors appear in the news. Your prospects will eventually need to decide between you and them, so being aware of why they should choose you is vital.

Why your personal brand is so important in B2B social selling

People buy from people, so although your company's brand positioning is important and will provide a backdrop for social selling relationships, your personal brand, and that of other key employees, is also important. Consequently, an interdependent brand builds a social selling strategy that embraces the contribution made by employees and builds on the synergy between it and the personal brands of its sales professionals, experts, business development directors and marketers.

How to develop and build your personal brand

Your personal brand is the unique combination of skills and experience that enable you to demonstrate a consistent and differentiated presentation of yourself. We all have a digital footprint and may have multiple representations of ourselves on the different social platforms we engage with. However, in terms of social selling, your personal brand should be the professional representation of you, a combination of your personality, interests and passions in relation to the work that you do. Your personal brand is you, not a cookie-cutter employee representative of your company. It should be based on your expertise and interests, and while being a strong support to your current business, it will also be transferable when or if you move to another organization.

Therefore, when thinking about your personal branding, consider what you want to be known for. Do you have a particular area of expertise or interest, what role do you play in the organization, how would you be able to add value to your community?

Successful entrepreneurs are brilliant at personal branding and use it effectively to complement and supercharge their company's positioning and competitive advantage. For example, Paul Armstrong (Armstrong, 2022) is the founder of HERE/FORTH, a technology advisory (HERE/FORTH, 2022). His business helps other organizations understand how to take advantage of disruptive technology today and for the future. He has built a strong personal brand positioning on his expertise in tech, but it is his high energy and brutally honest and open approach in assessing that tech that makes him stand out from his competitors. His personal brand supports and strengthens HERE/FORTH but has enabled him to branch out into other ventures.

When thinking about developing your personal brand positioning, consider both what is inherently unique to you and important about you.

- Important about you:
    - This first element of your personal brand should be something that is important to you, your business and your buyers. It is an area where you can add real and credible value. Do you have a particular expertise, perhaps you are the designer, engineer, inventor, owner or scientist in your business? Maybe you have some specific technical knowledge or have created a new methodology?

- Unique to you:
    - This is the element which enables your personality to shine through, the reason why people will want to engage with and follow you. It could come through in the way you express yourself but also in the issues or topics you comment on and support. Are you authoritative, witty, incisive? Do you have a strong passion for the environment, equality or mental health awareness?

Paul Armstrong is a disruptive technology expert – that is what is important about him. What is unique is his no-nonsense, honest and incisive analysis and the boundless energy used to impart his views. Together they create a unique and powerful personal brand.

The personal branding agency Jago (Jago, 2022) specializes in supporting individuals to define their personal brand and build a strategy to maximize its impact. They have some useful 'rules' to help focus your personal brand creation and deployment. Download and use the checklist below to remind you what to focus on.

RULES OF PERSONAL BRANDING CHECKLIST (O'KEEFFE, 2021)

1 Have a focus:
- Decide what your key message is & stick to it.
- This will make it easier to create content around your personal brand & help others define you.

2 Be genuine:

- o Your personal brand should be an easy daily filter that you create content and reach out to your audience with.
- o Make it easier on yourself by being you.

3 Tell a story:

- o The most personal way to tell your story is through video.
- o Make use of your smartphone & lean into the camera more.

4 Be consistent:

- o This could be your message, something visually or personality wise.
- o Don't let inconsistencies undermine your personal branding.

5 Be ready to fail:

- o The very best brands always come from continuous trial and error, mistakes & failures.
- o This is relatable and inspiring. People understand reality is far from instant perfection.

6 Create a positive impact:

- o Steadily grow a community around your brand.
- o Always keep in mind the impact you leave on others.
- o Your reputation is your brand.

7 Follow a successful example:

- o Study trends and popular individuals on different social platforms.
- o Learn from people that are doing it well and implement it by putting your own stamp on it.

8 Live your brand:

- o Make your actual lifestyle and brand one and the same.
- o It should be an authentic manifestation of who you are and amplify what you believe.

9 Let others tell your story:

- o Word of mouth is the best PR.
- o Creating value for your audience will result in them sharing and becoming your brand advocates.

Reproduced with permission of Ryan O'Keeffe and Steve Richards, Founders of Jago (O'Keeffe, 2021).

Your strategy may focus on one individual in the business, perhaps the CEO or founder, using their personal brand to support social selling, or you may deploy multiple sales professionals with their own networks, with each focusing on a different area of the business and bringing their unique interest areas into their conversations. Much will depend on the size of your business and the number of people actively involved in social selling; however, every person who social sells for you should be doing so using a consistent and authentic approach centred in a planned personal branding positioning.

Why your buyer is so important in a three-way interdependent brand relationship

The third element in the interdependent brand relationship is your buyer. Their values, motivations, interest areas and behaviours should influence and impact the way you represent yourself and your business. These factors will have a direct impact on your decision on how to position your business in relation to your competitors, or what areas of expertise might be best to highlight in your personal brand. Understanding the drivers that affect your buyers will help your brand strengthen its ability to remain important and connected, and crucially to become the centre of a buyer community. You can gain these insights by speaking directly to buyers, using social listening and other research and analytics, and monitoring the conversations and comments in social media.

How to develop content to attract attention and gain trust

As established in *Social Media Strategy* (Atherton, 2020), there are a number of ways to organize your content to ensure you focus your efforts in a consistent and useful way. Two tools are particularly useful for social selling and work best when used together. They are content pillars and the content value exchange model. The former will help you decide what topics you want to talk about and the latter, the format and style of your content.

Your marketing or sales enablement team is likely to be managing your corporate social profile and posts and creating other content to support you and this will form the spine of your social selling content. But through your social selling dialogue you are 'the voice of the prospect' (Neal, 2022) and should work collaboratively with them to ensure you have the right content for your audience. In addition, you will want to curate and create your own content and deciding what and how to do this will be easier if you use an established methodology.

Using content pillars to support your social selling

Content pillars are thematic groupings that together articulate the differentiating position of your business. They can be created at an organizational/department level or at a personal brand level and provide a compelling reason as to why your buyer should choose you over your competitors. Because social selling is conducted via your own (or your team's) personal social channels, each person will need to define their own content pillars. These pillars will in part come from the business's content pillars but will be demonstrated via each individual personal brand. Figure 4.5 articulates some examples of how content pillars may manifest themselves across the organization:

- Company/department level:
  - In this marketing services provider (MSP) example the organization has identified four areas of expertise and competence that differentiate it from its competitors and are important to both the business and its buyers. They are data expertise, technology expertise, its stance on equality and diversity, and the unique product (agile platform) it has created and owns the IP for. Each of these areas is a content pillar and therefore the business will build an SEO strategy that optimizes these areas and create content across all channels to build credibility and authority in these areas. This content will be managed and delivered at a brand level via the website, corporate social media and other owned channels.
- CEO/founder/MD level:
  - Social selling occurs at a personal level via an individual's personal social channels. Often the leader of the organization is highly connected and influential. They may have a larger following than the business and should have a much more engaged community. They want to promote the business but if they talk about everything their impact may be diluted. They also want to be true to their own principles and interests. Why they set up the business and how they lead it is likely to

be an important driver for them. In the example in Figure 4.5, when defining their personal brand content pillars, the CEO has decided to focus on how they lead and the unique product the business offers. Their leadership pillar fits inside the company's equality and diversity pillar so they will be able to use some company content here. However, they will also be able to share their own opinions and curate other content that they feel is important. Their second pillar is the unique platform. They will talk about this but in terms of why they think it is important and relevant, rather than just sharing corporate content.

- Individual level 1:
  - At this level you could be a salesperson, business director, expert or marketing professional. In a small organization you may be the only frontline salesperson alongside the CEO, but in a larger organization there may be several people at this level. Whatever your organization size, you are likely to head a department and therefore have a particular area of expertise. Perhaps you are responsible for data or technology in the organization, like the individuals shown in Figure 4.5. In this instance each person will talk about the unique product the business offers but also share, curate and comment on either data or technology content.

- Individual level 2:
  - In a larger organization you may have multiple people who are interested in the same content pillars. However, they are unlikely to share exactly the same opinions and preferences within the pillar. At this level the business can benefit from a more specialist approach, perhaps one person is interested in data privacy and another in artificial intelligence (AI). These diversified interests, within a company pillar, add depth and breadth to the business positioning and differentiate the individuals within the organization. However, in every case, the core unique agile platform and its benefits are always featured.

When building your own social selling strategy, ensure each individual builds their personal brand around their perspective of your corporate content pillars. The content pillar approach ensures a consistency across even the largest organization, but it also empowers the individual to add their personal approach and build their personal brand. Remember, in a small business you may only have one person involved in social selling, but you can still take the same approach. In this case, even though you may only

FIGURE 4.5 Applying content pillars across the organization – an example

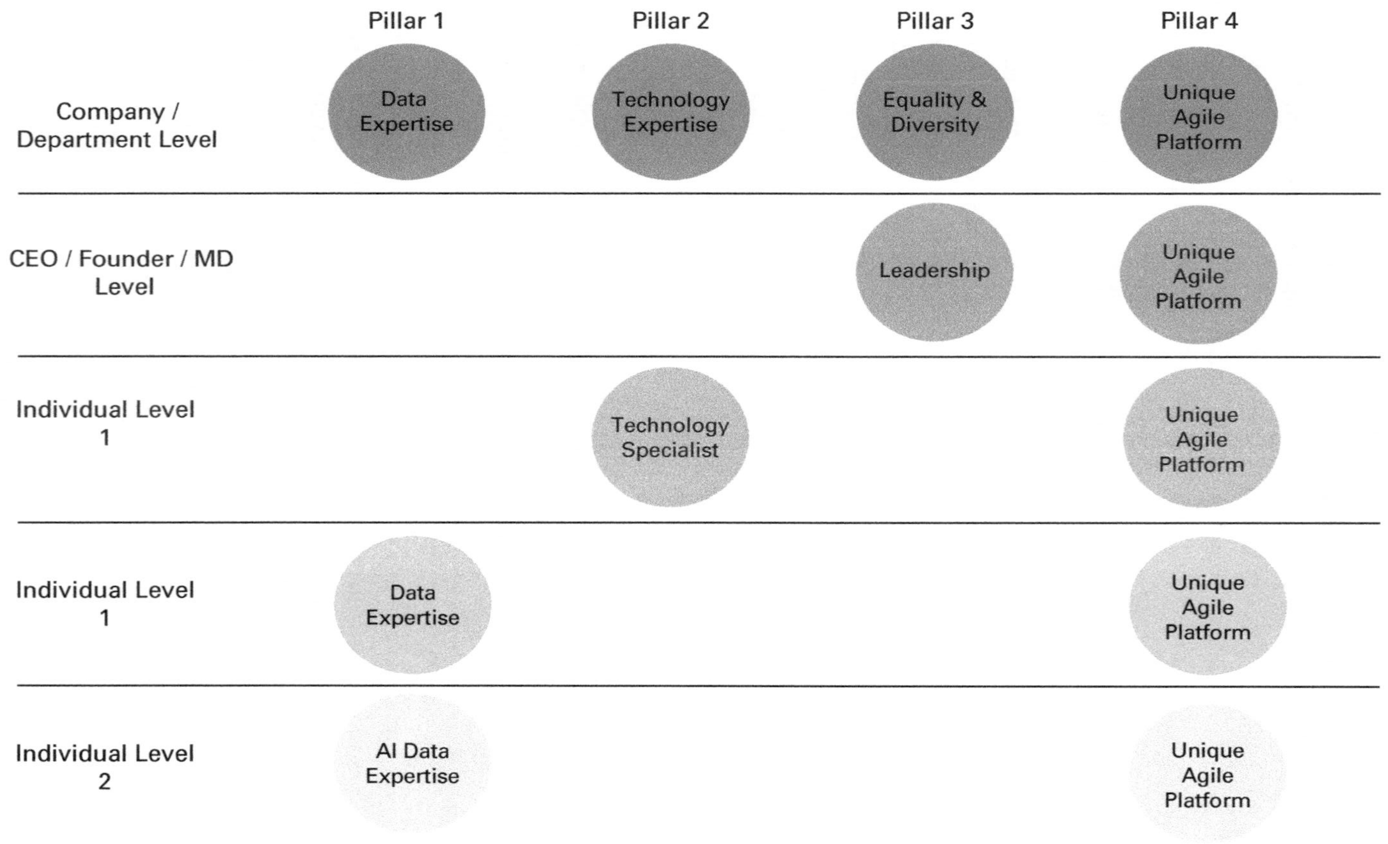

	Pillar 1	Pillar 2	Pillar 3	Pillar 4
Company / Department Level	Data Expertise	Technology Expertise	Equality & Diversity	Unique Agile Platform
CEO / Founder / MD Level			Leadership	Unique Agile Platform
Individual Level 1		Technology Specialist		Unique Agile Platform
Individual Level 1	Data Expertise			Unique Agile Platform
Individual Level 2	AI Data Expertise			Unique Agile Platform

TEMPLATE 4.2 Applying content pillars across your organization

		Pillar 1	Pillar 2	Pillar 3	Pillar 4
1. Identify your company level pillars 2. Pick 2 pillars per person for their social selling content 3. The pillar that each individual chooses should be related to their expertise / interests	Company / Department Level	●	●	●	●
	CEO /Founder/MD Level	●	●	●	●
	Individual Level 1	●	●	●	●
	Individual Level 1	●	●	●	●
	Individual Level 2	●	●	●	●

have one or two company pillars, the person conducting social selling should build their personal brand nested within the company-level pillars.

Download and use Template 4.2 to think about how you strategically apply content pillars across your organization and your social selling team. By using a holistic approach, there is a consistency across the business which has a number of benefits, including improved SEO, access to relevant, centrally created content, and the ability for different individuals to meet the different needs of any buying committee.

In the case study, Copy House shows how they use their MD's personal brand to amplify the company's strong brand positioning.

CASE STUDY
Copy House: Using personal brands for social selling

Copy House is a B2B content marketing agency specializing in the technology and FinTech sectors. Its clients include Meta, Klarna, Lendflo, Travelex and Money Dashboard. The business has grown dramatically since repositioning to specialize in content marketing, technology and FinTech brands. Their success is also highly attributed to the personal brand of MD Kathryn Strachan, which is used to amplify the company's reach and impact.

Copy House recognized that by using personal brands they could showcase the company culture and what happens behind the scenes of the business. By identifying their clients' needs, personalizing content and empathizing, they demonstrate the company's character and have strengthened relationships with potential consumers.

Strachan is constantly active on social media and focuses heavily on networking. She uses platforms such as Twitter and LinkedIn to show both the ups and downs of her personal life and work. Not only does she post about her achievements and the great things happening at Copy House, such as their recent expansion into Europe (Copy House, 2022) and their numerous award wins, she also posts the setbacks – for example, the difficulties of hosting and running events when your Wi-Fi connection is lagging or balancing your work and family commitments when running a successful business.

Showing these real-life situations and insights into her leadership and management challenges allows her to connect with her audience and show them that it's not always smooth sailing. There is a person behind the screen, and as we know, each person has their own wants and needs.

'It's about being honest with your audience. Showing them that we're all human and not every day is a good day' (Strachan, 2021). Creating this genuine personal brand shows your audience the character and values held by the company. So, although it's not a hard sell, it does indirectly entice them and allows them to learn more about you and your business. Research shows that 53 per cent of customer loyalty (Ouellette, 2022) is built through this marketing approach of sharing personal insights as well as thought leadership content.

Creating this relationship could be the difference between someone selecting your brand or choosing a competitor's.

Now that Copy House has dramatically expanded, senior leaders in each department aim to build their personal brands too. Although building this brand and seeing results can take time, it is a worthwhile investment as it creates that trust and credibility between the business and prospect on multiple levels of the business, not just with the MD.

Reproduced by kind permission of Copy House (Kusak, 2021)

Using the content value model to support your social selling

One of the biggest challenges to effective social selling is ensuring that you have a backbone of strong and relevant content that your team can use to support their social selling. Building relationships on social media can be daunting and Chapter 10 talks about how you can create a supportive and

FIGURE 4.6 Mapping the seller's pathway to the buyer's journey

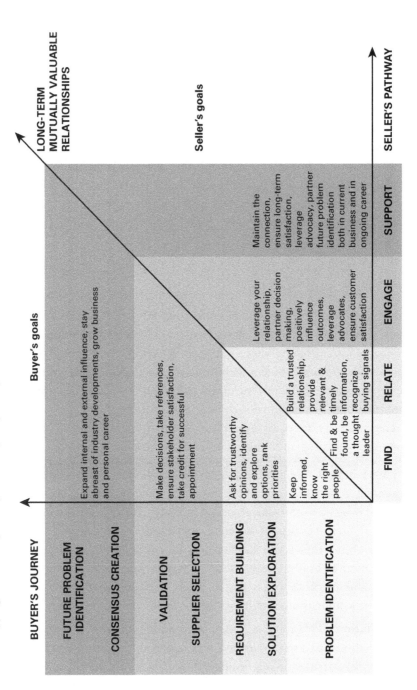

BUYER'S JOURNEY

FUTURE PROBLEM IDENTIFICATION

CONSENSUS CREATION

VALIDATION

SUPPLIER SELECTION

REQUIREMENT BUILDING

SOLUTION EXPLORATION

PROBLEM IDENTIFICATION

Buyer's goals

Expand internal and external influence, stay abreast of industry developments, grow business and personal career

Make decisions, take references, ensure stakeholder satisfaction, take credit for successful appointment

Ask for trustworthy opinions, identify and explore options, rank priorities

Keep informed, know the right people

Find & be found, be a thought leader

Build a trusted relationship, provide relevant & timely information, recognize buying signals

LONG-TERM MUTUALLY VALUABLE RELATIONSHIPS

Seller's goals

Maintain the connection, ensure long-term satisfaction, leverage advocacy, partner future problem identification both in current business and in ongoing career

Leverage your relationship, partner decision making, positively influence outcomes, leverage advocates, ensure customer satisfaction

FIND

RELATE

ENGAGE

SUPPORT

SELLER'S PATHWAY

collaborative culture to build confidence and success. However, if your team is the car, content is the fuel and creating content based on value is the way to supercharge that fuel.

The content value model starts with your buyer and their journey. At every stage they face challenges and have questions that enable them to make decisions and move to the next stage.

Matched to this journey is your seller's pathway (Figure 4.6). How will you find buyers and be found by them? How will you build trust and inspire and motivate your prospects?

The answer is through creating valuable content. Valuable content must be relevant and useful to your buyer, it isn't hard selling, but it does drive engagement and action. Importantly, every piece of content should sit within one of your content pillars and be created for a specific stage in the buyer's journey.

What makes valuable content?

Valuable content is based on meeting your buyers' needs. In the buyer's journey there are seven need states: problem identification, solution exploration, requirement building, supplier selection, validation, consensus creation and future problem identification. As a social seller you want to create and curate content that meets these needs and ensures you are an important part of your buyers' consideration process.

There are six types of need-based content. The first three are more emotionally focused and the remainder more rationally focused:

1 **Entertainment** – Enjoyable content which is often highly sharable. This content is useful at the early stages of the journey, perhaps even before a buyer is ready to start the process. They may engage with you and follow your content because of a shared interest, they enjoy how you present ideas or the topics you discuss. In social selling your personality will contribute to how enjoyable your content is. This content should also be easy and quick to consume, so video content, short personal views, podcasts, animations and infographics work well here.

2 **Inspiration** – This content is compelling and innovative. It is unusual and motivating, sparking discussion and acting to introduce your buyer to new ideas, trends or opportunities. Central to you creating a thought leadership position are your content pillars. Inspiring content requires

you to take a position and be seen as a trusted and knowledgeable voice. This content is especially useful at the problem identification stages of the buyer journey and could take the form of white papers, research, comment pieces, interviews, webinars and blogs.

3 **Support** – This content shows you care and that you empathize with your buyer and their challenges. Sharing your personal challenges and stories humanizes your content and creates additional emotional connections. From simple things like happy birthday messages and good luck GIFs to providing relevant content for a whole buying committee, supportive content can be used across the journey but is particularly useful at the consensus-creation stage and beyond the sale.

4 **Education** – This type of content is often called 'How to'. It is particularly useful at the solution-exploration and requirement-building stages where you can really help your buyer understand the range of possibilities and what each can do for them. Your content should enable the buyer to learn something new and be able to more confidently make a decision. Post-sale, educational content can also help with onboarding. In social selling product demonstration videos, jargon buster explainers and FAQs are great examples of educational content.

5 **Conviction** – Most useful at the supplier-selection and validation stage, this type of content is persuasive and reassuring. Case studies, testimonials and recommendations are powerful ways to give new customers the confidence to pick you.

6 **Information** – Decision making requires facts and stats. Your buyer is likely to be asked to justify why they have chosen you and demonstrate commercially it is the right decision. Comparators, benefit tables, projection models and proprietary information can be powerful communicators and are useful at every stage of the journey. One way to demonstrate your abilities and thought leadership will be by ensuring you have a strong knowledge base about your buyer's needs, their sector and problems, and your own solution.

Combining the content pillar approach with the content value model will enable you to consistently talk about topics you and your buyer care about and deliver relevant and motivating content for every stage of their journey. In Chapter 6 you will see how this translates into an actionable plan.

CASE STUDY

Copy House: Using relevant content for social selling

Copy House is a B2B content marketing agency specializing in the technology and FinTech sectors. Its clients include Meta, Klarna, Lendflo, Travelex, and Money Dashboard. Although some businesses' marketing techniques consist of hard sells, Copy House prefers a more indirect social selling approach that nurtures leads and educates prospective buyers.

Copy House operates on an 80/20 split, meaning that 80 per cent of the content they publish via social media is about thought leadership, events, awards, company culture, etc. The other 20 per cent is demand generation (selling). This can include a campaign advertising the launch of their content design service or an ad to book your free 30-minute consultation.

Through this approach, B2B customers can familiarize themselves with Copy House long before deciding whether they should acquire the agency's services.

For example, by posting on social media, prospects and customers can engage with content. They are able to read case studies, understand why their services are so important, know what the company values are and so on. Prospects can also view where they may be going wrong in their own marketing strategy and learn via the thought leadership content posted by Copy House.

In fact, 92 per cent of B2B buyers (Ouellette, 2022) are willing to engage with a sales professional who is a known industry thought leader, due to the knowledge and experience they provide.

By constantly posting on social media, Copy House is keeping potential customers up to date and aware of what they have to offer. This way, although they may not be ready to purchase a particular service at that time, when they are ready to buy, Copy House is at the forefront of their mind.

They will already have a deep understanding of what the business is, what it sells and how they benefit from it. This method encourages an indirect relationship between Copy House and the prospect, helping Copy House secure sales without the pushy and hard sell tactics.

'Having this constant flow of content keeps our potential customers educated on who our brand is and what we do. So, let's just say in four months, or in eight months' time, they're ready to purchase, they'll think, "Oh yeah, I know Copy House, I know that they produce thought-provoking content for technology and FinTech brands and I'm a technology or FinTech brand that needs content"' (Kusak, 2021).

So social selling helps keep that momentum and communication without being invasive. Unlike other marketing channels that are more direct, social media can focus on the long-term investment and is more subtle about sales. This is perfect in B2B.

Reproduced by kind permission of Copy House (Kusak, 2021).

Ultimately, by creating a strong, differentiated positioning for your business with clear content pillars you will be able to identify how each individual can support the overall thought leadership using their personal areas of expertise. In addition, the personal brands of each individual will be enhanced by association with the organization's brand and the personal brands of their colleagues.

This synergy is an important factor in ensuring the maximum impact from your B2B social selling strategy.

Bibliography

P Armstrong (2022) @paul__armstrong, twitter.com/paul__armstrong (archived at https://perma.cc/3EPP-SA4Y)

J Atherton (2020) *Social Media Strategy: A practical guide to social media marketing and customer engagement* (1st edn), Kogan Page, London

B2B Marketing (2018, July 26) Direct Line for Business campaign aims to 'humanise' business insurance for SMEs, www.b2bmarketing.net/en-gb/resources/news/direct-line-business-campaign-aims-humanise-business-insurance-smes (archived at https://perma.cc/72PQ-GEXW)

L F Binet (2017) *Media in Focus: Marketing effectiveness in the digital era*, IPA, London

Copy House (2022) Copy House, copyhouse.io/introducing-copy-house-europe/ (archived at https://perma.cc/K8P5-DYBH)

Direct Line (2021) Direct Line for Busines, www.directlineforbusiness.co.uk (archived at https://perma.cc/8MMF-WQLV)

S D Glynn (2018) *B2B Brands in the Human Era*, Lippincott, New York

S Hemsley (2019, June 5) Why B2B brands need to invest in brand marketing, www.marketingweek.com/b2b-brands-invest-brand-marketing/ (archived at https://perma.cc/L9H8-GDPY)

HERE/FORTH (2022) www.hereforth.com (archived at https://perma.cc/R8H2-HZFW)

Interbrand Thinking (2021a) Using social listening to find why rising brands resonate with niche audiences, interbrand.com/thinking/using-social-listening-to-find-why-rising-brands-resonate-with-niche-audiences/ (archived at https://perma.cc/LFT2-QW4Z)

Interbrand Thinking (2021b) What is a brand? interbrand.com/london/thinking/what-is-a-brand/ (archived at https://perma.cc/DBC9-HBND)

Jago (2022) wearejago.com (archived at https://perma.cc/6R8P-ALQQ)

K Kusak (2021, December 1) Marketing Manager, Copy House

E Neal (2022, January 7) Head of Outbound, The Marketing Practice

R O'Keeffe (2021, December 2) Founder, Jago

C Ouellette (2022, January 7) optinmonster.com/social-selling-statistics/ (archived at https://perma.cc/JS9G-L257)

S Sinek (2016, September 20) Simon Sinek start with why – TED talk short edited, www.youtube.com/watch?v=TDi4hzRIrgc (archived at https://perma.cc/GZQ5-ZQRP)

D Stephens (2019, December 3) In brands we trust: Why companies are the new communities, www.businessoffashion.com/opinions/retail/in-brands-we-trust-why-companies-are-the-new-communities (archived at https://perma.cc/D7PR-YLJ4)

K Strachan (2021, November 22) Founder, Copy House

The Gender & Sexual Therapy Center (2019, November 29) Moving from codependent to interdependent relationships, gstherapycenter.com/blog/2019/11/25/moving-from-codependent-to-interdependent-relationships (archived at https://perma.cc/H7B7-CNTR)

TrueStart (2021) Good for you. Naturally. www.truestartcoffee.com/blogs/wild-for-life/health-benefits (archived at https://perma.cc/4U75-V7NP)

YouTube (2018) Keeping up with your world – Direct Line for Business, www.youtube.com/watch?v=4outMGEoOVo&t=1s (archived at https://perma.cc/G3BL-VXLM)

05

Campaigns: how to take an integrated approach to B2B social selling channel selection

What are the best channels for B2B social selling? Use the channel characteristics comparison to identify the most important channels for your business goals. This chapter will enable you to confidently decide where and how you need to invest your social selling time and resources.

Where to start with channels for B2B social selling

Chapter 2 introduced the ABC strategy process which starts with your networked audience, where each contact is part of a number of professional and personal interconnected units. The second stage is the mature interdependent brand, which is experienced through the three-way relationship of the company brand, your personal brand and your buyer. This chapter considers your channel selection, which is central to how you will deliver your social selling campaigns. Remember, although your campaigns should be divided into separate plans for delivery purposes, they are experienced by your buyers as continuum of symbiotic experiences and dialogue.

This continuum spans the entire buyer's journey and therefore exists in social media but also in multiple other touchpoints and experiences. When selecting your channels for social selling purposes, an integrated approach is therefore necessary, as you will need to consider the interplay between your personal and corporate social channels, paid social advertising, email, telesales, face-to-face and virtual meetings, SEO, your website and other online assets. Planned effectively, each channel will support the journey and benefit from the synergy between them, allowing your buyer to communicate with you via the right channels for them at a relevant time.

Social selling doesn't mean spending all your time on social media. It means understanding where social media can support and amplify your existing sales and marketing approach. The best results come from integration, as shown in the case study below.

CASE STUDY
The Marketing Practice (TMP): A sustainability-focused social selling programme for a major telecommunications company

TMP is a global B2B marketing agency which specializes in creating growth for technology companies using social selling, ABM, demand generation, partner marketing and targeting as a service. Its clients include Salesforce, Citrix and Telefonica. This case study demonstrates how they worked with a client to integrate email, LinkedIn and telemarketing in a synchronized campaign. The results achieved an 11 per cent conversion rate of contacts to leads.

Client objectives

This telco business has a number of content pillars, one of which is sustainability. Recognizing that this issue was core to a number of potential new customers, the campaign was created to initiate and develop conversations around the topic of sustainability which would generate meaningful leads.

The campaign targeted both private and public sector companies and created a new conversation for the telecommunications company and its prospects. It built strategic relationships at a board/senior management level, while aligning with the company's solutions to support organizations with their overall sustainability agenda.

The approach

Target accounts were chosen based on their affiliation with high-level sustainability groups and three stages of comms were used:

- Stage 1: Email deployment
  - The emails were signed off and deployed by a senior sustainability colleague in the social selling team. The first email focused on awareness and the second on consideration.

- Stage 2: LinkedIn connection requests

   o To follow the email thread, LinkedIn connection requests were sent to the same contacts. For a more personal connection, the content of the copy subtly referenced the email thread, with the main aim being to expand the social selling team member's network to include similar sustainability-minded people.

- Stage 3: Calling

   o All the target accounts were followed up with a phone call with the aim of securing a 30-minute meeting with the CSR team. Prior to calling, the social seller researched key information on the individual and their business on LinkedIn.

The results

The results dramatically exceeded benchmark performance. Out of 160 connection requests sent, 51 people accepted, giving a connection acceptance rate of 32 per cent and exceeding TMP's benchmark of 15 per cent. Fifteen responses were received from the sustainability team member's connection request, giving a response rate of 30 per cent and exceeding previous response rates (around 6 per cent).

A total of 18 meetings were generated from 162 targeted contacts.

- Nine opportunities were generated from the LinkedIn connection requests and another nine from the calling, providing an overall campaign lead>opportunity conversion rate of 11 per cent. LinkedIn alone saw a lead>opportunity conversion rate of 6 per cent.

Note: this case study has been included with permission from The Marketing Practice (Stephenson, 2022).

How to identify the right channels for your B2B social selling strategy

When deciding which channels to use you will need to consider a number of different factors; however, the most important one will be to understand where your audience are and how they behave in that environment, as discussed in Chapter 3. Each social media channel is a distinctly different ecosystem, with unique attributes, tools and user behaviour. For your social selling activity you will need to identify the channel(s) where you can best find and be found by your audience and build meaningful relationships. The best channel(s) for social selling may differ from your best social media marketing channels, but they will need to work in tandem with each other.

For the best channel selection decisions for your audience:

- **Go where your audience is.** Prioritize by how many of your target audience use each channel and how much time they spend there as well as how appropriate the channel is for your purposes. For example, LinkedIn can be particularly useful for researching buyer interests and connections but not all sectors or markets use it equally. For example, 'Marketers love LinkedIn but if you look at the CTO, or the head of legal or financial services, they aren't there every day. Many haven't even fully filled in their profile. So, if you are aiming for reach and frequency go where the audience is. Follow the data – tech buyers are active daily on Facebook and Twitter' (Howell, 2022).

- **Maximize your resource effectiveness.** Limit the number of social media channels that you use to ensure you have the time and other resources available to optimize results. Think about how your corporate and personal channels will connect so that you can maximize impact through integration. Ideally pick one core social media channel for your business for social selling and only use others to support if needed. For example, SAP invest globally in the LinkedIn platform and Sales Navigator, but individual markets and individuals can choose to add additional channels for social selling depending on their buyer and personal preferences (Liden, 2022).

- **Focus on objective achievement.** Ensure the channel(s) can support meeting your core objective. Do you want to deliver leads or build awareness? Are you trying to build a community? Are you trying to identify new contacts or engage with existing ones? Is there a particular part of the buyer's journey or seller's pathway you are tackling? For example, 1.8 billion people use Facebook groups every month (Martin, 2022). Because they are opted-in communities, engagement is high and you can tailor content around key areas of interest, and also gain valuable insights. In addition, Facebook prioritizes groups in the newsfeed. A great example of an active group is run by the social media agency Social Minds. The group provides a community space primarily for the agency's podcast listeners. It is 'where the best social minds in the industry meet, discuss new episodes, ask, and answer questions, connect with our guests' (Social Minds, 2022).

- **Take advantage of channel synergies.** This is how well or easily the channel(s) integrate with other touchpoints or communication. For example, Meta own Facebook, WhatsApp and Instagram so you can easily link all three accounts, enabling additional contact methods and content sharing.

- **Consider each channel's personality.** Each social media channel has its own personality, and they lend themselves more closely to certain types of content and behaviour. Match the particular social media environment to how you want to demonstrate your personal brand. For example, Twitter is great for continuous topical conversations and your followers can subscribe to your newsletter from there, LinkedIn is the most professional ecosystem and ideal for building thought leadership, whereas Instagram and TikTok can help you bring your personality to life with highly engaging short-form video.

- **Improve performance with integrated tools.** The specific tools and options each channel offers vary so select one that can meet your needs. For example, LinkedIn's Sales Navigator is specifically designed to support social selling and at the advanced levels provides a consolidated view across the whole business and the full sales team.

- **Ensure the content and format meet your audience needs.** Establish how and where your audience prefers to engage with and explore content. For example, the channels offer options for live events in various forms, but does your audience want to attend a live audio event on Twitter Spaces (@TwitterMedia, 2022) or will the live audio and video events on LinkedIn be more appealing (Harvey, 2022)?

The Immediate Future case study shows how important channel selection is in your social selling strategy.

CASE STUDY

Immediate Future Facebook live: Using Facebook for social selling with a global technology brand (Howell, 2022)

A UK-based independent social digital consultancy, Immediate Future, build and deliver award winning data driven social media strategies for brands including IBM, Fujitsu and Motorola. Here, their CEO shares a cases study from a global technology brand.

The approach to Facebook is different from a more business-focused platform such as LinkedIn. When using Facebook, remember that you're interrupting your customer. Your buyers are connecting, watching, being entertained, and posting to family and friends.

So, you need to interrupt with something entertaining, interesting or useful to the audience. Just as you switch off from an ad that's boring, people will flick past mundane content. And just like TV, when you really like an ad, you watch it and watch out for it. Like the Oxo family, Heinz Beans and Hovis. They tell emotive stories. And even in B2B, the story and the emotion are your way to reach your audience.

A global technology business ran a large European industry event bringing together thought leaders in the sector to challenge, champion and consider the future of technology. Immediate Future ran a series of live interviews similar to a BBC News Click. Punchy and to the point, the interviewees included subject matter experts, B2B influencers and professors that would appeal to C-suite buyers.

By researching and listening to each buyer segment and persona, content was created that connected the brand's expertise with the problem the buyer needed to solve. Experts from each field agreed to talk about these issues. Two days of back-to-back interviews were published live on Facebook. Entertainment and expertise were wrapped in a news-style delivery that was punchy, exciting and very watchable.

The viewing figures equated to someone watching all eight series of 'Game of Thrones' back to back 17 times. A phenomenal result in two days. The campaign delivered a pipeline in multi-million euros.

Understanding the characteristics of each channel in a social selling context

Table 5.1 summarizes some of the key differentiators for the six most popular channels used in B2B social selling: LinkedIn, Facebook, Twitter, Instagram, TikTok and WeChat/WeCom.

The choice about which social channels you use will depend on where you operate in the global economy, the sector you are in, and the behaviour and needs of your audience. For example, if you are working in China then LinkedIn has <5 per cent market penetration and the majority of this is

TABLE 5.1 The key social selling differentiators for the channels LinkedIn, Facebook, Twitter, Instagram, TikTok and WeChat/WeCom

Channel	Best markets	Content and tools	Key B2B buyer audiences	Buyer behaviour insights	Integration opportunities	Best for...
LinkedIn	Global but USA, Netherlands, Australia, Canada, and UK reach >60% of adult population. China and Pakistan <6%.	Increasing use of video and live events as new creator and collaboration tools developed. Sales Navigator is a bespoke tool built to support social selling. Notifications of job movers and promotions and content updates support timely and relevant conversations.	The go to platform for business professionals to network, seek and share industry related content, and build reputation.	Only 4% of B2B buyers had a favourable impression of a salesperson who reached out cold, but 87% did when the salesperson was introduced via their professional network (LinkedIn, 2022).	Microsoft owned, integrates well into social selling CRM platforms. Links to Twitter. Sales Navigator enables joined up ABM and sales team delivery.	The cornerstone channel for most business' social selling strategy. Building a thought leadership personal brand.
Facebook	Global but Peru and Philippines reach > 90% of population aged >13 years. Columbia, Mexico, Vietnam, and Thailand >80%. Nigeria <20%.	Facebook Groups offer the opportunity for online community building in a private space. A wide range of apps, content creation tools and livestreaming options available.	>48% of B2B decision makers use Facebook for finding new vendors (Jacob, 2022).	Hyper-local, 2/3 weekly Facebook users visit the pages of local businesses (Csutoras, 2022; Golden, 2021). Decision makers connect with work colleagues and share content with them.	Meta owned – accounts can link to WhatsApp, Messenger, and Instagram. Informal connections with other businesses work well for local businesses	Finding prospects with ads. Nurturing local or interest-based communities. Affordable for SMEs.

(continued)

TABLE 5.1 (Continued)

Channel	Best markets	Content and tools	Key B2B buyer audiences	Buyer behaviour insights	Integration opportunities	Best for...
Twitter	Global but Japan and Saudi Arabia reach >60% of population aged >13 years. Egypt and Indonesia <8%. India <3%.	Use Twitter Lists to monitor and engage more relevantly with customers, prospects, and competitors. Twitter Spaces and newsletter options widen opportunity for increased engagement.	68% of business professionals use their mobile to educate themselves with business-related news (Window, 2022).	Buyers follow thought leaders on Twitter for up-to-date, opinionated information.	Easy to share your LinkedIn content on Twitter.	Great for social listening to understand your audience and stay ahead in thought leadership.
Instagram	Global but Turkey reach >70% of population aged >13 years. Brazil and Argentina >60%. India <22%.	Highly visual and hashtag-led generates high engagement from interested followers. A wide range of apps and content creation tools.	>50% of millennials are active on Instagram (Simmonds, 2022).	Instagram is synonymous with inspiration – inspire potential buyers to find out more. 80% of Instagram users follow at least 1 business (Hopper HQ, 2021).	Meta owned – accounts can link to WhatsApp, Messenger, and Facebook.	Showing more of your personality. Easy to have multiple profiles so you can keep your professional personal brand separate.

TikTok	Global but Saudi Arabia reach >87% of adult population. Malaysia and Thailand >60%. Japan and Pakistan <15%.	Informal, fun, and informative video content with high visibility for interesting content. Use locally specific hashtags to connect with local professionals and business leads.	Increasingly used by millennials who make up 73% of the B2B buyer audience (Choudhury, 2020).	TikTok content is highly shared across other platforms and the hashtags make it easy to share your content with other businesses.	Like SEO the keyword selection helps focus consistency on content pillars.	Showing your character and expertise. Easier to gain visibility organically than other platforms.

Q&A comments function.

WeChat WeCom	Primarily China with reach of >78% of 16-64-year-olds. Hong Kong >53%. USA penetration of 18–24-year-olds is 23%. The home screen for smartphones in China.	WeCom for business includes: CRM sales platform, video conferencing and appointment scheduling, posting ads and sharing thought leadership (We Chat Moments), in-platform payment (WeChat Pay), and live streaming (WeChat Channels).	The primary social media route to the Chinese market. Employees Buyers	Prefer to receive information via informal WeChat groups.70% use mobile when looking for new suppliers but move to desktop for purchasing and accreditation (Golden, 2021).	Platform is a fully integrated system if using WeCom. Unlike LinkedIn, the company information created by sales staff belongs to the business and is retained when employees leave.	The primary social media route to the Chinese market.

NOTE

1 With the exception of WeChat, the market penetration figures are sourced from the Digital 2022: Global Overview Report (Kemp, 2022). The report is published annually in full and with quarterly highlights. It includes detailed social media and other digital statistics at a country and global level.

2 The WeChat market penetration figures are sourced from the WeChat Revenue and Statistics Report (Iqbal, 2022).

3 The following channels are banned in China: Facebook, Google, Twitter, Instagram, Snapchat, Yahoo, Slack and YouTube. However, China's special administrative regions, Hong Kong and Macau, can access Facebook, as they operate under the Chinese mantra of 'One country, two systems'.

considered to be individuals working for global non-Chinese organizations. In China, WeChat is the most widely used social network and its completely integrated ecosystem is the blueprint that Meta and other platforms have followed. WeCom is the enterprise arm of WeChat and offers the same levels of integration. It allows businesses to communicate with their employees, customers and prospective buyers via a range of microprograms (apps) and tools. The vision for WeCom is to facilitate all employees, not just sales professionals, reaching out and connecting with customers and prospects.

> 'Regarding WeCom, if it is positioned as a communication tool within the company, I think its scene and meaning will be much smaller, and it will only generate greater value when it is extended outside the enterprise. The subsequent new changes at WeCom are based on a new concept: I hope that every employee of the enterprise will become a window for enterprise services. People are services and they are certified services.' Allan Zhang, Founder of WeChat (Ross, 2020)

Although LinkedIn is by far the most popular social selling platform (outside China), there are some interesting opportunities offered by the other channels, particularly for building your personal brand. If you have a particular aptitude or interest in certain channels or types of content creation, then you could use them to show your personality or differentiate yourself in a memorable way.

How to integrate personal and business channels for social selling

When starting to use social selling in your business, start simple and keep it simple.

- **Select one channel.** This will be the organization's backbone for content creation and thought leadership. For many businesses this will be LinkedIn, but your buyer behaviour or location may determine another channel choice. Use the considerations mentioned earlier to make your choice; go where your audience is, maximize your resource effectiveness, focus on objective achievement, take advantage of channel synergies, consider each channel's personality, improve performance with integrated tools, and ensure the content and format meet your audience needs.

- **Establish a strong business page/profile on that channel.** Post regularly with useful, engaging and valuable needs-based content. Use your content pillars to ensure consistency. Provide compelling reasons to encourage followers and interaction. Tie keywords and hashtags into your SEO strategy.

- **Encourage, train and support your sales team and leaders to build their personal brands.** Strategically decide how to synergize the combinations of expertise and interest within the team to ensure maximum breadth within the consistent brand pillars. Support with content from the central team but empower individuals to create their own content, share opinions and develop a recognized thought leadership positioning.

- **Use targeted ads to support visibility.** Boost awareness across the platform with your target audience with some paid advertising.

- **Consider other social media channels for specific purposes.** You may decide to add channels such as Twitter to support events in real time or a Facebook group to build a discussion forum. Individuals may also decide to be active in another channel because they have a particular interest or expertise there.

- **Test out the specialist in-platform tools.** Many channels have tools to support you. For example, LinkedIn Sales Navigator offers free trials for individual sellers or can help you set up a company-wide approach.

- **Embed social media into the whole customer journey.** Recognize that social media will not be where the complete conversation happens. When will you encourage moving this to another touchpoint? How do email, telephone and face-to-face fit in?

By keeping it simple you are much more likely to convince the team to support your social selling initiative and achieve your objectives. People are often unsure about starting, either because they feel unconfident or because they don't feel social selling is necessary. Often, the most difficult people to convince are your most successful sellers because they feel they don't need it. When SAP introduced social selling to their global sales team, they recognized that salespeople were highly motivated by revenue targets, so they knew they had to demonstrate how social selling could help individuals achieve their sales quota and be more successful. The case study shows how they did this.

CASE STUDY
SAP: proving social selling works at SAP (Linden, 2022)

The market leader in ERP software, SAP enables businesses of all sizes to become more agile, improve operational efficiency, raise productivity, increase profits and enhance customer experiences. When introducing social selling to the business, SAP used two different methods to clearly demonstrate its power to the global sales team.

1 By conducting a head-to-head test

SAP (SAP, 2022) is a multi-million-dollar global busines with many different divisions across the world. It was therefore able to conduct a head-to-head test by identifying a specific division and testing whether social selling worked.

- **Step 1: Test division selected** – Many of SAP's products and services have very long sales cycles and can take two or more years from initial contact to sale. To provide results in a more timely way, the initial test was conducted in the inside sales division. This division has a shorter sales cycle as it offers smaller packages. Prior to the test telesales was the primary channel.

- **Step 2: Test teams selected** – Two teams were identified that were comparable in revenue, size and financial performance. Both were in Southeast Asia and both had LinkedIn Sales Navigator. Both teams felt they were doing social selling but hadn't had any formal training or taken a strategic approach to implementation.

- **Step 3: The test** – A different approach was taken with each team:

  o Team 1 was given 3–4 days of SAP's social selling training programme. They learned how to do social selling effectively; not to spam, not a hard sell, but actually joining conversations, building the rapport to develop the relationships.

  o Team 2 was allowed to continue as before.

- **The results** – Nine months later Team 1 had generated seven times more pipeline value than Team 2. The training had introduced Team 1 to a different way of selling, helping them discover the true power of social selling.

2 By looking at social data on LinkedIn

Every person who uses LinkedIn can access their social selling index (SSI), which provides a real-time assessment of their overall presence and activity on LinkedIn.

SAP analysed LinkedIn and sales data in selected teams, correlating individuals' sales performance with LinkedIn's SSI. LinkedIn defines a social seller as having a score of >70. When SAP looked at all of their salespeople using LinkedIn Sales Navigator, they found that those who had an SSI of >70 were much more successful. They had:

- shorter sales cycles
- achieved on average 160 per cent of their quota, which was much higher than the overall average

The measurable results convinced managers to put their team through the training and were supported in implementation with peer-to-peer learning. The star sellers were asked to tell their story to their peers as it was much more convincing to hear it from a fellow salesperson than from marketing.

By selecting the most appropriate social selling channels you can focus your team and your resources in a consistent and powerful way to drive sustainable and impressive additional revenue and customer loyalty. In the interview below, Danny Bermant, Director of CaptainJV and social selling expert, shares his insights into channel selection and integration, and using LinkedIn for social selling.

INTERVIEW
Danny Bermant, Director, CaptainJV (Bermant, 2022)

Can you define social selling?

It is the process of using social media to find, connect with, understand and nurture sales prospects.

What are the best channels for social selling?

The channels vary depending on your business and goals. The most important thing is to be effective, regardless of the platform you're on. However, in general, LinkedIn is most relevant for B2B organizations, as most of the businesses they are targeting will be present there. LinkedIn has made networking much easier and more systematic. It used to take forever trying to get hold of people by phone or to set up meetings. With LinkedIn and platforms like Zoom the logistics are easy, international relationships can be as strong as local ones, and you can find people who are likely to be great connections efficiently and quickly.

How does social media fit in with other channels used in social selling?

Social media is not an end in itself but rather a means to an end. LinkedIn is very effective for prospecting, but it is best used in conjunction with other non-social channels. I'm keen to get the conversation offline as quickly as possible, so for example, where I'm leveraging LinkedIn to achieve introductions, I will try to move prospects to a Zoom or phone call. I also advocate moving prospects onto email. You can look up their email on their LinkedIn profile, so, when my prospects receive an email from me, I'll mention that we recently connected on LinkedIn to provide context. They may also have seen my LinkedIn posts, which will increase their recognition. Once I have identified someone I'd like to talk to and have been introduced by someone in my social media network, I move to a largely email- and Zoom-based relationship.

What are the most effective ways to generate connections on LinkedIn?

The main behaviour to focus on in your social selling is giving value in advance. I am overwhelmed with people who want to connect to me, and they try very hard to write an engaging message, but you can see right through that they want to sell. It's done to such an extent on LinkedIn that in order to stand out from everybody else you really have to work hard on your connection message. What's my unique role? What can I do to help my target audience to solve their problem? People are much more likely to respond if you're offering to help them with something.

For example, during lockdown a business leader reached out to his network on LinkedIn and said, 'I'm writing a report on how people in my industry and their businesses are adapting as a result of Covid. I'd love to hear your opinions.' This is the type of content people respond positively to. They respond where they see value. The primary thinking process of someone on the receiving end of LinkedIn messages is 'What's in it for me?' So, you have to think very carefully. If you were in their shoes, how would you respond to your message? Unfortunately, most people who are active on LinkedIn don't think that way.

Are there other channels besides LinkedIn that might be useful for social selling?

Facebook can be useful either as a stand-alone or as an additional channel to LinkedIn and is particularly effective in:

- **Reaching non-habitual LinkedIn users** – Facebook ads can be used to reach certain sectors and individuals who are infrequent LinkedIn users, or who have jobs which mean that they mainly use social media for personal and relaxation purposes. For example, doctors who are treating patients tend not to look at social media other than for personal use but can be targeted with relevant Facebook ads. In a recent healthcare sector campaign I ran, it was easier to get their attention using Facebook ads than via LinkedIn. The doctors clicked on the ad and were able to opt in for more information which could then be sent to them and start the social selling relationship.

- **Creating a community using Facebook groups** – Facebook groups are extremely popular in business and can be far more active than most LinkedIn groups. LinkedIn groups were early to arrive but there's no dynamism. In a Facebook group somebody will post something and then there will be a whole flurry of comments and members will join in the conversation. Facebook groups seem to have a much tighter remit, they feel like they've got a real function that they're trying to deliver. Whereas often the LinkedIn groups seem to be covering a wide subject range, such as social media or procurement, Facebook groups seem to be much more targeted, with a much tighter remit.

What makes a successful social selling approach?

The company that succeeds is the one that has spent the most time researching what is bothering their client. What is keeping them awake at night, what are they trying to do, what are they trying to solve, whether they are where they need to be? The more tuned in you are to what your prospective buyer is grappling with, and the more you address that in your content, the more likely they are to pay attention to you.

How do you balance the time spent researching people and their organization, which is implicit in social selling, with getting on the phone or going to meetings and trying to convert a sale?

It is vital that you assess the resources you have in terms of time, money, tools and people. People are often over-ambitious on social media. Remember:

- Social takes time. Make the most of your limited time:

  o You may not have time to create lots of content. But you can be active on LinkedIn, for example by sharing third-party or industry content with your own comments and views.

  o Don't spend lots of time one-on-one prospecting on LinkedIn. Instead look at your top five or six clients and their network. See who they're talking to and ask them to refer you.

- Start with your core objectives:

  o Most companies have lots of ideas of what they want to do in terms of content type, tool usage, etc. Don't start with the ideas, rather think about the core outcome you need to achieve and the easiest way you can get there. For example, with limited resources the one thing you can do is be active on LinkedIn. To grow your LinkedIn network, start by connecting with your work colleagues, your clients and your suppliers. As you grow your network you will start to see who's talking to who and who's connected to who. You can then start to identify potential opportunities for referrals. It doesn't take up a huge amount of time, but it's worth mapping out what to prioritize with the limited resources you have.

- Don't overcomplicate:

  o People often tend to overcomplicate. They focus on advertising, random networking meetings or hiring someone to post on social media, rather than focusing on the 'low-hanging fruit'. Start with the simplest method first. Which of your friends or clients are connected to people you want to work with? Leverage your social media network to get introductions. And then, only if you have more resources available, start thinking about more complicated options.

Once you have identified the core channel(s) for your social selling strategy you will be ready to start creating a plan. The next chapter pulls together each element covered so far and shows you how to build this into an effective but manageable plan.

Bibliography

@TwitterMedia (2022) Twitter Spaces, media.twitter.com/en/articles/products/2021/twitter-spaces (archived at https://perma.cc/D5R8-TL6X)

D Bermant (2022) Director, CaptainJV [interview] (1 January 2022)

M Harvey (2022) LinkedIn is launching live audio and video events, my.socialmindshub.com/#linked-in-is-launching-live-audio-and-video-events (archived at https://perma.cc/7PNZ-69RJ)

K Howell (2022) CEO [interview] (13 December 2022)

M Iqbal (2022) WeChat revenue and usage statistics (2022), www.businessofapps.com/data/wechat-statistics/ (archived at https://perma.cc/YZC9-638J)

S Kemp (2022) Digital 2022: Global Overview Report, datareportal.com/reports/digital-2022-global-overview-report (archived at https://perma.cc/QY58-G3DZ)

M Liden (2022) Vice President, Head of EMEA Marketing Transformation Office [interview] (18 February 2022)

M Martin (2022) How to use Facebook groups to grow your business and engage customers, blog.hootsuite.com/facebook-groups-business/ (archived at https://perma.cc/N99P-2N5U)

L Ross (2020) Everything you should know about WeChat Work (WeCom), www.chooseoxygen.com/en/blog/everything-you-should-know-about-wechat-work (archived at https://perma.cc/59FE-HLZ9)

SAP (2022) SAP UK and Ireland, www.sap.com/uk/index.html?url_id=auto_hp_redirect_uk (archived at https://perma.cc/FXD5-T9FF)

Social Minds (2022) Social Minds Facebook Group, www.facebook.com/groups/351364439135606/about (archived at https://perma.cc/H8EC-CVK4)

S Stephenson (2022) Associate Director Social Media, The Marketing Practice [interview] (6 January 2022)

06

Campaigns: building and implementing a B2B social selling plan

Every strategy needs a delivery plan. This chapter which shows you how to organize and deliver your strategy with example plans and templates to ensure an effective customer journey from lead generation to nurturing and sales conversion, through to enduring relationship building. Plus, useful tactics that can enhance the effectiveness of your plan.

The essential components of an effective delivery plan

As Bermant noted in the previous chapter, 'social takes time, make the most of your limited time' (Bermant, 2022). By creating a plan and sharing it across the wider team you can ensure that you consolidate your efforts in the areas that will have the most impact and maximize the synergies of an integrated approach.

By working through the previous chapters, you should have the core elements of your strategy decided, including:

- clear articulation and understanding of the objectives and KPIs
- agreed timeframe for delivery
- detailed understanding of your buyer and their networked audience
- articulation of your brand differentiation, both for your business and yourself

- core content pillars and how they will be deployed at an organizational and personal branding level
- primary channel for social selling and any secondary channels that might be useful

Your plan will pull these together to enable a co-ordinated delivery and deployment that meets both your long- and short-term goals. Therefore, you will need to deliver both overarching and specific campaign activity by ensuring you have the right content for every stage of the buyer's journey and campaigns targeted to meet the goals of the seller's pathway. Clear targets, focused content and active measurement and management ensure the successful deployment of your plan, as Nigel Church discusses in this interview.

INTERVIEW
Nigel Church, CEO, Emerge Digital (Church, 2021)

A Microsoft partner and award-winning technology provider, Emerge Digital supports businesses in IT and technology innovation as they move through digital transformation. Their clients include Gloucestershire Rugby, Infosec and Cytoplan. Recognizing the power of social selling, they have integrated it into their new business strategy with organizational-level content pillars and data-led decision making driving the plan. Their CEO shares his thoughts on this important development.

How is social selling important to your business?

Many businesses use social selling just to build awareness, to get their name out there. But we need leads out of this. So, the integration of social selling with social advertising, SEO and the website is all about driving leads, and ideally sales-qualified leads.

How do you balance short- and long-term goals?

Ideally, we want to attract long-term partners. So, it's important to be known for our full offering, from managed IT services to digital transformation. It's always a balance. We want to communicate what we're about, what the business delivers and what our vision for customers might be. But we also don't want to miss an opportunity because we're too big picture. We use data to help understand where someone is in this journey and use a prospect qualification process to determine how much time, effort and energy we should invest in each prospect. One new customer may initially look very much like another, they have both just bought a cyber security product. But their attributes, characteristics and behaviours can indicate whether they have the potential to be long-term partners.

How do you use data in your social selling activity?

We use a combination of goal setting and data insights which are overlayed to make decisions for:

- **Intent:** We look at intent data because we want to understand where people are on their buyer journey and then, how to engage with them.

- **Personalizing conversations:** Tracking software on the website tells us who is coming to the website and is overlayed against our website goals to understand how we should be behaving. For example, if our data analysis tells us that Company A has visited our cyber security page on the website 30 times in the last three weeks, and seven different people from the organization have been looking at information on Microsoft Advanced Threat Protection, we know there is no point in talking about digital transformation. Rather, we have to talk about Microsoft Advanced Threat Protection and our capabilities in that area.

- **Targeting:** Managed IT services are usually bought by IT departments, but digital transformation affects every part of a business. So, we look to target both influencers and buyers by marketing to the organization via targeted LinkedIn advertising and connecting with several people in the same business. We might want to speak to the CEO, but if we can't, we can still influence key individuals in the buying group of a prospect organization.

What value do you put on engagement in social media?

We use an engagement matrix to indicate when it is the right time for us to reach out to a prospect. It considers information such as number of visits, number of engagements, length of time between engagements, etc. Ideally, we don't want the customer to be too far down the buying journey before we reach out because we want to influence the buying process. A good sales process is where we've been engaged early and exerted some influence. For example, the prospective buyer used our online learning resources to develop their RFP. We think engagement is important because we don't want to be just chasing leads, we want to be useful and encourage prospects to reach out to us.

How important is content in the plan?

It's important to send the right message at the right time to the right person. Content needs to change depending on who you're speaking to you. The content is critical. It can feel a bit overwhelming, a complex 3-D matrix of who to speak to, what to say and when. But testing isn't expensive, and you can keep trying until the message resonates. It would be nice to get it right first time.

How do you tailor content in the plan?

The content is king and needs to support the customer journey. For example, a recent lead, which we tracked with our lead-tracking software, visited our website, then spent a few minutes reading a particular case study, then clicked the live chat button and booked an appointment. When we talk to them, we will be interested to understand where we touched that organization before, was it on social media or did we benefit from our SEO?

It's important that prospects find the content they need in social and on the web, but that each area integrates to support the journey. The potential customer benefits from the content, then we benefit from the call to action and the ease of the call to action. The three elements coming together in one moment creates a lead. By tracking the journey, we can assess areas that might need additional content. For example, if we identify a conversion issue, we can start creating more relevant content and developing our brand reputation to improve this.

Balancing short- and long-term goals

For many sales and marketing professionals long-term brand-building investment can be hard to justify when short-term sales activation brings faster returns and is easier to implement and measure. However, both elements are vital in generating long-term sustained success. In 2017 the IPA published Binet and Field's analysis of marketing effectiveness on the long-term success of brands. The work highlighted the differences and benefits of these two types of activity, with brand building setting the scene and priming the relationship on which the offers and persuasive messages of sales

FIGURE 6.1 The roles of brand building and sales activation for B2B

BRAND BUILDING	SALES ACTIVATION
Creates mental brand equity	Exploits mental brand equity
Influences future sales	Generates sales now
Has broad reach	Tightly targeted
Long term	Short term
Emotional priming	Persuasive messages
Builds trust	Harnesses trusted relationships
Creates authority	Deploys position of authority
Useful and inspiring content	Decision supporting and reassuring content

The figure is an expansion of Binet and Field's definitions for brand building and sales activation (IPA, 2017).

activation can springboard into higher conversion rates and stronger results. Their magic ratio for success was to spend 60 per cent on brand building and 40 per cent on sales activation (IPA, 2017). In B2B the term demand generation is usually used to describe the brand-building activity where you ensure organizations are aware of you, interested in the content you offer and are building trust. Sales activation is sometimes referred to as lead generation or lead activation (Figure 6.1). This is where you capture contact information and nurture leads into sales.

Binet and Field's work was largely conducted on B2C brands; however, more recently, they relooked at their analysis from a B2B perspective and found very similar results. B2B brands which invested in both types of activity performed much more strongly than those that ignored or significantly reduced the proportion of brand building relative to sales activation. In fact, for B2B they concluded that the most efficient balance between brand building and sales activation was a 46:54 ratio (The B2B Institute, 2021). The Institute of Practitioners in Advertising (IPA) also found that running both brand-building and sales-activation campaigns together for B2B was six times as effective as running acquisition campaigns alone (The B2B Institute, 2021).

So, what does this mean for B2B social selling? How much of our time should we spend investing in our brand building and how much on sales activation? In our seller's pathway this brand building ensures we can be found, are trusted and buyers want to build a relationship with us. The sales activation focuses on finding potential buyers and leveraging that relationship to generate a sale. To know how much time to invest in each, we need to take three factors into consideration:

1 The length of your sales cycle:

   o B2B sales in general have a much longer sales cycle than B2C brands. Some businesses are also locked into lengthy contract terms or making a change takes time as it will require other infrastructure or organizational adjustments. For this reason, it is estimated that only 5 per cent of B2B buyers are ready to buy at any moment in time (Wray, 2021). Clearly, if you focus your content or campaigns solely on sales activation you will risk ignoring the needs of most of your connections and followers. The balance is important and by understanding where your buyers are in their buyer's journey will enable you to flex the mix of emotional priming and sales-generation content.

2 The source of leads:

   o In the old world a sales professional may expect to be 'given' 'warm leads' from marketing or you may have met your potential buyers at an event and started to build a relationship face to face. In B2B social selling you will still gain leads from marketing activity and in-person meetings, but you will also be identifying and nurturing your own leads via social media, sometimes for years before and after a sale. In addition, you need to consider not only your business's brand but also your personal brand and how it connects to that of your business. As you seek to find contacts and be found by active buyers in social, build trust and authority, and provide useful, inspiring information, you can utilize brand-building content through your personal profile and conversations to ensure you and your business are a favoured choice as buyers move from problem identification and into the more active purchasing stages of their journey.

3 The nature of social media:

   o Finally, let's consider the nature of social media itself. In the same way you wouldn't walk up to a stranger at a conference and immediately try to sell them your business services, you need to introduce yourself and your business in a socially acceptable way online. Remember, not everyone is in active supplier-selection mode and depending on which social channel they are using they could be engaged in more personal than business activities. Your personal and corporate brand-building content and engagements are powerful ways for you to nurture relationships and look for signals as to when a more sales-activation approach is required. Recent research has underlined the importance of thought leadership content in affecting decision making, with 54 per cent of decision makers spending more than one hour per week consuming thought leadership and 65 per cent of buyers reporting that a piece of thought leadership significantly changed their perception of a company for the better (Edleman and LinkedIn, 2021).

For the above reasons look to invest time and effort into both brand-building and sales-activation activity to ensure you reach and interact with potential buyers at every stage of the buyer's journey.

Creating and using a content repository

To deliver your social selling strategy you will need to have a repository of core content created by the business for each content pillar and each stage of the buyer's journey. To understand where you may have gaps it is useful to create a content repository to store all your content information and audit the current position. Your CRM system may include a content database or repository, but if not, you can download and use Template 6.1 as a starting point.

Your content repository should be created and maintained by a central team or person. This will normally be the marketing team. However, the information should be accessible to everyone involved in social selling or other sales activities across the business. It should include the following information in a database that can be searched and sorted:

- **Content pillar name** – Each of your content pillars should have a name. You will want to ensure that you have enough content for each pillar as individual social sellers are likely to focus on only one or two of the business's pillars when building their own personal brands.

- **Content type** – Include the content type as you will want a range of content to be available, such as video, infographic, case study, blog, webpage, gif, etc. If you are including videos, state the length of the video as this will be important when deciding where it can be used.

TEMPLATE 6.1 Content repository template

CONTENT PILLAR NAME	CONTENT TYPE	CONTENT TITLE	BRIEF CONTENT DESCRIPTION	CURRENT LINK	IDEAL FOR PROBLEM IDENTIFICATION	IDEAL FOR REQUIREMENT BUILDING AND SOLUTION EXPLORATION	IDEAL FOR VALIDATION AND SUPPLIER SELECTION	IDEAL FOR CONSENSUS CREATION AND FUTURE PROBLEM IDENTIFICATION	CONTENT CREATION DATE	CONTENT EXPIRATION DATE
AAA	blog	blog title	key highlights	insert link	Y/N	Y/N	Y/N	DATE	date/ evergreen	specific shortcode
AAA	video	video title								
AAA	infographic	infographic title								
AAA	web page	web page title								
AAA	case study	case study title								
AAA	etc	relevant title								
BBB										
BBB										
BBB										
BBB										
BBB										
BBB										

(continued)

TEMPLATE 6.1 (Continued)

CONTENT PILLAR NAME	CONTENT TYPE	CONTENT TITLE	BRIEF CONTENT DESCRIPTION	CURRENT LINK	IDEAL FOR PROBLEM IDENTIFICATION	IDEAL FOR REQUIREMENT BUILDING AND SOLUTION EXPLORATION	IDEAL FOR VALIDATION AND SUPPLIER SELECTION	CONSENSUS CREATION AND FUTURE PROBLEM IDENTIFICATION	CONTENT CREATION DATE	CONTENT EXPIRATION DATE
CCC										
CCC										
CCC										
CCC										
CCC										
CCC										
DDD										
DDD										
DDD										
DDD										
DDD										
DDD										

- **Brief content description** – Summarize the highlights or importance of the content so it is easy for the reader to understand why they might want to use it.

- **Current link** – Put in the general link here. Ideally this will be a short code link such as a bitly (Bermant, 2022).

- **Ideal usage by buyer's journey stage** – Highlight the part of the buyer's journey that the content is most useful for with a Y or N. Some content could be useful at more than one of the following stages:

  o problem identification

  o requirement building and solution exploration

  o validation and supplier selection

  o consensus creation and future problem identification.

- **Content creation date** – State the date the content was created and available for use.

- **Content expiration date** – Some content is time sensitive, such as a 2023 trends blog. Other content can be evergreen, such as a case study. Either include an end date for the content or state that it is evergreen. This will highlight where content needs to be reviewed and repurposed or deleted. Make sure you periodically review the evergreen content too.

- **Campaign usage short code link** – For every campaign where the content is used create a short code link that includes the core information about the usage, such as content pillar, content type, channel and campaign. Information on how to structure this is included in Chapter 7.

When you come to deploy your social selling strategy, as a social seller you can access the content repository and use it as the backbone of your social selling activity, picking relevant content to support your personal brand building and to share and discuss with prospects. Although you will also create your own posts and curate external content within your pillars, the repository will give you easy access to your company's content and useful information and tools to support your buyers.

Planning business-level content with the hero, hub, help model

Once you have audited your current content using the repository you may find that you have some gaps. This is normal, so don't worry. However, as you start to execute individual campaigns you will be continually creating or repurposing content and will naturally start to fill the gaps. Although some content is time sensitive, much of what will be created will be evergreen or long lasting, so the investment in creation can be reaped over a significant length of time.

Because the core content should be created at an organizational level, it is useful to do this in a structured way and for specific time periods or campaigns. For example, you may plan content quarterly or bi-monthly, or create content for a specific event or audience. In each case, using the hero, hub, help (HHH) model will ensure your content effectiveness is maximized and resource usage is minimized.

Hero content is the encapsulation of the big idea, the key piece of content created for the specific campaign. It might be more expensive to produce but it will hold together the other content being used over that period. Hero content is typically thought leadership content and is usually time sensitive, adds real value, and therefore is highly sharable and engaging. Examples of B2B hero content are a white paper, new research, an event or webinar. The content will be designed for a specific audience and tailored to meet their needs. It could be sector specific or created for a particular challenge your buyers face. Hero content is great for demand generation/brand building, helping you and your business to be found by buyers and building your reputation and trust as they identify their problem and explore possible solutions.

Hub content is the relationship building, nudge content, the elements that support the overall campaign, and used to remind and encourage your followers to engage. Hub content could be short videos or animations, testimonials and recommendations, gifs and blogs, podcasts, or images. For example, if your hero content is a piece of new research, the hub content could include a short animation of the key outtakes, various graphs of specific findings, a blog and a feature in the company podcast.

Help content is useful content that is always available to be found by your potential buyers. It supports them throughout the buyer's journey and could include interactive content such as a requirement builder or audit process. Case studies, checklists, toolkits, information sheets and top tips are all good examples of help content. Look to create help content that is focused on your buyers' needs at each stage. What are the questions they most want answered? How can you help improve their experience and make it easier to choose you? In your persona you will have considered the questions your buyer asks at each stage of the journey and these insights will be invaluable in creating your help content.

As you deploy your content, make sure it is also optimized for the different social media channels. In the following case study, Copy House demonstrate their highly targeted approach to content delivery.

CASE STUDY
Copy House: taking a hyper-personalized approach to social selling

A B2B content marketing agency, Copy House (Copy House, 2022a) specializes in the technology and FinTech sectors working with established brands and start-ups across Europe. Its clients include Meta, Klarna, Lendflo, Travelex and Money Dashboard. Their approach to social selling optimizes the integration of personal branding, thought leadership and a strong focus on consistent content pillars. In 2021, they achieved a growth rate of over 280 per cent.

Copy House takes a hyper-personalized approach to social selling which means they only post on platforms relevant to their audience, specific content is posted at specific times, and each platform has a unique approach to maximize engagement via its algorithm.

Channel choice and post timings

As a B2B technology content agency, the most relevant platforms for their audience are LinkedIn and Twitter. But to maximize impact and engagement, both platforms are treated differently. For example:

- **Twitter** – Used to share day-to-day updates, events, achievements and so on. Posting occurs numerous times a day on Twitter to get the community talking and involved in current events within the industry.

- **LinkedIn** – Posts are published once a day, five times a week to ensure the posts do not compete with themselves. The channel is used to showcase the most important company and industry updates, content advice and announcements.

Channel content and algorithm optimization

Because the audience engages with content in different ways depending on the channel and time of day and the algorithms prioritize specific engagements, it is important to take this into account when deploying a campaign. For example, for Christmas 2021, Copy House counted down to Christmas with their '12 Days of Christmas Content Marketing Tips' campaign (Copy House, 2022b) and took a different approach on each channel:

- **Twitter** – Each day, posts were published showcasing each tip in the lead up to Christmas (Figure 6.2). To keep the campaign fresh across multiple posts per day, some were stand-alone posts, others were a gateway into further insights and aid.

- **LinkedIn** – Although this worked well for Twitter, LinkedIn required a different approach (Figure 6.3). Research indicated that the LinkedIn algorithm favours carousel posts as they encourage a physical click from the user (Haq, 2021). Therefore, on LinkedIn a single post summarized the tips in a carousel format (Figure 6.4). This was also accompanied by a blog post for more depth and detail. This method made the post more interactive and visible, and ensured the tips didn't compete with each other on LinkedIn.

By integrating channels, adapting the content to make the most of different platform tools and audience behaviour, and having a consistent approach, Copy House maximizes its impact on social media.

FIGURE 6.2 Sample tweet from the '12 Days of Christmas Content Marketing Tips' campaign

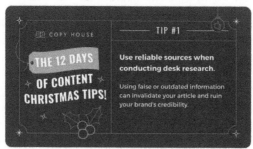

FIGURE 6.3 LinkedIn post from the '12 Days of Christmas Content Marketing Tips' campaign

Copy House
1,880 followers
3mo · 🌐

🎁 🎄 We have been busy counting down to Christmas on our Twitter with our 12 Days of Content Christmas Tips, gifted by our busy Copy House-elves themselves! 🎄 🎁

Today, we are excited to share all of our tips in one place to get you in the true festive spirit!

Our tips show that just like Santa, brands need to understand who their audience is, what their needs are, and take the proper steps in their content strategy to position themselves as the solution provider their audience needs. 🎅

Check out all of our content tips below, and if you'd like more information on each tip, read our latest blog: https://lnkd.in/eBdtGNXx.

#contentmarketingagency #12daysofxmas #contentmarketingtips #techmarketing #b2bmarketing #copyhouse #thecopyhouseway

FIGURE 6.4 LinkedIn carousel from the '12 Days of Christmas Content Marketing Tips' campaign

Your HHH plan will provide the backbone of your social selling campaign and be deployed at a business level. However, your individual sales professionals will need to be aware of the plan as they can use it to support their own activity in building their personal brand and engaging with individual buyers.

In a recent campaign around digital transformation, Emerge Digital created a transformation animation as hero content for use on social media and on their website. To support it, a range of hub and help content was available to the sales and marketing team, including an online assessment tool, case studies in key target sectors, checklists and blogs. The leadership team also created a range of posts and videos for use on their personal channels which they used in conjunction with the corporate content.

Curating content as an individual social seller

With a strong backbone of content in place at a business level and an up-to-date content repository, you can plan your own social selling activity by curating the business's content and non-competitive third-party content that fits within your content pillars and helps demonstrate your thought leadership. Your curation is key. What do you choose to share and comment on? What is your opinion? Why is the content useful to your audience? These factors will determine how relevant you are and the content you share will help build trust in you and your business. Because content shared at this individual level is much more widely seen and highly engaged with than corporate content, it is important that you feed back to the business on which content is most valuable and important. As Neal states, social sellers 'are the voice of the prospect' (Neal, 2022).

Effective social selling tactics to include in your plan

There are many different types of social selling tactics. The following examples offer a range of options to improve insight, targeting, personalization, engagement and reach.

Using LinkedIn groups for insight

LinkedIn groups are great for understanding the issues of a sector or audience and can deliver compelling and powerful insights that can be quickly used on active campaigns. The case study below shows how Erica Neal from The Marketing Practice (TMP) put this into action.

CASE STUDY

The Marketing Practice: using LinkedIn groups to support lead generation in the manufacturing sector (Neal, 2022)

The client offer was a digital transformation solution for supply chain management. The content and campaign messaging had been successful in several sectors but was struggling to gain traction in the manufacturing sector.

After conducting some insight gathering it was apparent that talking to manufacturers about digitally transforming their supply chain was an oxymoron because manufacturers historically grow through mergers and acquisitions. This means that they typically have numerous legacy back-office systems that don't talk to each other because they have come from several different businesses that have been merged.

To understand what they were actually talking about, and the language used, Neal joined a relevant LinkedIn group focused on manufacturing and supply chains. Because group members are kept informed each week with an email summary of the key topic areas, Neal was able to identify that one of the hot topics of group conversation was around what they called 'a Frankenstein ERP (Enterprise Resource Planning)'. The group used the term to describe all of their different legacy solutions that were stuck together with gaffer tape. Manufacturers knew they needed to transform, but they couldn't find one solution that would fit across their multi-platform complexity.

Neal suspected that some new messaging around the language expressed in the group might be more effective so tested out her theory with a few initial calls with prospects, who were supply chain directors across Europe. Neal brought in this idea of a Frankenstein ERP. It resonated with them all: they knew they needed to be agile but felt trapped.

Neal then met with the TMP strategist and they redefined the problem as 'the agility trap'. An email was sent out immediately which resulted in high engagement and leads.

Using groups for this insight to action approach can be replicated in many other scenarios. From a social selling perspective, groups are very effective. They enable you to understand your network, how they talk and how they define their challenges. You can then demonstrate that understanding back to them by using their language and fresh insights which will make all the difference on the call, social post or email they next receive from you.

Using LinkedIn Sales Navigator to improve personalization

During the Covid pandemic many salespeople dialled down the amount of outbound calling and increased email usage as central switchboards were less likely to be manned with homeworking. With office workers on average receiving 120 emails per day (Templafy, 2020), it is even more crucial to ensure your emails stand out in the inbox and, more importantly, are relevant and useful to the recipient. Recognizing this challenge, TMP used Sales Navigator to research their audience prior to sending emails:

> 'We had to really strengthen our written capabilities to demonstrate personalization, so out of all the emails that a prospect receives in a day, ours are the ones that stand out. Somebody's LinkedIn profile is a resource to get to know that person before you contact them. I want my team to be that different contact that a prospect gets. The email that just sets us apart because we have demonstrated that we've taken the time to look at them as an individual, and what their organization is doing, and then aligned our proposition. It means that we're doing all of the thinking and heavy lifting. All our prospect needs to do is say thanks for taking the time to actually think about this for me.' (Neal, 2022)

Sales Navigator offers additional insight opportunities and allows sales professionals to create saved decision-making groups or campaigns. These tools can be used to provide insights to personalize individual emails or to support a call to a gatekeeper or potential buyer. The importance of somebody's LinkedIn profile and the information about them in the wider public domain are so vital to create relevance that it seems counterintuitive not to use them and just go straight into a sales pitch and hope for the best.

At TMP they use a 3×3 approach to maximize the effectiveness of outbound activity by focusing time and effort in a concentrated way.

THE MARKETING PRACTICE – CREATING RELEVANCE WITH THE 3×3 APPROACH (NEAL, 2022)

By spending three minutes finding out three things about your prospective buyer which are personal to them or relevant to your proposition, you can tailor your outreach to be more relevant and effective:

- 3 minutes of research
- 3 top-level pieces of information
- 3 conversation starters.

TMP use LinkedIn Sales Navigator, Google, the News tab on the target company's website and other social media channels for their initial research. In addition, there may be information in your CRM from previous conversations or account intelligence on their existing products or contacts.

Conversation starters work best when you refer to the buyer rather than yourself. Look for their achievements, such as a presentation they have delivered, an award they have received, a conference they attended, a blog post, or a cause they support. Alternatively, consider referring to a recent promotion, length of tenure at the company, a recommendation, or an endorsement.

Using hashtags and mentions to improve engagement and reach

Hashtags should be an important part of your planning. Your hashtags should be aligned to your contact pillars and keywords and used strategically with a focus on the result you want to achieve. Mentions are also great for widening reach and alerting key individuals and other businesses about your posts. Follow the guidelines below:

- Make sure your hashtags are legible and memorable.
  - Don't #go #crazy #so #you #look #ridiculous.
  - Don't #havelongwordstringsnoonecanread.
  - Create branded hashtags.
- Use hashtags to support your SEO strategy and increase visibility.
  - Link to your keywords and content. The social platform algorithms all use some relevancy criteria to decide who to show your content to and to prioritize its importance in the feed. The more closely your

audience, content, keywords and hashtags are related, the bigger the impact your posts or shares will have.

- Be mindful of the best practice levels of how many hashtags to use.
  - Twitter: 1–2.
  - Instagram: circa 20.
  - Facebook: 1–3.
  - LinkedIn: Up to 3.
  - TikTok: max it out.
- Widen impact by varying the hashtags from the original post when you reshare or comment on a post.
  - Don't overshare the same content across your business with no additional comments or independent views.
- Use mentions to alert people and businesses to your conversation.
  - Only mention someone who will respond quickly to a mention. The algorithms like conversations, so when someone you mention ignores you, it will have a detrimental effect on your visibility.
- Don't use too many mentions.
  - On LinkedIn, the best practice is a maximum of five. Make sure the content is relevant to them as mentioned above for hashtags.

Using personal profiles to improve impact

On LinkedIn, most activity, the sharing and commenting, happens not from a brand post but from an individual's posts. Someone who you're connected with, or somebody you know shared it with you, it's a person-to-person conversation.

On Facebook, the C-suite are often connected with their work colleagues and will share interesting business-related information with their board. They are connected with each other and so use their personal profiles on Facebook to share in a non-business environment. In our social life many of us are connected to our work colleagues in the same way.

LinkedIn company pages are not the best place to hold a conversation, but they make a great shop window and a content spine for your social selling plan. Posts that are being commented on by your employees or customers have much greater impact and that is why it matters so much that your leaders or experts have strong profiles and a clear personal brand.

'Straight shares aren't great for the algorithm. You need to start a conversation. Typically, a company page will post and ask colleagues to share it. When they reshare, engagement is 75 per cent to 85 per cent less than an original post with one image. A reshare is one of the worst kinds of posts you can do for the algorithm. At the start of 2022 it was eight times more effective for an employee to comment on a company page post,' says Laura Hannan at Pitch 121.

So, if your CEO has a strong network, ensure they comment on your company page posts as it can be a quick way to highlight what your company is doing and drawing attention to it. You could even consider using a tool such as Lempod (Lempod, 2022), which allows you to set up specific conversation pods, to help with this.

Integrating social and other channels to improve campaign effectiveness

Social doesn't work alone. You may use social media to find new buyers, or they may reach out to you because of your profile in their network; however, you will still need to use other channels such as face-to-face and virtual networking and meetings, phone, text, email and LinkedIn InMail to continue and support the buyer's journey. In the next chapter we will look at some tools to help with this as well as some recommendations on sequencing your deployment. In the interview below, Katy Howell of Immediate Future shares her thoughts on integration.

INTERVIEW

Katy Howell, CEO, Immediate Future (Howell, 2021)

Howell and her fellow directors lead the team at Immediate Future (Immediate Future, 2022), an award-winning independent social digital consultancy that works globally with clients including IBM, Blackberry, Thompson Reuters, Staples and Motorola.

How do you balance short- and long-term goals?

We really believe in Les Binet and Peter Field's philosophy of thinking longer term to ensure delivery in the short term. Unfortunately that's the bit that's missing in a lot of B2B. Everybody is focused on tomorrow, not the future. Consequently, with short-term thinking, the pool of opportunity gets smaller and smaller, and becomes less and less productive.

The opportunity in social media is to build brand, create context and develop relationships that matter. That nudge and nurture connection to the endgame. In social you have this chance to present yourself in the early stage of the funnel. To open the doors just a bit, so the sale is easier. You're looking to create thumb-stopping content, that speaks to the buyer problems, not to your services.

How do you integrate marketing and sales to increase impact?

It's important, too, to create a rhythm to your social. You need to think about all the triggers and motivations that will nudge nurture through the funnel. Nobody makes a B2B decision on one post. So, you're building a stable of sequential stories. For example, it could be a series around credibility and trust:

1   This is who we are and why that matters to the buyer – be entertaining and interesting
2   This is how we solve problems – the insight that proves expertise
3   Here's what it feels like to work with us – the people behind the business
4   This is why we are credible – the case studies and testimonials

The series could be anything from talking heads to humorous animation. For a recent client we targeted financial directors with a jokey/sarcastic campaign. It pokes fun at marketing speak, which is appealing to FDs. This campaign is about understanding the audience, understanding what it is like being on their side.

By building a marketing foundation and retargeting and remarketing constantly, it ensures that when your salespeople, or your subject matter experts, or your leadership team start to reach out, the door is open to start a conversation. The potential customer goes, 'Oh yes, I've heard of them, they do that report on XXX.' That's where you want to get to – a consistent, co-ordinated approach.

What is your view on using paid and organic social media to support social selling?

At an awareness level, organic can have an impact on channels like LinkedIn or Twitter. However, organic only on Facebook and Instagram has virtually no impact as there is a significant limit on who you will reach among your own followers. Despite this, consumer channels do work for B2B and can be effective if you get the content and context right.

There is some value in doing organic well on LinkedIn, but anybody who is just doing organic isn't serious about social. It's a bit like putting up a few posters in your local city centre and hoping somebody sees them. Paid is your opportunity to target places in the buyer's journey, interests and psychographics. That way you can deliver the right message at the right time in the right context.

Organic works when we start to move to one-to-one relationships, then it's a completely different ballgame:

- You and I are connected to each other.

- We will have a conversation; did you see this, or have you seen that?

- Now we're building a relationship that is one on one and it doesn't require me to use paid.

Who should be responsible for thought leadership?

Social selling plays a wider role, it is relationship building, but it's also establishing one's own singular credentials and this is where thought leadership comes in. It might be that your sales team don't want to be thought leaders, but that doesn't mean that they can't comment on thought leadership. It can be as simple as going out with what is in the industry news every morning.

Thought leadership should sit with the experts and leaders within your business. It needs to reside in their social voices. Thought leadership matters when it is deep. You need to know the kernel, the thing that your business is going to be a thought leader in – that you as an individual will spearhead for your organization and sector – and you can then become the leader in this specialism.

How do you determine what you should lead on as an individual representing your company?

We start with listening to our audience and then move on to build up social personas. How are these people behaving on social? What are they interested in? What are they doing? What matters to them? Then look at how that fits with what matters to you, your business and your own interests. Finally, decide how you're going to overlay your opinions and help those you speak to to understand your industry sector.

How do you enable thought leadership?

It's absolutely all about cultural change, and cultural change from the top. You can't really outsource thought leadership. You can delegate some of the writing or scheduling to somebody else, but the thinking and opinion must come from you. After all, you are going to be the thought leader and you will need to own that if you are going to be authentic.

To be effective it needs to be part of a job role, ensuring you carve out time to talk about the business with a voice that is yours. Often, that's okay if you are senior and can work it into your day, but if you're in sales and must make 100 calls a day, if time for thought leadership isn't built in, it will never happen. You not only have to build in time, but also set KPIs around it and give people the time to deliver. In my experience, people really underestimate how long it takes to build a thought leadership profile.

When deploying your campaigns, focus on the core objectives, plan in a structured way over campaigns or blocks of time, focus on your content pillars and the synergies between corporate and individual profiles to maximize impact for your effort and resources. At the business level, create a regular cadence with focused content to support a hero, hub, help deployment and share this with the wider team. At an individual level, consider how you can utilize the corporate content to support your thought leadership and personal brand and provide timely and useful information to your buyer network. In the next chapter we will look at some example tools to help increase efficiencies.

Bibliography

D Bermant (2022) Director, CaptainJV [interview] (20 January 2022), bitly.com (archived at https://perma.cc/J4WA-CCFZ)

N Church (2021) CEO, Emerge Digital [interview] (13 December 2021)

Copy House (2021a) Copy House Twitter, twitter.com/copy_house_ltd/ status/1468522005481807873 (archived at https://perma.cc/J679-YYZX)

Copy House (2021b) LinkedIn, www.linkedin.com/posts/copy-house-ltd_12-days-of-content-christmas-tips-activity-6879737078247165952-x346/ (archived at https://perma.cc/9AKV-ZBG4)

Copy House (2022a) Empowering technology brands to challenge the status quo, copyhouse.io (archived at https://perma.cc/V4U3-C8BF)

Copy House (2022b) 12 days of Christmas content marketing tips, copyhouse. io/12-days-of-christmas-content-marketing-tips/ (archived at https://perma.cc/ ERA6-TCDZ)

Edleman and LinkedIn (2021) 2021 B2B thought leadership impact study, USA, Edleman and LinkedIn

L Hannan (2022) Co-Founder, Pitch121 [interview] (6 January 2022)

Z Haq (2021) Why you should be making more carousel posts on LinkedIn, contentdrips.com/blog/2021/02/why-you-should-be-making-more-carousel-posts-on-linkedin/ (archived at https://perma.cc/RM4G-Q3T9)

K Howell (2021) Director, Immediate Future [interview] (13 December 2021)

Immediate Future, 2022. Immediate Future Homepage. [Online] immediatefuture.co.uk (archived at https://perma.cc/L2BS-D6XJ)

IPA (2017) *Media in Focus Report*, IPA, London

Lempod (2022) Lempod homepage, lempod.com (archived at https://perma. cc/7NW2-K4R8)

E Neal (2022) Head of Outbound, The Marketing Practice [interview] (7 January 2022)

Templafy (2020) How many emails are sent every day? Top email statistics for businesses, www.templafy.com/blog/how-many-emails-are-sent-every-day-top-email-statistics-your-business-needs-to-know/ (archived at https://perma. cc/4E2Y-5C2X)

The B2B Institute (2021) The 5 principles of growth in B2B marketing: Empirical observations on B2B effectiveness, business.linkedin.com/content/dam/me/ business/en-us/amp/marketing-solutions/images/lms-b2b-institute/pdf/LIN_ B2B-Marketing-Report-Digital-v02.pdf (archived at https://perma.cc/ SEF5-6QDE)

H Wray (2021) 95% of B2B consumers aren't actively looking to buy, my.socialmindshub.com/#95-of-b-2-b-consumers-arent-actively-looking-to-buy (archived at https://perma.cc/BMW9-CWEA)

07

B2B social selling tools

How to select the best tools to improve efficiencies, increase insight and transform results

> There are lots of tools on the market which can save time and resources, but how can you make sure you are spending your money wisely? This chapter considers some solutions, provides checklists to aid decision making and explains the benefits of integrated CRM, in addition to discussing the pros and cons of using LinkedIn Sales Navigator.

What are social selling tools?

There is a wide range of tools to support your social selling activity that are designed to increase productivity, the transparency of sharing information, automating repetitive tasks and generally easing the complexity. They are useful but can be expensive, so make sure you invest in the right ones and always remember that social selling is about relationship building. Therefore don't sacrifice the personal touch for automation efficiencies.

As Liden says, 'Automation is the future, it's part of data driven marketing. It's being intelligent, it can make you more efficient, save time, and save costs. Marketing and sales are more complex so your algorithms and the science behind automation have to become much more sophisticated, so that people don't feel like they are being spammed. It should always be the right message at the right time, and then people don't mind if it's generated by an automated process' (Liden, 2022).

The main types of social selling tools you might want to consider are discussed below and links to the companies referenced are included in the appendix.

- **CRM** – Customer relationship management systems are the backbone of sales and marketing deployment. Many are offered on a SaaS (software as a service), monthly-fee basis and there are numerous options which range in price and features. Your CRM system should be the first technology you invest in. It brings your marketing and sales intelligence together in one place and enables you to put your buyer/customer at the heart of your delivery with a transparent shared view. Depending on your budget, the size of your team, ability to customize the interface, and requirements, you may want a state-of-the-art CRM ecosystem such as Salesforce (Salesforce, 2022) or Microsoft Dynamics (Microscoft Dynamics 365, 2022), or a plug and play such as HubSpot (HubSpot, 2022) or Pipedrive (Pipedrive, 2022).

- **Prospecting and sales intelligence** – These tools enable you to source and manage accurate and compliant information and insights on prospects. If you operate in multiple markets, make sure that the data sources are compliant in them all as due to varying data protection laws, some solutions are market specific. There is a wide range of options available here, including globally-compliant data sources such as Cognism (Cognism, 2022), GDPR-compliant sources such as Vainu (Vainu, 2022), platform-specific tools such as LinkedIn Sales Navigator (LinkedIn, 2022), and in-depth analysis tools such as ZoomInfo (Zoominfo, 2022) and Dun & Bradstreet (Dun & Bradstreet, 2022).

- **Sales productivity** – These tools help reduce time wasted on admin tasks and simplify the buyer's journey by removing some of the stoppage points and putting them in control of the next steps. They include a range of options from automating meeting bookings into your diary using Calendly (Calendly, 2022) to qualifying leads prior to automated appointment booking with Chili Piper (Diffenderfer, 2022), automating testimonial creation with Trust Mary (Trust Mary, 2022) and creating on-brand proposals with Turtl (Turtl, 2022). By delivering a quick and relevant interaction with the buyer when they require it, the salesperson cuts out time-wasting missed calls and emailing back and forth, and the buyer's experience is improved.

- **Marketing automation and ABM** – An ABM approach requires a personalized and co-ordinated delivery across multiple touchpoints and the networked audience of individuals in your target companies. Many businesses use marketing automation technology to support their ABM activity with account-based intelligence, advertising and personalized content. This technology is often an extension of their core CRM technology, for example HubSpot (HubSpot, 2022) and Salesforce (Salesforce, 2022) offer these additional options. Alternatively, a bespoke ABM tool can be used in addition to your CRM platform, such as Demandbase (Demandbase, 2022). However, this type of technology isn't just limited to ABM, it can be used more widely to save time on social media posting, email follow-ups and other personalized content opportunities. Tools such as Sendible (Sendible, 2022) and Hootsuite (Hootsuite, 2022) are great for automated social media posting, scheduling and streamlined content creation.

- **Sales enablement and digital sales rooms** – As more of the sales process moves online, the opportunity to engage directly with customers, reduce buyer friction, share content and meet virtually in digital sales rooms has become more important. Some tools are extensions of CRM platforms, such as groove (groove, 2022) which is accessible to Salesforce users. Others are designed for sales enablement specifically and offer a digital sales room experience. They can be added into your existing suite of tools and include global market leader in sales enablement Seismic (Seismic, 2022) and the leading digital sales room Get Accept (Get Accept, 2022).

- **Customer success** – These tools are designed for beyond the sale to help preserve and extend revenues and deliver customer satisfaction. As social selling considers the post-sale relationship to be equally important, these tools could be a useful option. Examples include ChurnZero (ChurnZero, 2022), ClientSuccess (ClientSuccess, 2022) and planhat (planhat, 2022). All start with onboarding and try to ensure the customer experience is improved by providing actionable data and insights on customer health, usage/uptake and key triggers.

- **Configure, price, quote (CPQ)** – This sales automation software speeds up the sales cycle by automating key processes. The enterprise-level CRM systems such as Salesforce (Salesforce, 2022) offer these tools as options but there are alternative solutions available such as dealhub (dealhub, 2022) and Proposify(Proposify, 2022).

Note: the tools mentioned in this chapter are all detailed in the appendix at the end of this book.

How to select a CRM tool for B2B social selling

As your CRM tool will be the most important technology you use it is essential you make the right choice. Always consider the following factors when making your decision:

1 **Functionality** – Make a list of what you need the system to deliver as a minimum and what other options would be desirable. Think about what you need not only today but also over the next few years as ideally you won't want to make a change. For example, do you need marketing and sales integration, are you taking the system across markets and multiple sales teams, do you want to schedule posts from the system?

2 **Ease of use** – Consider the interface for your users and how much training will be required. If it is difficult to enter and retrieve information, the data will be incomplete or inaccurate and therefore the system won't be useful.

3 **Customization options** – Consider how much tailoring you require for your business. Many enterprise businesses use Microsoft Dynamics 365 or Salesforce because they want a high level of customization. Smaller businesses find SaaS offerings more affordable and perfectly suited to their needs.

4 **Implementation time** – Usually linked to the level of customization, most SaaS offerings can be live almost immediately.

5 **Customer service** – Make sure you have access to support. Check reviews and take references before you invest.

6 **Price** – Not the most important factor but certainly important to ensure you get an acceptable ROI.

You can use the principles in these considerations for other technology and tool decisions too.

LinkedIn and automation

For many organizations LinkedIn will be the core channel to market for your social selling activity, so how can you ensure you are making the most of the tools associated with this platform?

LinkedIn is a professional network that encourages social selling but does not want members to be spammed. It therefore has strict rules which you agree to follow when you join as both a company and an individual. If you are seen to be flouting these rules, your account can be banned. The most common reasons for having an account banned are sending too many connection requests, having too low a reply rate to connection requests, and using automation tools that have led to your account being flagged for suspicious activity.

Despite this risk there are hundreds of LinkedIn automation tools available on the market, many of which will claim to be 'safe' to use because their activity is restricted to 'reasonable' volumes, is randomized to 'mimic human behaviour' and they are cloud-based so are less easy for the algorithm to detect.

If you are considering using an automation tool alongside LinkedIn, be sure that you use it with caution. Only use tools which support the positive behaviours endorsed by LinkedIn (relationship building, networking and adding value), and if you are warned by LinkedIn that your account is temporarily restricted, take action immediately to stop using automation tools and check in with LinkedIn support to find out why.

The most effective and 'safest' automation tools for LinkedIn demonstrate LinkedIn best practice. Use the guide below for all your LinkedIn activity and to check any automation tool decisions against.

LINKEDIN USAGE BEST PRACTICE CHECKLIST
A guide to ensuring the best performance on LinkedIn for social selling

Use this guide to help make the most of your LinkedIn profile, but also as a checklist to consider when choosing an automation tool. Make sure that if do use automation tools they operate within LinkedIn guidelines.

1 Optimize your profile for social selling

Make sure that your personal profile is focused on your customer or prospect. In social selling you are not using your profile to be found by recruiters, you are using it to build your personal brand, to ensure you appear as interesting, trustworthy and useful to potential buyers. Remember that when you send out a connection request, your profile, and potentially your company profile, will be checked out and used to help decide whether they will accept.

A strong profile will increase your social selling index (SSI). To ensure your profile is interesting and credible:

- Know who your audience is, complete your profile with your ideal buyer in mind, what keywords will resonate with them, what characteristics or background information will be relevant. Telling them how great you are at selling is unlikely to be as important as how much you have helped other organizations with the same problems.

- Complete all your personal information including education, skills and interests.

- Make sure you appear as human and let your voice and personality speak consistently in each section of your profile. This includes having a memorable and distinctive profile headline and an 'about' section that is succinct and focused on the most important factors.

- Include how your company's products and services can solve the problems faced by your ideal buyer.

- Make sure your profile is visually appealing. This includes a professional and approachable profile picture, a meaningful background such as a company banner, and the use of rich media in your featured section.

- Demonstrate thought leadership by becoming a trusted adviser. As a rule of thumb post three times more valuable content (educational, useful, inspirational, supportive, etc) than you post about your company or products.

- Follow relevant hashtags and join groups that are important to your ideal buyer, complete a persona for them as shown in Chapter 3 so you are as relevant as possible. Being part of the same group provides another reason for that person to accept a connection request.

- Create a custom URL – mine is www.linkedin.com/in/julieatherton

- Welcome connections: do you want followers or connections? Include a range of contact details to make it easy for people to get in touch in the way that they prefer.

2 Maintain your SSI at >70

Your SSI is corelated with social selling effectiveness and top social sellers are more likely to have a score over 70. Maintaining a score of >70 is a quick and easy way to check that you are conducting enough activity on LinkedIn and balancing it across the four areas considered important to the algorithm: establishing your professional brand, finding the right people, engaging with insights and building relationships. An additional advantage of maintaining a high SSI is that LinkedIn limits the number of connection requests you can send to <100 requests per week, but if your score is >80 you can sometimes send more. And people with a high SSI are less likely to be banned by LinkedIn.

3 Build an ideal audience gradually

Relevancy is important to the LinkedIn algorithm; it wants to ensure your content is relevant to you and your audience. Consider who is in your LinkedIn network: is it dominated by colleagues, recruiters, salespeople, or by people who match your ideal buyer profile? You can ask LinkedIn for a copy of your data in the 'data and privacy' link found when you click on your profile picture. Regularly review the make-up of your connections and followers and try to increase the proportion that meet your ideal buyer profile.

As you build up this network of ideal buyers, warm up your account. Don't go from zero connection requests to 100 immediately, although you can send out up to 100 requests per day. The automation tool Closely (Blackwood, 2021) recommends capping at 50 per day and warming up in the following way:

- Days 1–5: up to 10 connection requests and messages per day
- Days 5–15: up to 20 connection requests and messages per day
- Days 15–25: up to 30 connection requests and messages per day
- After 25 days: up to 50 connection requests and messages per day

Remember, LinkedIn will be suspicious if you have too many outstanding longtail connection requests. Delete these by clicking on 'My Network' in the LinkedIn navigation bar, then clicking on 'See All xx' above your list of invitations. By clicking on 'Sent' you will see all the outstanding invitations you have sent out and can decide to withdraw those that have been there for a long time.

4 Personalize your outreach

When you do send out connection requests make sure they are personalized and give a reason for the outreach and why that person might want to connect with you. Don't include a sales message, make sure you are adding value, and don't send a sales message as a bounce-back message to a connection request acceptance. Remember, you are building a long-term trusted relationship, not driving short-term sales. Use a consistent tone of voice with your profile and always sign off. To ensure you can send a personal message with your connection requests, go your potential buyer's profile to make the request rather than just clicking the 'Connect' button on the 'People you may know from xxxx' list.

There are lots of ways to make your connection request timely and relevant, including reaching out after:

- attending the same meeting or event
- engaging with someone's content or they have engaged with yours
- they have visited your profile. You will have more visibility of who has visited your profile if you use Sales Navigator
- joining the same group
- connecting with someone else in their organization. People are more likely to accept a connection request if you are connected to other people they know well

5 Engage with your network

Concentrate on building relationships by ensuring your content is relevant and timely and adds value to your connections. Start your own conversations with interesting or useful content and don't start selling in the first, second or even third message. You will want to ensure that your connections feel positive after every interaction, your mantra is how can you help them, not when will you buy from me?

Remember that your reputation as a thought leader and the profile of your personal brand will encourage your network to engage. Monitor and test different messaging approaches and content to ensure you make the most of every opportunity and join groups, leverage industry data and non-competing content, and share ideas in comments to really get to know your connections.

Remember, the decision to use any form of automation on LinkedIn should not be taken lightly. All automation incurs some risk that your profile could be banned. Do not use automation to spam.

The case for and against using LinkedIn Sales Navigator

LinkedIn Sales Navigator (LinkedIn Sales Solutions, 2022) is the bespoke tool created by LinkedIn to support social selling. Costs vary depending on

TABLE 7.1 LinkedIn Sales Navigator key features comparison

Feature name	Feature description	Subscriptions with this feature	Potential benefits for social selling	Potential problems for social selling
Advanced lead and company search	Improved LinkedIn search to enable you to find the most relevant prospects.	Core, Advanced, Advanced Plus.	By enabling more focused searches and saving specific search lists, an alternative 'homepage' for LinkedIn concentrates effort on the important connections.	This is useful but if it is the only feature you use probably doesn't justify the cost. You can save LinkedIn searches to an external spreadsheet for use again if you do not have Sales Navigator.
Lead recommendations	Suggestions customized for you. Recommended people to connect with in your target accounts.	Core, Advanced, Advanced Plus.	Prioritize and qualify your sales preferences ensuring you consider the wider buying group and influencers.	Make sure you give a valid reason for asking to connect that is useful to your prospect and not just you. It may be tempting to start selling straight away because you have a stronger relationship with the other people you are connected to on the account. Remember you need to build a relationship with each person individually.

(continued)

TABLE 7.1 (Continued)

Feature name	Feature description	Subscriptions with this feature	Potential benefits for social selling	Potential problems for social selling
Real-time sales updates	Real-time and relevant updates on your accounts and leads, including job changes, anniversaries, etc.	Core. However, Advanced and Advanced Plus also include buyer interest alerts.	Sending a personal message in response to these alerts shows you care and helps keep you front of mind. Job changes are particularly important as your customers may want to buy your services in their new role and you will also want to make sure you build a relationship with their successor.	Think about timings and plan sequences carefully. You may well want to change things when you move jobs but probably not on the first day. Put yourself in your buyers' shoes: how can you help in their new role?
Notes	The notes can be synced back to your CRM. Use them to organize your leads and accounts with tags and additional notes.	Core, Advanced Plus, Advanced.	A useful way to sort information and ensure that multiple stakeholders in your organization can all share information on an account or buyer.	When working with a wider sales team, agree together any specific information that is important to enable a more transparent understanding.
CRM integration	Automatically saves leads and the accounts you are selling to and logs your Sales Navigator activity into your CRM.	Advanced Plus.	A great way to track and measure the impact of LinkedIn on sales and to provide an overall view of the account or buyer.	Make sure you take advantage of all the information available, and that the CRM is up to date. It can be frustrating if there is conflicting information on LinkedIn and your CRM.

Feature	Description	Plans	Value	Advice
InMail messages	Sends emails into LinkedIn members inboxes even if you aren't connected with them.	Core, Advanced, Advanced Plus. 50/ month.	Provides access to > 500 million members. The InMail can be targeted and personalized for different groups.	It can be tempting to use this feature as you can reach large volumes of prospects. Be careful, an inbox full of sales messages from people the recipient doesn't know well feels like spam. Ideally connect first and then use your personal account to send messages.
Smart links presentations	Enables presentations to be viewed within LinkedIn.	Advanced, Advanced Plus.	This enables you to track who is engaging with your content, providing useful insights on what is working for your audience.	Although your audience doesn't need to leave LinkedIn to view your presentation, make sure this is a benefit to them and it makes sense to receive presentations in this way before you use it.
TeamLink	Collaborate with your team with visibility of your company's combined network.	Advanced, Advanced Plus.	Use this function to identify people you know who are connected to people you want to reach out to. Ask them for an introduction or mention them in your connection request.	Make sure that you open and honest when you mention other connections. For example, only say someone has recommended you connect if they really have. Implying a stronger relationship with mutual connections than really exists is not appropriate.

(continued)

TABLE 7.1 (Continued)

Feature name	Feature description	Subscriptions with this feature	Potential benefits for social selling	Potential problems for social selling
Email integrations – Outlook Web and Sales Navigator Application Platform (SNAP) (LinkedIn Business Solutions, 2022)	Look at the LinkedIn profile information for your contacts in your Outlook inbox.	Core. However, Advanced and Advanced Plus have access to SNAP which allows integration into multiple additional tools.	This feature is particularly useful when people share their full contact details. It can save you time as you don't need to move between Outlook and LinkedIn to see their profile information.	Use additional contact information with care. You will have to disclose if asked how you obtained their phone number or email address and should be ready to do so.
Who's viewed your profile	See the full list of everyone who has viewed your profile in the last 90 days.	Core, Advanced, Advanced Plus.	Sending a connection request just after someone looks at your profile can increase the likelihood that they will say yes. This feature also gives you great insights as to whether your target buyers are engaging with you and looking to find out more about you.	Think carefully about the timing and content of your responses to actions. You want to respond quickly but don't want your messages to feel automated or 'stalky'. Remember you want to add value.

whether you are using it as an individual, as part of a sales team or on a customized licence agreement. If LinkedIn is your primary social selling channel, you may well want to consider whether Sales Navigator could help you improve your targeting, data insights and engagement levels. According to LinkedIn, sellers using Sales Navigator see a 15 per cent increase in their sales pipeline, 42 per cent larger deal sizes closed and 59 per cent of their revenues influenced (LinkedIn Sales Solutions, 2022).

The LinkedIn Sales Navigator features

The tool has a number of features which can be accessed at the various subscription levels of Core, Advanced and Advanced Plus. Table 7.1 highlights the different key features and considers how these might be useful to you and where problems could arise. Many organizations, including Ericsson and Emerge Digital, invest in fully integrating LinkedIn with their Microsoft Dynamics or Salesforce CRM to provide a measurable sales pipeline and full transparency across the business. Table 7.1 compares the key features for the three levels of Sales Navigator adoption.

Additional automation options

Probably the best combination is a mix of automation and the personal touch. That way you can focus your time on engagements that look interesting or have been pre-qualified while still making sure you reach a larger audience of potential buyers. Laura Hannan, co-founder of Pitch121, is an advocate of this approach and a LinkedIn expert. In the interview here she gives her views on LinkedIn, SEO and automation.

INTERVIEW
Laura Hannan, Co-Founder, Pitch121 (Hannan, 2022)

Pitch121 is a fully managed service that takes the LinkedIn profiles of key individuals in a business and uses their personal profiles for brand awareness and social selling. The leadership team often have their profiles managed because they don't find the time to do it all themselves. Personal leadership profiles are used to drive awareness, network with peers and more easily achieve those 'have a chat' meetings. Laura Hannan founded Pitch121 with Fergus Parker in 2017 after spotting a gap in the market for personal LinkedIn management.

How do you define social selling?

Contrary to what the name implies it is really about relationship building and is used not just to drive new business sales but for partnerships, upselling and long-term account management. It is about starting a conversation, helping out where you can, and when people see you can add value, then you can move into the sales conversation.

Social selling delivers awareness (personal brand and company brand), lead generation and lead nurturing.

What are the priorities in social selling?

Typically, we find that larger companies focus on awareness KPIs and smaller companies on sales KPIs. The need to see returns in terms of revenue for small companies tends to be a much shorter timeframe than in larger companies. However, with more time to engage deeper and wider in an organization you can gain the bigger, 'harder to win' clients.

It's a balance, we understand the need to be quick to deliver meetings and support SMEs to get to the end result as quickly as possible. With a large company, the marketing team recognizes that LinkedIn company pages can only do so much. For example, a personal profile of an MD will give ten times the reach of a company page post and so they're keen on using social selling for awareness. And in the end, awareness leads to revenue, but if you sit and wait for your leads to all come to you, you won't get the returns you could get. Awareness plus follow-up on a one-to-one basis is the key. It isn't an either/or.

Why did you choose LinkedIn as the social selling platform for your business?

We decided quite quickly to stick to LinkedIn because it has so many features and it really pulls marketing and sales teams together. You can do a lot of the early stage selling on the platform. It's not that the other platforms aren't useful, but LinkedIn has a high ratio of relevant users and we know who they work for, and in many cases we can find out what they are wanting to talk about.

However, we wanted to marry up the social side of things, which is very conversational (warming people up, building that relationship) with a more direct sales route.

By integrating LinkedIn and email from the same profile you build trust and have the best of both worlds – awareness building and conversation starting in social media complementing the more direct transactional conversations you get from email.

How useful is LinkedIn Sales Navigator?

Sales Navigator is a really good tool for being more efficient and is especially useful for:

- a directory to improve your searches
- saving specific searches as lists
- tracking updates on target companies and being alerted when your decision maker moves roles, is mentioned in the news or has put out a post
- creating an alternative 'home page' in LinkedIn with only saved contacts which helps focus your activity and effort on the people you are selling to. It means that you don't get distracted 'looking' rather than 'working'.

How does Pitch121's FANBase tool work with LinkedIn Sales Navigator?

Sales Navigator is great at telling you who people are, but not so great at collating what you have done, who has liked your post in the past, whether you've sent them a message about your next webinar or not, etc. So, FANBase and our email delivery platform sit on top of Sales Navigator, like a CRM with some additional functionality.

Sales Navigator lets you save all the people that you're trying to work with whether you're connected to them or not. Your Sales Navigator home feed only has the people that you've saved and so it's much more effective to focus your efforts there.

FANBase goes to this home feed and filters the feed to look only at what your leads have posted today. It's a person-to-person relationship on LinkedIn, so we don't worry too much about the company updates as they are probably only engaging with the social media managers.

Our tool ensures we don't miss an opportunity to engage in that post, so you are timely and efficient. For example, if somebody has posted a month ago and you like the post and then try to connect with them, it's too long ago. Whereas if the post has just gone up and you like it, and you're only the second person to like it, and nobody else has commented, they're going to notice you and be a little bit thankful that somebody engaged with their post that they spent time on.

In addition, the impact of their post will be greater because the algorithm likes the interaction. So, when you get in touch with them moments later to say 'your post just came up in my feed, I gave it a like and I'd like to stay in touch', then it's a bit of the Law of Reciprocity, you've done a little thing for them and they do a little thing for you, i.e. accept your connection request.

Do you use LinkedIn InMail?

No, we don't use LinkedIn InMail at all. It is a good alternative to sales messages in the inbox as you can reach a higher volume, but we've never found either to be very effective. People just don't like to be sold to on LinkedIn. They are looking to network and you just have to be a bit more empathetic, looking to help out rather than approaching with only your sales agenda.

Everything we do at Pitch121 is organic. We start with a social touchpoint, for example view their profile or like their post, and then we connect. It's messaging, posting, following up on people who liked your post or profile, and then email: 'Hey, we've been connected for a while. I would love to learn more about what you do. We're doing this, let's have a chat.'

We do set up meetings from LinkedIn itself, but they are much more value-based, for example, 'We should have a virtual coffee' or 'Let's swap some ideas', that kind of tone.

On email it's a little bit more transactional and direct: 'These are the services we offer. Are you interested in having a chat about XYZ?'

Sales messages in the inbox only work if someone is open and looking for your services right now. Most people aren't, they may be elsewhere in the buying journey, or not in it at all. And, if you have an ignored sales message, it's difficult to follow up on that. Chasing in the inbox is even worse, going from disappointment at getting a sales pitch not a conversation to annoyance that this person is interrupting my inbox with annoying chasers.

A more human, empathetic approach is needed. 'I noticed that you…', 'I liked your post about…' '… actually, you might be interested in this report. Happy to share…'

Many salespeople find it hard not to drive straight to the sales pitch. But they risk burning future relationships by selling too quickly either in the inbox or via InMail.

Everyone on LinkedIn is there in a business capacity; people are open to networking and buying from each other. The human approach helps you as a salesperson to earn the right to sell to them.

How important is automation versus human interaction in the social selling process?

I'm not anti-automation where it can bring efficiencies and a more well-timed approach or sophisticated approach. Working LinkedIn for sales takes time. However, it is automation that has facilitated generic messages with poor targeting. When this happens, it is a case of lack of thought, training or empathy on the side of the person setting up the campaign rather than the technology itself that is at fault.

Our process is led by the target customer, which means that contacts are more likely to convert later. I often see a lot of time spent on post creation, and some also spending time on amplifying, but the way to really get results is the follow-up and this is where a combination of automation and personal management really works using templated and personalized interactions. For example: 'Thanks for liking my interview post today <name>. I'd like to stay in touch!'

This is a great start to a conversation, initially about the post probably, but then it can be turned around: 'I saw that you are hiring for sales at the moment, not the easiest! How's that going for you?'

We lead the journey by the interaction using automation and templated messages blended with human interactions. Template usage goes wrong when you see it used for DSM (direct sales messages) such as 'So here's what I can do for you'. People just ignore it (unless they are one of the few that might actually need that offer, at that moment).

However, more conversational templated messaging that continues the conversation works well:

'Just, you know, going out on a limb here, but maybe it's worth us having a chat one day.'

'Yeah sure.'

'Great, are you around next week?'

Ideally, we look at what prospects are doing and talking about and respond to something they have done first, rather than us contacting them with our sales agenda. If you interact with somebody's content before you connect and use that as the reason to connect, you'll see a minimum 10 per cent uplift in your connection acceptance rate. Finding a reason to connect is important, so using a relevant reason based on the prospect's own activity makes sense and works.

How important is the link between social selling and SEO?

LinkedIn and search are closely connected, with 22 per cent of LinkedIn traffic coming from search (Social Pilot, 2022). LinkedIn company pages seem to be the best ranked on Google but personal profiles are quite well indexed, and some but not all articles get indexed. In the past, LinkedIn posts didn't rank on Google, but they do now occasionally.

To maximize the integration with search, think about how you post. For example, write an article for your website and (once indexed) duplicate it on your LinkedIn profile. Consider changing the headline to ideally be indexed for a different key phrase. You could repeat on Medium.com or Reddit too.

Promoting your article could increase visibility further as articles with more engagement are more likely to be indexed on Google. Although LinkedIn posts don't rank often on search, tweets do. I'm not a big Twitter user, but when I post on LinkedIn, I automatically share the same post with my Twitter account. I do this mainly with the aim of getting that content onto Google via Twitter.

How can you improve your SEO with keywords?

There are a number of places on LinkedIn where you can add keywords to improve your rankings on both a LinkedIn search and a Google search. They are:

- your URL
- the title of your profile picture and banner
- your headline
- your 'providing services' if you have it and your keyword is one of the services listed
- your summary/about section
- experience, particularly your job title
- skills
- media links and descriptions of content from your 'Featured' section and all the way through the additional sections
- having your keywords as part of your company name on LinkedIn – this is also quite smart from a Google perspective.

You can easily get a keyword into your profile a dozen times without it affecting readability, and similar to SEO, it is better and easier to rank for one or two keywords with repetition rather than adding 12 different keywords.

Automation plus personalization – the perfect mix

Whatever channel you use for your social selling, remember it is a personal human interaction and needs to feel authentic and relevant. The case study here gives some examples of how to mix templated/automated activity with personalized/tailored content to be timely and relevant and to add value to your prospective buyer.

CASE STUDY

Pitch121: maximizing lead generation with automation (Hannan, 2022)

Pitch121 (Pitch121, 2022) work with a range of clients from SMEs to large corporations. Using their FANBase tool they maximize the impact of LinkedIn by testing and continually improving their outreach conversations using personal profiles. With a combination of templated conversation starters and nudges and personalized interactions they continually increase connection acceptances and qualified lead generation results quarter on quarter. Q1 2022 saw a year-on-year increase of meetings booked of over 300 per cent.

The following conversation examples have all delivered great results.

Example 1: Branding agency outreach conversation sequence

Newly funded start-ups often need to work on their brand positioning and comms so are a great prospect for branding agencies. This branding agency used a combination of templated conversation starters and personalized messaging to trigger an initial meeting.

Figure 7.1 shows the messaging sequence over a three-week period which resulted in a meeting being set up with the prospective buyer. The first two outreach messages were templates. Once the buyer engaged, a personal tailored message was sent. This methodology enables the seller's time to be focused on those buyers who have engaged and are more likely to convert.

Example 2: C-suite outreach conversation sequence

It can be difficult to gain the attention of the C-suite as they are so busy and their appointments are often gatekept by a PA. LinkedIn has the advantage of bypassing gatekeepers. Asking members of the C-suite to be interviewed on your podcast can be a compelling way to start a conversation. Senior leaders are often happier to initially meet for an interview which will help promote their profile than for a creds

FIGURE 7.1 Example outreach conversation sequence from a branding agency

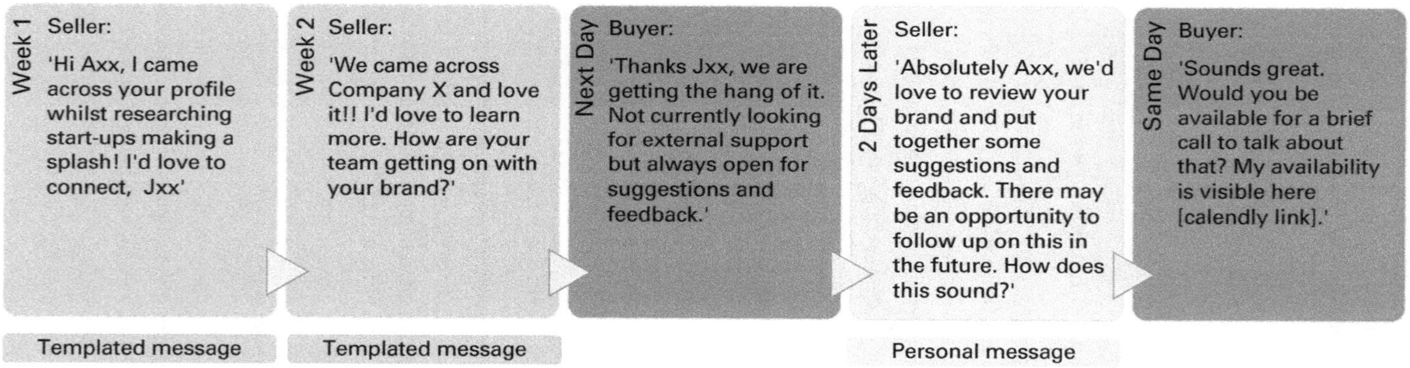

Seller:
Week 1
'Hi Axx, I came across your profile whilst researching start-ups making a splash! I'd love to connect, Jxx'

Templated message

Seller:
Week 2
'We came across Company X and love it!! I'd love to learn more. How are your team getting on with your brand?'

Templated message

Buyer:
Next Day
'Thanks Jxx, we are getting the hang of it. Not currently looking for external support but always open for suggestions and feedback.'

Seller:
2 Days Later
'Absolutely Axx, we'd love to review your brand and put together some suggestions and feedback. There may be an opportunity to follow up on this in the future. How does this sound?'

Personal message

Buyer:
Same Day
'Sounds great. Would you be available for a brief call to talk about that? My availability is visible here [calendly link].'

NOTE Test different versions of the templated messages to find the strongest conversation starters to ensure an acceptance rate of >25%.

FIGURE 7.2 Example outreach conversation sequence to a C-suite potential buyer

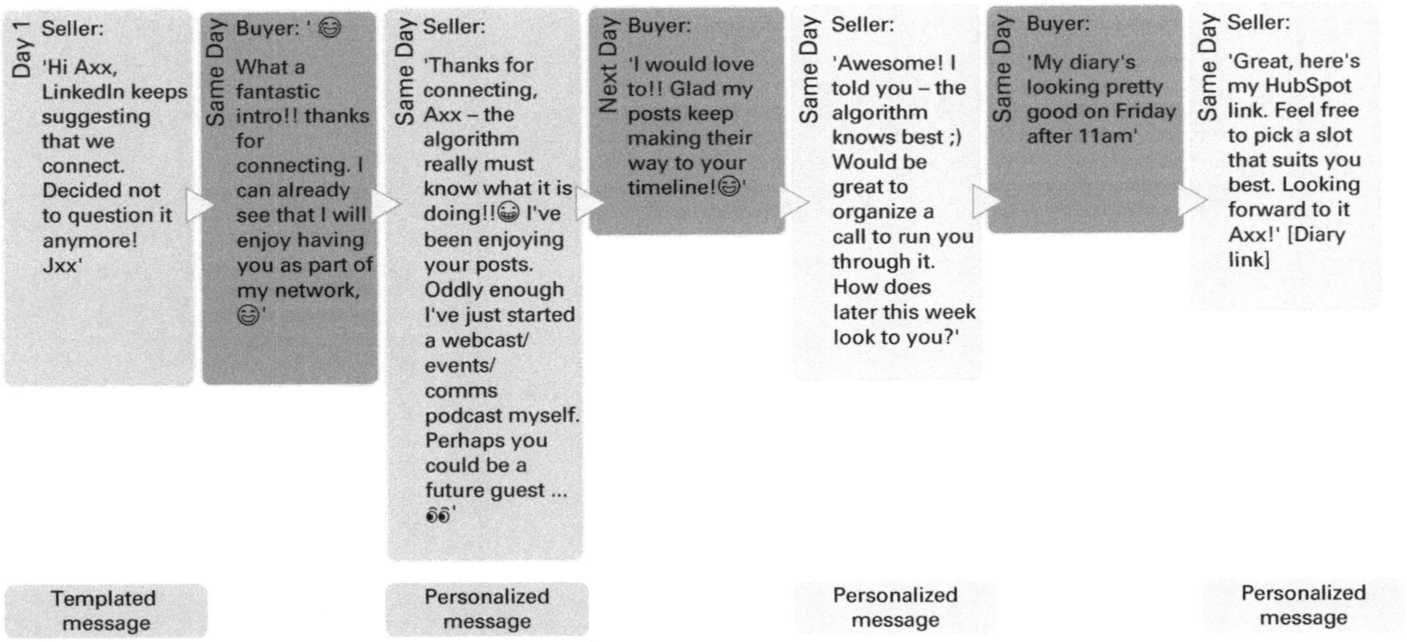

Seller:

Day 1

'Hi Axx, LinkedIn keeps suggesting that we connect. Decided not to question it anymore! Jxx'

Templated message

Buyer: '😊

Same Day

What a fantastic intro!! thanks for connecting. I can already see that I will enjoy having you as part of my network, 😊'

Seller:

Same Day

'Thanks for connecting, Axx – the algorithm really must know what it is doing!!😊 I've been enjoying your posts. Oddly enough I've just started a webcast/ events/ comms podcast myself. Perhaps you could be a future guest … 👀'

Personalized message

Buyer:

Next Day

'I would love to!! Glad my posts keep making their way to your timeline!😊'

Seller:

Same Day

'Awesome! I told you – the algorithm knows best :) Would be great to organize a call to run you through it. How does later this week look to you?'

Personalized message

Buyer:

Same Day

'My diary's looking pretty good on Friday after 11am'

Seller:

Same Day

'Great, here's my HubSpot link. Feel free to pick a slot that suits you best. Looking forward to it Axx!' [Diary link]

Personalized message

meeting. However, the session provides an opportunity for the buyer to explore their challenges and position their services in a value-adding way.

Figure 7.2 shows the messaging sequence over a two-day period which resulted in a meeting being set up with the prospective buyer. The first outreach message was templated and once the buyer engaged, personal tailored messages were sent. This sequence used humour to spark the initial conversation.

Tips on how to start and continue conversations on LinkedIn

There are multiple ways to start and continue conversations. Use the tried-and-tested list below to see what can work for you.

- Respond quickly.
- Compliment their business.
- Associate the compliment with your values/personality – add the word 'also' to talk about yourself while still talking about them. 'I see you also....'
- Sound excited and spontaneous – put personality into your messages.
- Show interest in them, making you likeable.
- Find common ground.
- Use posts to get people talking.
- Go the extra, check their website.
- Be playful with exchanges and mirror their behaviour, for example using emojis – keep the thread.
- Use open-ended questions.
- Use humour – 'the algorithm wants us to connect'.
- Plant the seed that you'll be speaking later.
- Move the conversation into your direction by acknowledging and then saying, 'I also find/have...'.
- Show you know your stuff without boasting through empathy, vulnerability, etc.
- Repeat what they have said to you.
- Take their negative and turn that into a positive ('We do the things you hate').

Tips on how to encourage connections to agree to a call on LinkedIn

Often the goal for an outreach campaign will be to set up an initial call. The list below provides some great ideas to move initial engagement into action through:

- value-led asks – happy to share some tips
- a (virtual) coffee – reduces pressure on the sales ask
- collaboration or mutual exchange (swap notes)
- a light and breezy approach, particularly about the game of LinkedIn
- framing the ask differently – able to then say, 'I'll show you what we've done for others'
- if not ready to buy, don't be put off – carry on with value add
- flattery, personally and company – without being too sucky!
- use of phrases that make the thought sound like a passing idea: 'Oddly enough/ weirdly/just thought/out of interest'
- making the ask less pressured by adding 'at some point/one day'
- resisting going into detail, very short benefit of a call and taking out of inbox
- interest in them when booking a call: 'I'd love to pick your brains'
- having a link to book a meeting
- being brave if you're having a good exchange
- softening direct asks with soft words, for example, if you have a free trial, don't offer it, say 'Perhaps I could offer a free trial'
- making the conversation sound like it will be a mutual exchange/collaboration
- finding a template that people respond well to and using it – check the template comes out in a timely manner
- restarting conversations to check in on how something went, as if it was sparked by their latest post that you've just seen.

Quizzes are a great way to prime participants before asking them to complete a lead gen form or sign up for more information. In fact, adding a lead form to a quiz can generate a 55 per cent opt-in rate (Hufford, 2020).

When you add these to a gamification platform, where teams and individuals can compete against each other and share results, you can potentially increase conversion rates even further. Leadfamly's gamification platform is used by both B2B and B2C brands and the case study shows how effective it can be.

CASE STUDY

Leadfamly: global enterprise technology firm – using Leadfamly's gamification platform to drive engagement, increase knowledge and generate leads

A global cloud storage vendor used both the company and their teams' personal profiles to launch a 'truth or myth' quiz on LinkedIn and challenged their audience to see if they could beat the experts.

A teaser video was embedded in the initial post which made it highly visible in the feed. The video asked if you were prepared to take the challenge. A click took you directly to the game which asked participants to test their data storage knowledge.

The campaign generated many thousands of gameplays and was shared as people 'challenged' their colleagues/peers to see if they could answer the quiz. It proved to be a very successful lead generator, capturing registration information and also an understanding of participants' knowledge about the subject.

Gamification lead gen with native video in the feed can provide great content marketing support to a B2B social selling programme. If you are investing in this type of tool, make sure you wrap around with other posts and reach out to your network from personal profiles and DMs to get them involved.

Remember, tools can be expensive, so don't take too many and make sure they really will add value. Always start with an organic approach, making sure your profiles are strong and your behaviour is focused on the most important prospects. If you do take paid tools, measure their effectiveness and don't be afraid to make a change if results tail off or are never achieved.

In the next chapter we will cover measurement in more detail.

Bibliography

A Blackwood (2021) LinkedIn 2022 safety guide, blog.closelyhq.com/linkedin-safety-guide/ (archived at https://perma.cc/JPM3-5CWW)

Calendly (2022) Easy scheduling ahead, calendly.com (archived at https://perma.cc/F6XR-Q5LN)

ChurnZero (2022) Fight customer churn, churnzero.net (archived at https://perma.cc/8DE4-5ZGD)

ClientSuccess (2022) The customer retention, growth, adoption, renewal, insights, success platform, www.clientsuccess.com (archived at https://perma.cc/DG8W-A9ST)

Cognism (2022) Fast-track your business growth with Cognism Diamond Data, info.cognism.com (archived at https://perma.cc/LD8V-VSFH)

dealhub (2022) Deliver one fluid sales motion, dealhub.io (archived at https://perma.cc/2CAC-WPX3)

Demandbase (2022) Your go-to-market, smarter, www.demandbase.com (archived at https://perma.cc/XW7X-SKU8)

K Diffenderfer (2022) Calendly vs. Chili Piper: Is Instant Booker right for you? www.chilipiper.com/resources/blog/calendly-vs-chili-piper (archived at https://perma.cc/DKD8-6A4R)

Dun & Bradstreet (2022) Sales & marketing solutions, www.dnb.co.uk/solutions/marketing-sales.html (archived at https://perma.cc/VCZ6-JCNS)

Get Accept (2022) Close deals faster digitally, www.getaccept.com (archived at https://perma.cc/XL7U-FLNC)

groove (2022) Supercharge your Salesforce®, www.groove.co (archived at https://perma.cc/WP4Q-DKEG)

L Hannan (2022) Co-Founder, Pitch121 [interview] (6 January 2022)

Hootsuite (2022) Social is your superpower, www.hootsuite.com (archived at https://perma.cc/U7HF-ACDZ)

HubSpot (2022) Get started with HubSpot, www.hubspot.com (archived at https://perma.cc/VJ8L-EB5L)

B Hufford (2020) 5 secrets to using quizzes for effective lead generation, www.activecampaign.com/blog/5-secrets-to-using-quizzes-lead-generation (archived at https://perma.cc/372B-D3R9)

M Liden (2022) Vice President, Head of EMEA Marketing Transformation Office, SAP [interview] (18 February 2022)

LinkedIn Sales Solutions (2022) LinkedIn Sales Navigator, www.googleadservices.com/pagead/aclk?sa=L&ai=DChcSEwiL8Jad1PX2AhWq6O0KHUoFBfEYABABGgJkZw&ohost=www.google.com&cid=CAESa-D2dLKMGHMD1wqbcROfqA4XrGu69AC7Imv4miuH2tG9_yF9bALrnt-9KGTow7SiaHESf_B4UdZ3eRT_hLrpsnDm7xFs2a9kCnPf51hsvQj7Q9jbs4SY4aCdLmsyGjzM7 (archived at https://perma.cc/D23V-5N7Y)

LinkedIn Sales Solutions (2022) SNAP partner directory, business.linkedin.com/sales-solutions/partners/find-a-partner#select-category (archived at https://perma.cc/8MTK-FQZZ)

LinkedIn (2022) Sales solutions, business.linkedin.com/ (archived at https://perma.cc/6BXV-KTKS)

Microsoft Dynamics 365 (2022) Microsoft Dynamics 365, dynamics.microsoft.com (archived at https://perma.cc/T57T-L26D)

Pipedrive (2022) The all-in-one sales platform for growing revenue, www.pipedrive.com (archived at https://perma.cc/L4VB-STQQ)

Pitch121 (2022) Creating conversations that convert, https://pitch121.com (archived at https://perma.cc/VY3K-AUH9)

planhat (2022) Unleash unlimited success, www.planhat.com (archived at https://perma.cc/M4JV-8X5D)

Proposify (2022) This is how you close, www.proposify.com (archived at https://perma.cc/F6H3-23VJ)

Salesforce (2022) More sales, better service, greater customer insight, www.salesforce.com (archived at https://perma.cc/4Y7A-82FA)

Seismic (2022) Smarter enablement better outcomes. seismic.com (archived at https://perma.cc/PP7W-6WZJ)

Sendible (2022) Manage social media at scale, www.sendible.com (archived at https://perma.cc/9WT5-TYUK)

Social Pilot (2022) 430+ social media statistics you must know in 2022, www.socialpilot.co/blog/social-media-statistics (archived at https://perma.cc/6SK3-98PC)

Trust Mary (2022) Collect testimonials and optimize your website to increase conversion rate, trustmary.com (archived at https://perma.cc/2PCB-W3L7)

Turtl (2022) Captivating personalized content at scale, turtl.co (archived at https://perma.cc/7VGG-YMZW)

Vainu (2022) Find your future customers with actionable business data, www.vainu.com (archived at https://perma.cc/837N-NJND)

Zoominfo (2022) It's our business to grow yours, www.zoominfo.com (archived at https://perma.cc/HMP5-3J7P)

08

Using B2B social media influencers

Making the most of influencer relationships

Influence is in the DNA of social media and this chapter unpicks the wide range of opportunities available to you. Learn how to find B2B influencers and gain tips on how to both work with influencers and become more influential yourself.

How social media influencing is changing

The world of influencers is changing as it matures. Although celebrities are still important to some brands, and payment per post still exists, for the majority of businesses their motivations for working with influencers have changed and therefore so has the type of influencer they choose. What has driven this transition is an increasing belief in transparency and authenticity, and a recognition of the importance of enabling creative autonomy when working with a creator network. This change can only be delivered by a long-term partnership and shared values and interest areas, both of which are much more likely to be delivered by smaller influencers, customers and employees.

In my 2020 book *Social Media Strategy* I discuss how influencers encompass a wide range of individuals, from top-tier influencers to employees. I also recognize that it is the increasing long-term partnership approach with smaller influencers and employees that is making a significant contribution to influencer growth.

Top-tier influencers include professional influencers and celebrities. They have large followings, can be extremely expensive to work with and will be followed by their community for lots of different reasons, one of which might be something in common with your brand or business. For example, in the B2B world Richard Branson could be considered a celebrity influencer. He is a famous entrepreneur and business leader. However, he is also famous for ballooning, commercial ventures in multiple sectors and going into space. If you were able to persuade him to influence on your behalf, you would risk being lost in the noise of his multiple interests.

In Figure 8.1 you can see how the size and scale of an influencer's community are correlated to their proximity to your brand and values. Top-tier influencers cannot know your business as well as your employees do and are less likely to be as focused on your specific content pillars (see Chapter 4) than a micro influencer you have picked for that reason. Therefore, the closer the influencer is to your brand, the higher the likelihood that their followers' engagement rate and interest in your content will be as well. As 42 per cent of businesses that use influencers prefer to use conversion to sale rather than

FIGURE 8.1 The relative size and brand fit of employees, customers and brand communities as influencers

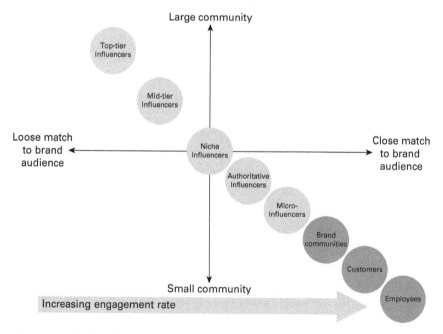

SOURCE *Social Media Strategy* (Atherton, 2020)

reach or engagement as a measure of success (Influencer Marketing Hub, in association with Refersion, 2022), this becomes ever more important to the influencer themselves as well as to you and your business.

What is a B2B influencer?

In this book we consider influencers in their broadest sense as anyone outside of the decision-making group who has an important impact on the outcome of a B2B purchasing decision. They could be a colleague, contact, customer, journalist or key opinion leader and they may affect different stages of the buyer journey depending on who they are and their connection with the buyer and other decision makers. However, each one has the potential to introduce, inspire, educate or persuade your customers to consider you as a potential solution.

B2B social selling is about a personal, individual-to-individual connection, but when we consider influencers in this wider sense, we can still include them in our strategy. The different types of influencers below can all support your social selling strategy and there is no reason why you cannot identify them and reach out to them on your social channels. The one criterion that unites B2B influencers is their expertise in and commitment to a specific content area or audience.

- **Key opinion leader (KOL)** – In B2B, KOLs and experts can almost be used interchangeably as their only difference is in the size of their following. As with celebrities, some influencers are famous for lots of different things, so it is important that you select a KOL who is a good fit for your business and ideally is recognized in the field that you operate within. As an individual social seller, you are less likely to build these relationships as they are more usually held via the PR and marketing teams; however, if you do, their ability to amplify your content is considerable. Your business may pay for a KOL to host a company event or be interviewed on your podcast, which might give you the opportunity to meet and connect with them or generate some interesting and unique content based on the experience.

- **Journalist** – Every sector has industry press, usually both off and online. It is a good idea to identify journalists who might be interested in your content and connect with them. They may interview you, ask for comments, or share content you have created if they think it is important to their audience. Remember to think about the news stories your customers might be interested in and the journalists they may follow. You may be selling your data agency's services and love following data journalists in the marketing press. However, your retail customers may be more interested in what *The Grocer* (The Grocer, 2022) has to say about data issues.

- **Industry expert** – Usually with a smaller following than a KOL, an industry expert may be very niche in their field of expertise, for example a LinkedIn industry expert such as Hannan (Hannan, 2022) rather than a social media KOL such as Vaynerchuk (Vaynerchuk, 2022). If the industry expert influences on your behalf in their niche area, they can have a significant impact on their network because of their specialist credibility on this subject.

- **Customer** – Never underestimate the influence of your customers in building credibility, acting as a reference and introducing you to potential buyers. The support stage of the seller's pathway is all about continuing relationships, encouraging recommendations and referrals, and staying connected so that you can remain a partner even when your customer moves on to a new role. Remember, B2B purchases are made cautiously, they can be very expensive and career-damaging mistakes if they go wrong, so buyers are often reassured by a connection who has a direct experience of your business.

- **Connection** – Networking is an important social selling activity and although many of your connections could well be potential customers, some will be useful introducers or partners who can influence their network on your behalf. Take a look at your own network and ask whether you have any connections that might be able to introduce you to potential customers. Don't forget to consider your university alumni, old school friends and former work colleagues as well as suppliers, those you have met at events or through connection requests.

- **Colleague** – Your co-workers from the CEO to the person delivering the projects are powerful influencers. Many salespeople don't deliver the actual business projects, so ensuring there are multiple connections across your business with potential buyers means that the credibility of your company can be reinforced by their profiles and posts. For example, Jago (Jago, 2022), the personal branding agency, uses both the business development director and the content creation director's profiles to promote different aspects of the agency. The synergy of their individual specialisms and personal interests increases amplification and gives a unique insight into the business and its culture. More junior colleagues can be encouraged via an employee advocacy programme to be an important part in sharing company insights, amplifying content, and providing an honest and less formal insight into the company values and culture.

From KOLs to colleagues, influencer relationships include both internal and external individuals. This internal/external dynamic is important when understanding the level of expertise for different influencers, as shown in Figure 8.2.

For example, customers and colleagues will be the most informed but perhaps only about specific parts of your business. Industry experts could be internal or external, and KOLs and journalists will be less informed of the details about your business, in part due to their external connection.

How to find and work with B2B influencers

In your social selling role, you aren't likely to be creating large-scale influencer partnerships but you can still take a strategic approach to considering the people in your network and the opportunity to work with them in this way.

FIGURE 8.2 Mapping B2B influencers by type

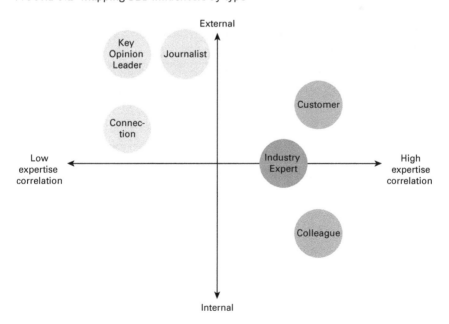

Start with the people closest to you and as you see results, move out more widely into your network:

- **Colleagues** – Make sure you are connected to your work colleagues in your business social channels. Your colleagues may be connected to potential buyers and you can ask for introductions. They may produce great content that you can comment on and share, or they may amplify your own activity. With a rich colleague network you can stay in touch with a wide range of people even if you or they move jobs.

- **Connections** – Regularly audit your connections, keep in touch with them either by joining in conversations on their posts, or by acknowledging birthdays, job moves and events. Ensure you always connect on social media with everyone you meet and check your connections before you reach out to a new prospect – you may be able to approach them with a recommendation.

- **Customers** – Don't lose the relationship once a sale has been made. Make sure you are connected with all your current and previous customers. Ask them for quotes, introductions and opinions, but carefully. Make sure there is a benefit for them. For example, inviting them to be interviewed for your company podcast raises their profile as well as supporting you. And remember, when they move jobs, you will be notified on LinkedIn and they could become a potential buyer or influencer in their new organization.

- **Experts, journalists and KOLs** – these are less likely to be used in social selling directly but if your marketing and PR team have created these connections, join in the conversations on social media, follow them and if you have the opportunity to connect, do so. The relationship will help you keep up to date on relevant information and trends, increase your confidence in engaging on interesting issues, and expand your credentials in thought leadership as you build your personal brand.

Social listening tools are a great way to find B2B influencers, particularly when you are working on a specific campaign or project. Figure 8.3 shows a sample of micro influencers identified within conversations about air source heat pumps. Many of them are experts in green energy and climate crisis. The analysis enables us to see:

- **Name** – who the influencer is. Each influencer is ranked, with the one suggested as the most interesting for the project and brand at the top.

- **Biography** – this is a short blurb about the influencer and their interests which will help you decide how closely they match your needs. You will need to investigate their actual posts and other information if you want to move ahead, but you can discount the ones that are obviously not relevant at this stage.

- **Affinity** – the percentage of the client's overall audience that follows the influencer. You may want this to be relatively low to enable you to reach new people via the influencer, or higher to independently reinforce your messaging with your own audience.

- **Reach** – the number of the influencer's followers on Twitter.

- **Social media** – the networks on which it is possible to obtain information on the influencer's profile. If the influencer looks to have potential you will need to dig further into their audiences on each platform, the content and their engagement rates.

FIGURE 8.3 A sample of potential B2B micro-influencers for air source heat pumps

Name	Biography	Affinity ⃝	Reach ⃝	Social media
Jeremy Leggett	Social entrepreneur & writer: climate, energy, tech, & the future of civilisation. Founder: Solarcentury & SolarAid. Latest book: The Winning of The Carbon War.	5.06% / 0.34%	23.4K	🐦 📷 💬 f in
Carbon Tracker	Financial specialists making climate risk critical to financial markets. #EnergyTransition #FossilFuels #StrandedAssets #Oil #Gas #Coal #Renewables #Climate	5.27% / 0.35%	44.4K	🐦 📷 💬 f
UK Green Building Co	UK Green Building Council	Together for a better built environment	5.41% / 0.36%	43.6K	🐦 📷 💬 f
Sarah Merrick	Wind-loving Walthamstow mum. Feminist. Disruptor. CEO + Founder of @RippleEnergy - making clean energy ownership a reality for consumers everywhere. ?	5.41% / 0.36%	6.2K	🐦 📷 💬 f in
Ed Hawkins	Climate scientist, University of Reading/NCAS	IPCC AR6 Lead Author	MBE	Warming Stripes: http://ShowYourStripes.info	Partner to @OceanTerra	Views own	5.56% / 0.37%	75.9K	🐦 📷 💬 f in
Good Energy	Switch to clean power from Good Energy — one of the biggest things you can do to tackle the climate crisis. Made from sun, wind and water since 1999.	5.84% / 0.39%	39.7K	🐦 📷 💬 f
Andrew Bissell	Founder CEO of @SunampLtd. Heat Battery pioneer (4x energy density, 15x power density). Passionate #EV and #EnergyStorage advocate. Political views all my own.	6.2% / 0.41%	2.7K	🐦 📷 💬 f
Adam Vaughan	Chief reporter, @newscientist. DMs are open. Email: adam.vaughan@newscientist.com. Get my newsletter via the pinned tweet.	6.2% / 0.41%	44.0K	🐦 📷 💬 f in

Reproduced with permission from Adroit (Adroit Data and Insight, 2022)

Because influencers in the B2B world do not just influence a sale, they are an authority within the industry and therefore they are more likely to be nano or micro influencers rather than influencers with millions of followers. Once identified, you can take a look at their social content and reach out by direct message or email to start a more formal relationship.

Larger organizations may use an influencer agency, such as SEEN Connects, not only to identify influencers but to also co-create content with them. These partnerships can be extremely useful as they usually result in a large amount of highly shareable and innovative content. You may also be given access to the influencers or content as part of the delivery plan.

In the case study here Joe Mowles shares how important it is to match the personality and values of the influencer to your brand. At SEEN Connects they use brand archetypes to help with this.

CASE STUDY
SEEN Connects: using archetypes to match influencers to brands (Mowles, 2022)

SEEN Connects (SEEN Connects, 2022) is an innovative influencer marketing agency with offices in the UK and the US. They work with influencers from celebrities to micro and their clients include eBay, Panasonic and LVMH.

SEEN Connects believe that the connection between the brand and the influencer is vital for a successful partnership. For them that connection is the foundation of trust which frees the influencer to use their own creative approach spontaneously and work in an authentic way on more scripted content. The brand doesn't want to be too directive because the influencer's followers love their personality and style. The connection is key because influencers need to solidify everything that you are doing as a business.

To ensure the brand and the influencer share the same values, interests and beliefs, SEEN Connects use Jung's brand archetype theory (Maidment, 2021) to match them. Everyone and every business is different and each archetype epitomizes different attributes (see Figure 8.4 for the full list of archetypes). By identifying both the brand and the influencer's archetypes and marrying them up with influencers, SEEN Connects create a much more authentic and believable partnership. Because the influencers are aligned with that brand's mission, the foundations are set for a solid working partnership built on shared values. The result: better content, which in turn creates better ROI, and ultimately happy influencers, brands and followers.

Archetypes in action

For example, an innovative accountancy software firm could be identified as exhibiting two archetypes, the sage and the hero. As a new entrant and challenger, they are on the side of the small business, trying to cut costs and processes, they are the hero trying to change the world. However, they are also sensible, thoughtful, accurate, the sage. It is accountancy, after all.

Matching influencers via archetypes leads to partnering with entrepreneurs, small and medium-sized enterprises (SMEs) which could try the accountancy software and then demonstrate it and talk about it on social media, predominantly LinkedIn. The connection of the entrepreneur, the hero, and the accountancy software firm, the hero, together with the real hands-on experience of using the service, creates an honest and authentic advocacy.

How to encourage customers and connections to influence on your behalf

As with all social selling, this activity is based on a positive value exchange. The content value model is discussed in full in Chapter 4 but remember that engagement and action will come from understanding and fulfilling an audience need with content that meets at least one of those needs – entertainment, inspiration, support, education, conviction, information. Knowing your customers and connections well, using social listening, monitoring how they engage with and create content will give you a good insight in how to approach them and the value to offer in exchange. For example:

- **Personal recommendation** – You can ask your connections for a recommendation in LinkedIn which will improve your profile. However, think carefully about what you want to appear. You may work in sales and hitting your targets is fantastic if you are looking for another job in sales, but in social selling you need to be more buyer focused. Ask for a recommendation about how well you understood their business, or tailored a solution for them, or responded quickly and efficiently, for example. In return think about what you can offer – a reciprocal recommendation is great so be sure to say why you want to recommend them in your request. The clearer you are about their benefit, the more likely they are to respond. You are showing you are interested in them, which meets the support need.

- **Case studies, testimonials or quotes** – These have a great value to you in endorsing your business or you, personally. However, if presented in a way that recognizes the individual customer or connection positively, they also can have a dual benefit for them. Present the request in this way and it is more likely to be approved.

How to utilize PR and brand-building techniques to become more influential

As you build your personal brand and become recognized for adding value to your network, two techniques from brand building and PR, considering your archetype and understanding the principles of a compelling narrative, can help supercharge your activities.

Using brand archetypes to find your tone of voice

When building your personal brand, it is important that your voice, your personality comes through in the way you present content and in your tone of voice. One way brands ensure consistency here is by understanding and operating within their brand archetype(s). Born from Jung's theories of collective unconsciousness, the 12 brand archetypes define deep unconscious human behaviour. When a brand is associated with an archetype it taps into the emotions that signal its culture and what it stands for. Each archetype's name signals those behaviours and beliefs. The archetypes are rebel, magician, hero, lover, jester, everyman, caregiver, ruler, creator, innocent, sage, explorer (Maidment, 2021). Each one represents a fundamental perspective:

1 Caregiver – being of service helps them support others.
2 Ruler – control and structure are the key drivers.
3 Creator – innovation drives them to deliver.
4 Innocent – optimistic and safe, they are carefree.
5 Sage – independent and informed, they have a strong understanding.
6 Explorer – a free spirit, they are open to possibilities.
7 Rebel – their fundamental driver is liberation, they want to leave a legacy.

8 Magician – their fundamental driver is a belief in being able to make big changes.

9 Hero – their fundamental driver is being the one who can lead the change.

10 Lover – loyal and committed, they want to get close to others.

11 Jester – they want to bring joy and seek connections.

12 Everyman – just a regular person, they want to belong.

In Figure 8.4 you can see how the 12 archetypes are also grouped by Jung's four core motivations of providing structure, seeking independence, delivering change and making connections.

FIGURE 8.4 The twelve brand archetypes

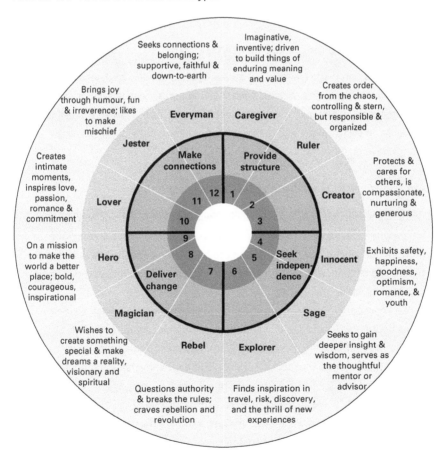

When thinking about your personal brand, consider the archetypes in Figure 8.4. Which one does your business personify? Do you match? Can you combine your personal archetype with your business's archetype to create a compelling and differentiated tone of voice for your content? For example, your business may be a ruler archetype, structured, ordered and in control. These types of organizations focus on measurement, can be authoritative and may seem somewhat unapproachable. Law and accountancy firms are often rulers and it's important that they have these traits considering the work they do. You, however, might be a creator, innovative and inspired. Combining this with the ruler will humanize the content you share and bring a unique perspective to the conversations you join.

In the interview here, Ryan O'Keeffe shares his thoughts on personal branding and how to express your personality alongside that of your business.

INTERVIEW
Ryan O'Keeffe, Founder, Jago (O'Keeffe, 2021)

A certified B Corp, Jago (Jago, 2022) guides business leaders to develop their personal brand, enabling them to build their networks, deepen relationships and grow commercial opportunities. A founder of the agency, O'Keeffe shares his thoughts on social selling and the important influence individuals' personal brands have on its success.

Are you using social selling to grow your business?

Yes, since we repositioned and relaunched our business it's all social. We have built a whole business by presenting ourselves on LinkedIn and keeping our network really tight. Our strategy wasn't to build a big network, it was to build a tight, close network in a specific sector and to have a lot of conversations going on about us within that network.

We knew our work was great. We knew people were loving what we were doing because we could see that with the net promoter scores (NPS). We wanted to see that validation and social proof by them putting their own comments about Jago into social. For people to have conversations about us within this space.

And it's worked, we have just been recognized as one of the most respected agencies in the UK. And we are the smallest, and the only one who just does personal branding. Most of them are huge agencies, and I can only think that one of the main reasons we have been selected, as well as the good work that we've done, is because people have seen us active on social. They have seen our points of view, what we believe in, and how we're different from other companies.

What profiles do you use to support the social selling of Jago?

Currently we use the two founders', myself and my business partner's, personal brands and our company brand, but we are developing five other people within the team to step up and put themselves out there. It's hard – like most people, they're fearful of doing so, fearful of being judged. They are questioning what they will be known for. What will be their own unique way, point of view and content pillars? All that good stuff. So, we need to take them through the process we take our clients through.

Why is social selling and personal brand building so important?

We have seen that it accelerates the trust-building process. Social validates you because prospects can see your content, see more information about who you are, check your company and personal website. It paints a story in their head. So, by the time you get to that prospect meeting, which is usually a Zoom call, the pre-consideration is done already.

For example, I recently had a first meeting with a prospect who had approached me. Rather than being an exploratory call, the prospect said that he was ready to talk numbers. In the initial call we met, talked about his requirements, agreed numbers and he became a client. When I asked why, he said that he had done all the pre-work before the call.

He made a decision so quickly because 'I'd already done my research on you and Jago. I saw the video on your LinkedIn about the story of how you set the business up, the trouble you had with your son. I saw your business partner with this proposition, video again, I'd been reading your content, and I saw you on a podcast which you featured on your LinkedIn profile. And I really liked what you guys stood for. This call today was really just to validate you are who you appear because I was ready to go ahead.'

So that's the impact. And that is the reality of what a lot of people are doing now in terms of working out who they want to work with. By the time they actually speak to you they have already done a huge amount of research.

Are there any other advantages in building your personal brand?

There are advantages for every size of business, for example:

- We have been perceived to be a much bigger business because we're out there consistently and regularly.

- A strong personal brand helps investors find you or support your pitch for investment.

- It transforms in-person networking. I remember walking into networking events as a salesperson, trying to meet people and introduce my business, but very few people would know me. Now I go into a networking event and people have seen me online. People are booking in time with me. They know I am at this event and want to see me. They have a level of trust with you already.

- It can help you attract the best talent when you hire from your network because of your personal brand.

How do you use content pillars to support your personal brand?

I think people are looking to keep things at a macro level. They're looking for competency, consistency and character through your content.

People know what they expect from Elon Musk when he comes to speak. Same with Richard Branson. You need to think about what you want to be known for and what's important before you start to activate yourself on social, otherwise it will just feel really diluted and not the real deal.

I keep it simple with content pillars around emotional intelligence, personal branding and leadership, including who I am outside of work. I'm a father of three, a husband and a football coach. These are the things that people start to warm towards. Social selling should be social, you should let them into your world. Knowing that I'm a father builds trust, and it might connect me with other fathers who are in business. So, there are certain things that I'm happy to reveal and tell my personal story, so they can get a sense of why I'm passionate about that particular area as well. Sometimes life events can trigger our professional motivations.

Whatever pillars you use in terms of your content, don't become fragmented because people won't know what to expect from you and you will start to lose trust. People want to know what they expect from you.

Why is emotional intelligence so important?

I've been fascinated with the correlation between good levels of emotional intelligence in different people and how that translates into performance and the ability to build trust.

From my personal experience, I am conscious of the fact that high levels of EQ help me understand and read the room. Even before I turn up, I need to prepare myself to turn up. Not just be present but be positive, focused and ready to engage in terms of a mindset and an approach to self-regulate how I might be feeling at that point. I could be experiencing a mixture of different emotions depending on how my day is going, but I am going to self-regulate that and bring balance and harmony to impact the relationships and interactions I have with other people.

And that's the key with the consistency of your personal brand. This is why we do it. Why you put yourself out there on social media. It's actually understanding how to bring consistency to your behaviour.

How do you demonstrate emotional intelligence in social when you can't make eye contact or read the room?

We're looking for people to feel the same way about you when they've seen you online, on social, as they do when they meet you offline.

That means being consistent with your content, your point of view. Making sure how you engage through written form and video is consistent and authentic to you as an individual. You will need to think about:

- How you comment and how you respond to other people's posts – ensure the quality of your thinking when it comes to engaging on other people's posts.

- Being social – don't just post and wait for the engagement on your post. Go out there and engage with your audience and peers, comment and engage on their posts, whether that's a question or a supportive and encouraging comment on what they might have achieved. This is important to the people you engage with. They'll be seeing your comments and the way you respond to things.

- Pausing before you respond – it gets challenging the more you establish your personal brand and attract more people that challenge your point of view. So, it's important you take a moment to pause before you respond. Use that gap to regulate and temper your responses so that you don't get involved in a back and forth that's exposed to the whole world on social.

Using storytelling to create compelling narratives

Effective communication is fundamentally about finding the information that will resonate with your intended audience. Of course, knowing your buyers' needs, preferences and priorities is critical in almost every aspect of social selling, but unless your content engages them, all that knowledge, research and investment in content creation falls straight into the gap that exists between your organization and your customers.

But building a bridge between you both is straightforward – albeit shockingly more esoteric and intangible than data, technical know-how or product knowledge could ever be. That bridge depends on your ability to fulfil the oldest and most fundamental requirement of humanity: the quest for meaning.

That might sound a bit grandiose if all you are trying to do is increase sales of your client's brand of air-conditioning units, but ever since the beginning of human development, we have been hardwired to look for a narrative thread in everything we see or experience. That narrative thread is how we process the world, what we use to understand it and, more importantly, how we learn from and pass knowledge on to others. From the first painted scenes of hunting on a cave wall more than 65,000 years ago to the discussion you may have had with your friend over lunch yesterday, there was a story being told.

We are, by nature, storytellers and that's why assuming your buyer only wants to know the facts about your air-conditioning equipment is a mistake. They want to find meaning in your content and by giving them that, in a story, you bridge the gap and engage in a way that sticks.

This storytelling is always very obviously present in the most memorable consumer advertising campaigns. Consider the often perplexing narratives behind a TV perfume campaign. They are simply nothing more than a glossy visual biography of the kind of people the creators see as epitomizing that brand. And because they are telling a story geared towards a specific demographic, that demographic will find meaning and familiarity.

The rules don't change when you are working in a B2B environment. Selling a product can often result in content that leans too far to the 'factual' and not far enough into the engaging narrative. We may leave our personal preferences at home when we become B2B customers, but we don't leave the fact that we are human there too.

In an interview with the *Harvard Business Review*, author of *Storynomics*, Robert McKee (HBR, 2022), goes some way to clarifying that conflict. He says that most business challenges are met with an intellectual response that details problems and solutions backed up with statistics and facts. It's an approach based on logic and while that may seem an entirely reasonable approach, if the solution relies on *engaging* humans, logic – or reason – alone is unlikely to suffice. Instead, he advises presenting that information as part of a compelling story. By uniting an idea with an emotion, you are engaging on a human level. You are telling a story.

But how do we know that our story is going to resonate? According to Christopher Booker in his 2004 book, there are only seven possible ways to do that. *The Seven Basic Plots: Why we tell stories* took Booker over 30 years to write and involved analysing the plotlines in thousands of works of fiction (Booker, 2019). In essence the plotlines cover seven different types of dramatic occurrence with can befall or bless human beings. And while there may be an infinite number of events that can happen, Booker contends that the basic dramatic narratives within which they can occur are finite. Those plotlines are:

1 **Overcoming the monster** – This type of story requires a goody (protagonist) and a baddy (antagonist). It is the fight of good over evil. The protagonist can be a single person (you) or a group of people (your brand/business), but you build a story of the battle you face conquering the baddy. Challenger brands find this a useful storytelling plotline as they position themselves fighting the status quo, perhaps cutting costs, being greener, cutting red tape, or just tackling business problems in a completely new way. For example, Starling Bank is always demonstrating how they champion their customer needs with their pureplay mobile and online service which is so much more relevant and cheaper for businesses than a more traditional bank (Cavagileri, 2022). As an individual you can also adopt this route. Perhaps your personal brand archetype is hero or rebel and you are standing up for issues important to your buyers.

2 **Rags to riches** – This type of story is all about overcoming adversity. You will need to show how, despite the challenges, you reach a happy ending. Many family businesses or entrepreneurs tell their story in this way. They may tell how they started with nothing but an idea and built an empire, or bring in their personal struggles faced in the journey to build a successful business. Richard Branson uses this type of narrative when he talks of how he dropped out of school at 15 and has dyslexia but managed to create and grow the Virgin business (LDRFA, 2022).

3 **The quest** – This story requires you (the hero) to be inspired or informed by something external which you recognize and requires you to make a change (or reverse) to the situation. Good examples here are when organizations or individuals realize the impact of a lack of diversity in the workplace or poor mental health and wellbeing and want to do something about it. Organizations such as BRiM (Black Representation in Marketing) (Advertising Association, nd) provide frameworks and tools to change the way that ads are made. You may be committed to a particular quest yourself and use your personal brand to support it.

4 **Voyage and return** – The plot here requires you to set out on a journey to find something and then return with new wisdom and experience. This plotline works well if you can share the discovery with your followers – perhaps it is a journey they are making with you. Sharing your personal journeys of discovery in this way can make compelling reading in your feed.

5 **Comedy** – Positive comedic characters and stories are engaging and often highly shareable. Think about how you could bring content to life in a more light-hearted way. However, be careful using this plotline in a B2B situation. You need to ensure that you are still seen as a serious partner who can deliver.

6 **Tragedy** – This plotline isn't often used in B2B social selling as it requires your main character to suffer a negative change of fortune. It is unlikely you will want to be dwelling on negatives in your content or personal brand building.

7 **Rebirth** – As this approach requires the main character to have a transformation from bad to good it is not an ideal plotline for B2B, unless your business has been guilty of bad behaviour in the past. For example, as the automotive industry recovered from the emissions scandals a rebirth narrative can help build trust in sustained change.

When it comes to writing compelling narratives there is a lot you can learn from corporate PR techniques as they are constantly trying to sell stories about their client organizations to time-poor and story-hungry journalists.

PR practitioners handle lots of content across traditional and digital platforms, dealing mainly with news which is the mainstay of media relations. But news content is still story telling even though the news form and the story-telling form are seeming opposites of each other. The one thing that unites them is the seven basic plot lines. In effect, all of the seven plot lines

FIGURE 8.5 The components of a compelling narrative

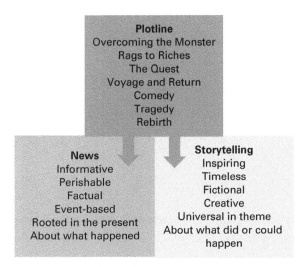

Reproduced with permission from A.J. Wood Corporate Communications (Wood, 2022).

not only make for a great news story but equally at least one of them *has* to be present in order for it to even qualify as a news story. They are also the foundations of storytelling which, as a form, is unconstrained by the demands of news media.

So even though the style or platform you choose for your content can vary, the presence of one or more of the seven plotlines will be essential in making it engaging (Figure 8.5). As corporate PR expert and former journalist Amanda Wood states, 'The best content creators understand at a visceral level that those plotlines have to be there for their material to transcend the norm. Examples of how this happens either accidentally or by design are to be found in every viral meme and in every memorable campaign. Humour, tragedy, transformation, triumph – we want to experience products in a human context and storytelling is the way we achieve that' (Wood, 2022).

Finally, always think about what you can do to add drama, interest, shareability and engagement. When writing your posts and comments there are some additional techniques that will make your content more interesting, shareable and relevant. Make sure you:

- know your audience and why should they be interested
- focus on your content pillars
- encourage sharing – include short codes, links hashtags, etc

- keep copy short and compelling
- include unique and new information
- plan your timing – when is the right moment to share or post?
- ask whether you need an unboxing moment
- always have a plotline – what is the hook that will grab my attention?

Even in a short post, keeping these factors in mind will make your content stronger. Perhaps your plotline can be developed in a single blog or over a series of shorter posts or videos.

CASE STUDY
WDADTW (what did Amazon do this week?): creating a compelling narrative as an influencer (WDADTW, 2022)

The brainchild of the author of *Disruptive Technologies* (Armstrong, 2017), this weekly newsletter and subsequent social posts provide compelling insights not only into what Amazon has done but what it means. As an expert adviser in the technology space Armstrong was continually being asked about Amazon. He realized that although there was a lot being written about Amazon, no one was pulling it all together, looking at their future, exploring the possible horizons and what they could mean, not only for Amazon but for other businesses.

Armstrong isn't afraid to tell it how it is and so is highly trusted by his audience. The result: up-to-date news content with an incisive commentary targeted at the huge audience who want to know not only what Amazon did this week but what they might do next and what it means for them.

Read a sample here: https://whatdidamazondothisweek.substack.com/about

---

Influencers are an important factor in B2B social selling and work best when you use compelling storytelling to synergize your personal brand with your company brand and that of other colleagues. Together, your combined thought leadership and support will influence the B2B buying decisions of your network.

Bibliography

Adroit Data and Insight (2022) *Social Selling Example Output*, Adroit Data and Insight, Cirencester

Advertising Association (nd) BRiM, adassoc.org.uk/brim/ (archived at https://perma.cc/9527-HRB8)

P Armstrong (2017) *Disruptive Technologies*, 1st edn, Kogan Page, London

J Atherton (2020) *Social Media Strategy: A practical guide to social media marketing and customer engagement*, Kogan Page, London, pp 158–182

C Booker (2019) *The Seven Basic Plots: Why we tell stories*, Bloomsbury Publishing, London

C Cavagileri (2022) Challenger and mobile banks, www.which.co.uk/money/banking/bank-accounts/challenger-and-mobile-banks-aj0mj7w688r5 (archived at https://perma.cc/D67A-R89A)

L Hannan (2022) Laura Hannan profile, www.linkedin.com/in/laurahannan/ (archived at https://perma.cc/GV99-6HVH)

HBR (2022) Storytelling that moves people, hbr.org/2003/06/storytelling-that-moves-people (archived at https://perma.cc/U9KE-DGSG)

Influencer Marketing Hub, in association with Refersion (2022) The state of influencer marketing 2022, influencermarketinghub.com/ebooks/Influencer_Marketing_Benchmark_Report_2022.pdf (archived at https://perma.cc/TSX6-P4HJ)

Jago (2022) Personal branding, wearejago.com/service/personal-branding/ (archived at https://perma.cc/L9GE-XD34)

LDRFA (2022) Famous people with dyslexia. Sir Richard Branson dyslexia coping tips, www.ldrfa.org/famous-people-with-dyslexia-sir-richard-branson-dyslexia-coping-tips/ (archived at https://perma.cc/2WJV-QWXG)

A Maidment (2021) Brand archetypes, marchbranding.com/buzz/brand-archetypes/ (archived at https://perma.cc/Y9CN-2RZM)

J Mowles (2022) Business director (celebrity and influencer), SEEN Connects [interview] (3 March 2022)

R O'Keeffe (2021) Founder, Jago [interview] (2 December 2021)

Ovo (2022) Brand archetypes, brandsbyovo.com/expertise/brand-archetypes/ (archived at https://perma.cc/JY7D-4C9F)

SEEN Connects (2022) Innovative influencer marketing agency, seenconnects.com (archived at https://perma.cc/YHV6-KTAN)

The Grocer (2022) Home page, www.thegrocer.co.uk (archived at https://perma.cc/QX2K-QL4G)

G Vaynerchuk (2022) Gary Vaynerchuk profile, www.linkedin.com/in/garyvaynerchuk/ (archived at https://perma.cc/6BH7-YKFG)

WDADTW (2022) What did Amazon do this week? whatdidamazondothisweek.substack.com/about (archived at https://perma.cc/N8MA-QL8F)

A Wood (2022) Director, A.J. Wood Corporate Communications [interview] (14 April 2022)

09

Monitoring and measurement

Measuring the effectiveness of your B2B social selling strategy

Delivering results is essential for success. Make sure your tracking and analysis provide meaningful monitoring and measurement. Use the ROI calculator to ensure you keep on track and learn how and what to measure in the short, medium and long term.

The difference between monitoring and measurement

It is important to understand the difference between monitoring and measurement and why you will need to do both. Monitoring describes the close observation and analysis of information. It can include taking measurements, but it also involves qualitative information gleaned from listening, watching and noting behaviour or cultural changes. Measurement is the quantitative assessment of data, determining whether you have met the objectives set. Monitoring is continuous, whereas measurements are taken at key points when their validity is relevant and important.

When you implement your B2B social selling strategy you will want to measure its effectiveness and monitor its progress throughout the process. Did it meet the hard targets you set such as driving revenue, increasing the number of new customers, creating a thought leadership positioning, launching into a new market or sector, or increasing your brand's share of voice (SOV)? These measurements are your effectiveness KPIs, they tell you whether you have achieved the objectives you set out in your strategy and enable you to know the value of your social selling activity. However, because social selling strategies and sales cycles can be very long, taking years in some cases, it is important to monitor performance throughout the process. Some examples of social selling metrics are:

- Measurement examples – number of sales or leads, ROI, total revenue, market share, net promoter score, conversion rates and, on a personal level, the number of new connections or levels of engagement.

- Monitoring examples – competitive position (who your competitors are, whether there are any new entrants, how their positioning compares to yours), demand signals (indicators of where your prospects are in the buyer's journey), brand strength and sentiment (the types of mentions you get), influence or interest (the level of engagement with your activity) and your SSI.

Chapter 2 outlined how to set SMART objectives and provided some example measurements for Bradley's Juice (Bradley's Juice, 2022) for each stage of the seller's pathway, as shown in Figure 9.1.

However, because each stage of the pathway will take some time to complete, Bradley's Juice should also monitor the indicators that will show their strategy is working, such as tracking engagement rates, assessing which type of content or offers work best, and monitoring who their competitors are and how they respond to market conditions and customer needs. Importantly, you will need to decide the KPIs that will determine the success or failure of your strategy and what you want to monitor along the way.

At Ericsson, Anita Veszeli is keen to ensure that objectives and KPIs are SMART. In particular, she focuses on them being realistic and achievable so that everyone remains motivated and encouraged to continue. When individuals start using social media for social selling, they don't measure its effect on leads or sales for at least six months. Rather, they focus on supporting social selling behaviour adoption and monitor SSI, follower growth and connections growth (Veszeli, 2022).

In the interview overleaf, Erica Neal and Sarah Stephenson share their thoughts on the importance of measurement.

FIGURE 9.1 SMART objectives and KPIs – an example for Bradley's Drinks

BRADLEY'S DRINKS

MY BUSINESS:
Bradley's Juice – a family-owned premium juice business in Somerset, England that sells B2B to restaurants, pubs and retail outlets.

MY BUSINESS MODEL:
Product-based. A manufacturer of a seasonal (food) product it is important to sell stock at key times of the year to meet seasonal demand and reduce inventory costs.

SMART OBJECTIVE	WHAT DO I WANT TO ACHIEVE?	WHAT IS THE TIME PERIOD?	WHAT DOES SUCCESS LOOK LIKE?	HOW WILL I MEASURE IT?
FIND	Identify and connect with new international wholesalers Be found by independent retailers	By end of xx Over next xx months	Key decision-makers in the wholesalers are aware of Bradley's juice	Number of new connections Number of new followers
RELATE	High levels of interest in our full range of products and our brand story	Ongoing but tracked monthly	Requests for product trials Interaction and sharing on social media Downloading specific content from website	Number of trials Taste trial feedback scores Number of social followers/ mentions/ shares
ENGAGE	Sign long-term contracts with new wholesalers Sell xxx units	By xxx	Obtain committed buyers for planned production units	Number of contracts signed Number of units sold Value of units sold
SUPPORT	Happy customers who spread the word Opportunities to expand the range of products they buy	Ongoing but tracked monthly	Existing customer satisfaction/ sentiment stable/increasing Increased take up of full product range	Monthly CSAT score /NPS score Ongoing Sentiment Analysis Number of new product taken/ customer

Reproduced with permission from **Bradley's Juice**.

INTERVIEW

Erica Neal, Head of Outbound (Neal, 2022), and Sarah Stephenson, Associate Director, Social Media (Stephenson, 2022), from The Marketing Practice (TMP) talk about the importance of monitoring and measurement for their clients

The Marketing Practice (The Marketing Practice, 2022) is a B2B marketing agency which specializes in the technology sector. Its clients include Salesforce, Citrix and Telefonica. Together Neal and Stephenson ensure their clients build and deploy effective social selling strategies in LinkedIn that integrate with other sales and marketing channels.

What do you measure organically?

Social selling is incredibly powerful when approached as an integrated solution. We use a mix of LinkedIn, outbound calling and email. Primarily all our activity is organic and we strive to send InMails to connections organically to increase response rates and ensure authenticity. For every client we set at least two benchmarks relevant to the type of campaign. For a social selling campaign our LinkedIn benchmarks might be for connection acceptance and message responses. A typical expectation here would be:

- connection acceptance rate of 10–15 per cent
- InMail or message response rate of 8–10 per cent.

Because the leads themselves won't necessarily come from LinkedIn, a lead target is set at an overall level for the campaign and based on previous results and client objectives.

What do you measure in paid?

Our use of paid media on LinkedIn is limited but we do recommend using paid with prospecting to drive awareness, lead gen or events. We use paid advertising to make sure that people are seeing what we're doing but we're not intruding by using InMail to non-contacts. For us, paid in LinkedIn should be advertising alongside the organic relationship building.

What paid does give us though is the ability to track customer journeys using the LinkedIn pixel and granular measurement of different audience activity.

How do you use metrics in different markets?

The level and type of LinkedIn activity and engagement are related to your culture so it's important to be aware of the cultural aspects when you're building a strategy and setting benchmarks and KPIs. For example, within the Nordic region, although LinkedIn use is very high, people post a lot less than in the UK and their activity is different across posting, commenting and their tone of voice:

- **Posting** – Individuals feel less comfortable with frequent posting in the Nordics, preferring to post once a week, compared to three to four times a week in the UK and USA.
- **Commenting** – Publicly posting comments in the Nordics is also low and tends to be limited to congratulation comments such as a new job, birthday or work anniversary. No business is done publicly. If you wanted to reach out to someone about a deal it should be done privately, as they would not comment publicly.
- **Tone of voice** – This also varies by region and so you should ensure you adopt the right tone of voice because the more authentic you can be when you're posting or sending messages, the better quality your leads will be.

How do you ensure the expectations you set are realistic?

We know that some sectors perform better on LinkedIn than others so when we are setting KPIs we need to ensure we take this into account. For example, retail campaigns perform well as people in this sector are more active with posting about different retail updates and trends. People who work in education and financial services are less active and typical of more risk-averse industries which don't network so publicly on the platform. However, although their public engagement rates may be lower, they still use the platform for research and recommendations and respond to outreach from relevant potential partners.

Why is it important to monitor how a campaign is progressing?

Our social selling activity focuses on building relationships that ultimately drive sales and revenues, but this can take time. Therefore, we need to ensure we are creating enough qualified leads by using a combination of channels: emails, phone and InMail. Rather than measuring the number of phone calls made or number of emails sent, we look at the number of engagements to understand effectiveness.

During the Covid pandemic our monitoring highlighted a change in buyer behaviour. We saw a decrease in engagement through Sales Navigator InMail, so we pivoted to ensure that we directly connected with prospects prior to engaging because an accepted connection request is an early sign about being willing to engage. We also moved, where possible, to phoning prospects rather than relying on campaign emails as this was a more powerful engagement. We monitored results at every stage of the campaign and compared against benchmarks and the campaign targets. For example, the level of engagement will be measured at each of the following stages:

- **Connection acceptance** – Aim for 10 per cent of target audience connect.

- **Outbound call** – On average one in eight LinkedIn profiles have a mobile number which can be rung to say thank you for connecting.

- **Email** – Ideally the next step is that the prospect asks for more information to be sent on email.

- **Nurturing** – The relationship moves to email.

- **Meetings** – These are set up, the lead is qualified.

- **Lead development** – The lead passes to the next stage controlled by the sales team.

How does monitoring support iterative improvements?

We use social media or telephone to have a real-time dialogue of feedback with prospects which means we are the voice of the prospect and are continually monitoring how they feel. If the prospect tells us, 'No, I'm not interested', we can ask why. In social media and on the phone we're able to really dig into the 'No thank you', whereas on an email it's just a no thank you and you're blocked from that contact.

At TMP we have created a monitoring process to loop back from the sales team to marketing:

- Sales and marketing meet weekly and sales talk about whether the key messaging is resonating with the audience.

- Sales hear how the prospect describes their problems and can tailor our messaging accordingly and try it out on different prospects.

- Sales let marketing know if we have used different messaging and which work best.
- Based on the feedback from sales the marketing messaging changes as well as the sales messaging and results.

This process was used in the TMP case study described in Chapter 6.

How to measure realistic objectives and KPIs

It is important to remember when deciding what to measure to not get too bogged down with multiple, detailed factors. You will want to know that you are on track to reach your goals and know when you have achieved them, but you should avoid wasting time navel gazing by being overwhelmed with detail. For example, rather than micromanaging personal branding effectiveness, use your SSI to provide an overview of overall performance.

However, if you do want to dig into more detail to ensure you are on track, use the seller's pathway stages and different metrics at each stage to assess progress:

- **Find and be found** – To ensure you can be found, brand awareness metrics are important and can include metrics such as views on posts, views on profile, company page followers, re-shares, comments and likes, companies and job titles that saw the posts, and website visitors.
- **Relate** – At this stage you are making connections and trying to build a relationship. Metrics such as connections out, connections accepted, replies to messages, calls booked, emails out and email responses are important.
- **Engage** – Here you will be leveraging your relationships with content and advice around decision making. Metrics that indicate interest in these areas are good indicators of progress and include webinar sign-ups, agreeing to be sent case studies or other company content.
- **Support** – With your existing clients or customers, you will want to remain front of mind and ensure you stay connected and engaged. Metrics such as referrals and ongoing content engagement are useful here.

In practice, there is a disconnect between the way salespeople are traditionally measured and targeted on monthly and quarterly sales versus the way you should be measuring social selling, which is much more long term and activity rather than sales focused. It is hard work, and you have to believe it can work by behaving consistently every day. It's definitely not a flurry of activity to drive a sale at month end. Relationship building takes time and effort and is hard to measure. For that reason, Hannan recommends measuring activities rather than sales:

'To really see the benefits, you need consistency over time, and it's tough for salespeople with monthly and quarterly targets to hit. I encourage them to look at weekly activities instead of monthly or quarterly sales results. It really is a numbers game. If you measure every stage, particularly the conversions, and you know what those stats should be to get the results, you can work back from your target to know what activities you need to do every week. To keep your salespeople motivated, at the end of the week, let them finish their activities, knowing that their job's done. "I might not have got my deal this week, but I know I've completed the activities I need to get there." If you do that consistently week in, week out, the results come' (Hannan, 2022.)

Once you are measuring activities you can easily track performance to see where you are losing people and the quality of the relationships. By using ratios in conjunction with activity measurement you can ensure quality and quantity. There is no point in congratulating someone who has sent out 200 connections if they've only had a 10 per cent acceptance rate. But by targeting on the acceptance rate as well as the activity, both quantity and quality are maintained.

Pitch121 use their Future Advocacy Network (FAN) definition in their metrics. A FAN is someone who could be a prospect, partner or future customer – regardless, you should treat them as someone who will, in the future, advocate your service to others. They then use the following sales funnel to measure progress by counting the activities and measuring the ratios:

- FANs contacted – the number of connection requests sent out.
- Connections accepted – the number of connections accepted.
- FAN responses – the number of FANs who have replied on LinkedIn or by email.
- Interest – the number of FANs who have expressed an interest in the business and its offer, which can be indicated by actions such as webinar sign-ups, asking to see a case study or being interested in a meeting or call.

Hannan believes that the most important factor is the percentage ratios rather than the numbers out. You do not want to be in a position where

FIGURE 9.2 Pipeline summary in funnel form for a retail ERP tech company

Pipeline summary

2 months

Fans contacted	1682	100%	**1682** Contacted
Profile 1	949		
Profile 2	733		
New connections	532	31%	**523** Connected
Profile 1	260		
Profile 2	263		
#FANs in conversation	221	42%	**221** Conversations
Profile 1	98		
Profile 2	123		
Interest	88	39.80%	**88** Interest
Profile 1	41		
Profile 2	47		

NOTE This pipeline summary is included with permission from Pitch121 (Hannan, 2022).

your ratios are low because then you would have to send more and more connections and messages. Therefore, the focus should always be on increasing the following ratios:

1 Connection acceptance rate = percentage of acceptance from connection requests sent.

2 Response rate = percentage of replies from FANs contacted.

3 Lead rate = percentage of interests from FANs contacted.

In Figure 9.2 you can see the ratios at each stage of the funnel for two different prospect groups (profiles 1 and 2). Although both groups end up with a similar number of interested leads at the end of the process (41 and 47), their pattern through the funnel has varied. Despite this, the high connection acceptance rates and levels of conversation and interest indicate a relevant, timely and high-quality campaign.

Keeping track of ROI

The balance between detailed measurement and high-level monitoring to embed positive social selling behaviours will depend on your organizational culture and goals. Chapter 10 discusses the cultural challenges in more detail and Hannan's interview in the previous chapter also considers the dilemma. However, many organizations do track from the connection to the sale via their CRM system and ultimately need their social selling strategy to deliver revenue and a strong ROI in order to be deemed a success. Using a dashboard which captures the key metrics can be a great way to track this type of performance.

Some suggested elements to include in an ROI-focused dashboard

The following elements are useful inclusions in an ROI-focused dashboard:

- Number of live leads and leads per month, including the level of qualification. Are the leads sales- or marketing-qualified leads? The former means they fit the criteria for a recognized buyer persona and have shown interest. The latter, that they are interested in receiving content but not ready or able to buy.
- Leads source – did the lead come from a specific channel or profile?
- Revenue – both delivered and those in the pipeline.
- Costs versus sales and lead value – note there may be some lag here on a monthly basis as high-value sales take time to convert.
- Actual ROI.

The figures in Figure 9.3 show how these elements could be presented in a dashboard for a fictitious business using example costs.

Monthly lead pipeline analysis shows the metrics for each sales-qualified lead (SQL) generated in a month with an allocated lead value of £6,857 per lead. This value has been calculated by knowing the average value of a sale and the average conversion rate from a SQL to a sale. With six leads in the pipeline, the value of forecast leads this month is £41.14K.

The figure also shows that one SQL has converted to a sale which is valued at £17.41K and that £3.47K has been spent on the sales and marketing activity this month. This spend will include content development costs and perhaps scheduling and management tools.

The figures here can be used to calculate ROI using the ROI calculator in Template 9.1. In this example there has been only one sale this month and all the costs have been associated with the sale although there are other leads in

FIGURE 9.3 Example dashboard metrics – monthly lead pipeline analysis

New Leads This Month

Lead Name	Lead Qualification	Source	Lead Suitability Rating	Lead Value	Sale Valu
	SQL	FS Website Contact Form	High	£6,857.00	£0.
	SQL	FS Website Contact Form	High	£6,857.00	£0.
	SQL	FS Email	High	£6,857.00	£0.
	SQL	Telemarketing	High	£6,857.00	£0.
	SQL	FS Website Contact Form	High	£6,857.00	£0.
	SQL	FS Live Chat	High	£6,857.00	£0.
	SQL	FD Referral	High	£6,857.00	£17,406.

£41.14K

Forecast Lead Value

£3.47K

Total Costs

£17.41K

Actual Sale Value

the pipeline. Even with all the costs allocated to a single sale, revenue is at four times the costs incurred. You could, if you wish, share the costs across leads and sales when calculating ROI and it is also useful to track ROI over time in a graphical format.

Download the Template 9.1 on page 207 to measure ROI for your activity.

As well as understanding revenue it is important to look at how the leads were generated. They may come from your website via different routes and it is important to look at which ones are most effective. In the example shown in Figure 9.4, lead sources include the website contact form, referral, email, live chat and telemarketing. You could also include meetings and other sources such as LinkedIn InMail.

Measuring by campaign and content

In addition, to understand overall revenue performance it is especially important in social selling to be able to track specific campaigns, content types and sources. I recommended using a tool such as bitly to build short codes with detailed information about the content. These codes enable you to track in detail the effectiveness of different elements. Figure 9.5 shows an example link-building logic system you could use to track content effectiveness. In the example three elements are being tracked: the source, content type and campaign. Every time a piece of content is used, the link to that content will include these three elements. Depending on where it is used and what type of content it is, a different set of information will be included in the code. The effectiveness of the different elements can then be measured independently, for example campaigns can be compared against each other or email can be compared with telemarketing.

Social listening, combined with Google Analytics, can provide additional insights. For example, it can be useful to understand where your brand is being mentioned. Figure 9.6 looks at both the volume of brand mentions and how they have changed year-on-year (YoY) for each social network.

Because personal branding and social selling emphasize your reputation and thought leadership credentials, it is likely that you would expect an improvement in brand sentiment over time. Figure 9.7 also uses social listening to show the change in sentiment for four different brands over the course of several months.

FIGURE 9.4 Example dashboard metrics – count of lead by source analysis

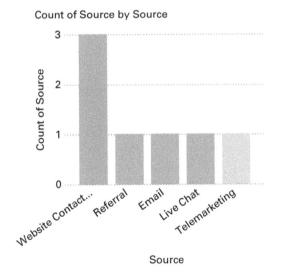

Count of Source by Source

Source

Planning for measurement

As discussed in Chapter 2, make sure you think about what you want to measure and how you will do so right at the beginning. Your measurement factors will depend on your objectives and what stage you are at in your social media transformation journey. You may want to set individual and team targets, but remember that social selling requires new habits and new ways of working so the KPIs should reflect this. Too much emphasis on monthly revenues at an individual level could hamper a social sales culture embedding in your business.

The final chapter considers the cultural challenges in more detail and recognizes how essential your leadership, mindset and confidence will be in delivering success.

FIGURE 9.5 Example link building logic system

Source	Content type	Campaign
LinkedIn	Video	Threatlocker
LinkedIn	Banner	Threatlocker
Dynamics	Email	Threatlocker
Dynamics	Landing page	Threatlocker
Dynamics	Event landing page	Threatlocker
Telemarketing	Email	Threatlocker
Referral partner	Email	Threatlocker
Referral partner	Ad	Brand awareness
LinkedIn	Carousel	Brand awareness
Google	Display	PPC
Google	Display	PPC

Used with kind permission from Emerge Digital (Stevens, 2022).

FIGURE 9.6 Volume of content by social network

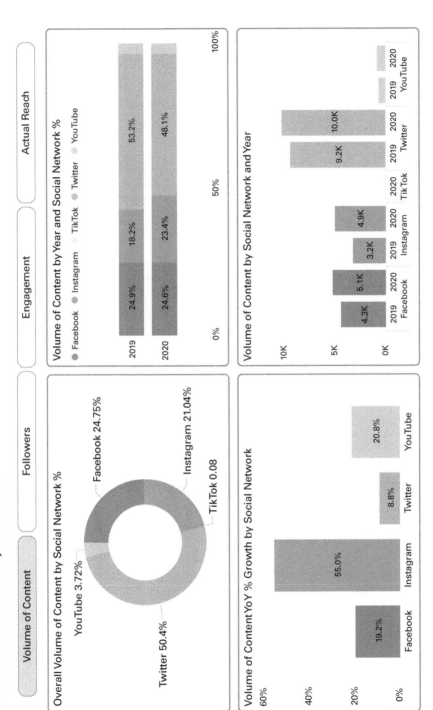

FIGURE 9.7 Sentiment analysis over time

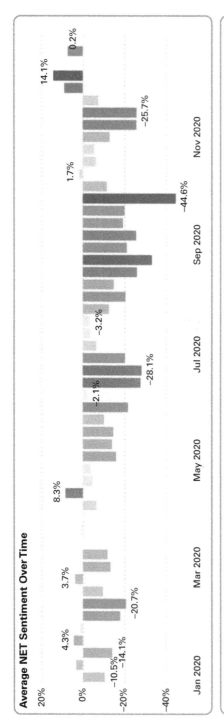

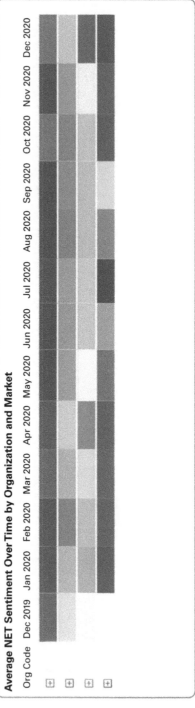

TEMPLATE 9.1 ROI calculator

ROI calculator				
	Sales in month	Sale value (revenue)	Costs	ROI
Sale 1		£ 17,406.00		
Sale 2				
Sale 3				
Sale 4				
Sale 5				
Sale 6				
Sale 7				
Sale 8				
Total		£ 17,406.00	£ 3,470.00	4.02

Use the template to calculate your return on investment (ROI) by month

Bibliography

Adroit Data and Insight (2022) Social selling example output, Adroit Data and Insight, Cirencester

Bradley's Juice (2022) Bradley's Juice, www.bradleysjuice.co.uk (archived at https://perma.cc/R822-73VV)

L Hannan (2022) Co-founder, Pitch121 [interview] (6 January 2022)

E Neal (2022) Head of Outbound, The Marketing Practice [interview] (17 January 2022)

S Stephenson (2022) Associate Director, Social Media, The Marketing Practice [interview] (6 January 2022)

J Stevens (2022) Marketing Executive, Emerge Digital [interview] (5 April 2022)

The Marketing Practice (2022) Goodbye silos, hello lasting success, themarketingpractice.com/en-gb/ (archived at https://perma.cc/V2NR-22EB)

A Veszeli (2022) Director, Social Media and Advocacy, Ericsson [interview] (18 February 2022)

10

Social transformation

Creating a B2B social selling culture in your business

Social selling is all about confidence and attitude. This chapter looks at the dynamics of an effective social selling team. Supported by original research into personal branding, it explores the behaviours that are essential to success and the importance of leadership and role modelling in creating a rewarding and supportive social selling culture in your business. A useful personal action plan for LinkedIn can help get you started.

Recognizing the need for social transformation

The term social transformation is usually used to describe the transformation of society due to globalization, technology, and societal and environmental factors. In this context it is used to describe the process whereby an organization starts to put social interactions and social media at the heart of its business strategy. Think digital transformation for social media.

For many organizations, social media is still a bolt-on to their core business activities. It may even only be considered purely as a media channel. However, future-focused organizations recognize the impact social media is having on business interactions at every level and have embraced both the opportunity and the challenges this brings. Anita Veszeli is ready to meet this challenge at Ericsson, with responsibility for social media 360 including social listening, governance, paid and organic, branded content and social selling. She states:

'To embed social selling in your business you need social media transformation. Many companies talk about digital transformations and have a digital transformation plan, but most don't have a social media transformation plan. Digital is really about the tools, and businesses going through digital transformation identifying the tools they need – collaboration tools, tools that talk to each other, the different tech. But social transformation gets underneath actually how people are behaving on social, how they are using it, how they make connections, this is something that is really needed today' (Veszeli, 2022.)

By recognizing the need for social transformation Veszeli understands how social media now impacts not only every stage of the buyer's journey but also the way we interact and engage as employees and influencers. If social media is siloed into a channel strategy, the opportunity to optimize the three-way interdependent brand relationship is lost. At Ericsson they have conducted a social media audit and plotted their social maturity for different factors. Their ambition is that by 2025 they will have completed their maturity journey and be a social-first business.

To deliver a successful social selling strategy you too will need to be cognizant of where your business is in its social maturity and where you will need to offer training and support, change the culture, define goals and specify new measurements. In particular, how do you embed social behaviour, increase the collaboration between marketing and sales, and empower employees to advocate for your business? The case study here shows how Ericsson are tackling this issue across their business.

CASE STUDY
Ericsson: implementing a social selling programme (Veszeli, 2022)

Ericsson is a Swedish multinational networking and communications business and 5G leader, creating groundbreaking technology solutions for businesses and consumers. Their social media and advocacy director, Anita Veszeli, defines social selling as 'the fostering of key relationships with customers or potential customers through social media, and the use of social media to prospect, connect leads back to their pipeline, and measure performance' (Veszeli, 2022).

At Ericsson, social selling is integrated – it's not about just using the social media platforms as media channels, they are also connected to all other sales activity. For example, LinkedIn Sales Navigator is connected to Salesforce, and the sales teams and marketing teams work together on social selling.

Ericsson took a maturity journey approach to social selling with realistic support and expectations at each stage of their social selling programme:

- **Step 1 – Social media maturity assessment:** This was conducted to show the executive where they were, where they should aspire to be and what was required to get there. The assessment gave a good overview of the business in different markets and identified people and departments that were more socially mature and could act as champions, and those that needed more direction, training and support. It also provided a roadmap and timeframe for success.

- **Step 2 – Enablement:** This stage lasted approximately six months. Starting with the basics, Ericsson encouraged the team to start using the relevant social media platforms in their markets. For the majority this was LinkedIn. Training and support were given to enable the sales team to feel comfortable posting, sharing and commenting on LinkedIn and knowing how to use Sales Navigator.

- **Step 3 – Embedding social behaviour:** To be effective the sales teams needed to change their behaviour and include social media activity as part of their daily routine. Behaviour change is hard, but the pandemic helped as the sales team were keen to use social media and social selling when more traditional channels were closed to them. At this stage measurement was by adoption metrics such as follower growth, connection growth and improved social selling indexes. A two-way feedback dialogue helped embed those daily practices so social became a new norm for them. Not something on top of their job, but part of their job. Members of the programme were given feedback and encouragement to promote best practice and learning. In addition, they fed back on where they were having success in terms of insights and interactions with customers.

- **Step 4 – Revenue generation:** No sales figures were looked at in the first six months. The sales cycle is long and it could have been discouraging to not see immediate results. Instead, the focus was on the positives and what the sales team could see was working. After the first six months, the programme went to the next level. All the daily routines have been embedded, and it's natural to be on LinkedIn engaging and sharing content or creating their own. At this stage the programme helped individuals with their community and started measuring how the pipeline had been affected. Measurement looked at lead value, lead source (marketing/sales/business development), the effectiveness of collaboration and sales velocity.

The Ericsson programme was designed to drive revenues but recognized that looking at pipeline and hard sales metrics too early would be a mistake as social selling takes time to embed relationship-building behaviours and integrate with other channels. For Ericsson, the measurable revenue value is approximately one year away from when a team joins the social selling programme.

Transforming your sales culture to embrace a social selling mindset

The process of social transformation is real. Social media has changed the way we communicate and build relationships, both personally and at work. It hasn't replaced conversation, but it has added a dimension. In organizations this includes the addition of increased internal security and collaboration through tools like Slack (Slack, 2022), to wider networking via LinkedIn (LinkedIn, 2022a), to insight and information gathering through external conversations on Reddit (Reddit, 2022) and Twitter (Twitter, 2022).

The impact of social selling is no less impressive, with 78 per cent of salespeople engaged in social selling outselling their peers (Oeullette, 2022). However, although many of us recognize how impactful it can be, actually delivering a social selling strategy in your business can be hard. According to Barney-McNamara, there are three important elements that contribute to successful social selling (Barney-McNamara, 2020):

- **The antecedents** – Having favourable pre-existing conditions is an important foundation. At an individual level, is your team confident in and positive about social media, customer orientated, entrepreneurial, tech savvy and extrovert? Do they use social media and technology regularly? How old are they and what is their level of sales experience? At an organizational level, where is your business in its social transformation journey? How orientated is your company strategy to social media, marketing, customers, sales and technology? How big is your business and how well has company behaviour adopted your social media and sales technology strategies? Finally, at an industry level, how competitive is your sector, is it orientated towards technology, and will the sector you operate in contribute to determining whether your business is ready to make the most of social selling?

- **Social selling activities** – These consist of personal branding, information exchange, networking and social listening. People respond to people, and you will gain the most interaction and involvement from peer-to-peer engagement, so it is especially important that all sales-focused members of the team build their personal brand. The better they build this, the more people they will be connected with and the more opportunities will be created for networking, information exchange and social listening.

- **Social selling outcomes** – If the antecedents are favourable and the social selling activities are undertaken consistently and well, then positive buyer engagement is created via strong value co-creation. This in turn generates high salesperson performance and social selling success.

Tech and marketing businesses are more predisposed to successful social selling than more traditional or non-office-based organizations. This is because they are by nature highly social media and tech savvy, are more likely to have younger, entrepreneurial workforces, and are selling to companies that also exhibit this behaviour. In these organizations, adopting and embedding the social selling activities should be easier, but it will still require effort. However, successful social selling can be a reality whatever your industry or starting situation, so long as you are aware where you are starting from and provide a clear framework and support to create a social selling mindset across your business.

Changing how you behave and how you measure takes personal commitment, a culture change in your organization and the ability to hold your nerve – it takes time. And at the heart of this culture change is a commitment to building the personal branding of your sales fronting team, whether they be business development roles, senior leaders or sales professionals.

The Ericsson case study is a great example of how a tech company is supporting this, with steps 1 and 2 focusing on the antecedents, step 3 on the social selling activities and step 4 where the success of the outcomes is measured. Importantly, Ericsson recognize the importance of embedding new behaviour and provide support to do this. Recent original research into the attitudes and behaviour around personal branding by the sales team of another global tech business shows how important this company-wide approach is.

The importance of leadership and management in supporting transformation

There is no doubt that to make any kind of transformational change, visible support and direction are needed by the company leaders and management.

Social transformation is no different and the research in the case study here highlights this importance for personal branding.

CASE STUDY

Global technology company research (Gallagher, 2021) – social selling: the supports and challenges to personal branding

Background

The original research was conducted in 2021 and focused on the sales team of a global technology business that was actively using social selling and wanted to see how they could improve its performance specifically in the area of personal branding. When the research was conducted the majority of the team were taking part in personal branding activities, but 27 per cent were not (Figure 10.1).

Methodology

A two-step approach was taken:

1 **Interviews**: seven semi-structured interviews with managers enabled an in-depth exploration of the topic and indicated the most useful topics for the survey.

2 **Survey**: 34 sales professionals from across the business completed an online survey. The group included a range of ages, genders, sales experience, and social and technology confidence and expertise. Overall, they believed that social media was a great way for them to build their personal brand (Figure 10.2).

FIGURE 10.1 79% of sales professionals agree that social media channels are a great way to build their personal brand

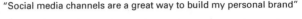

"Social media channels are a great way to build my personal brand"

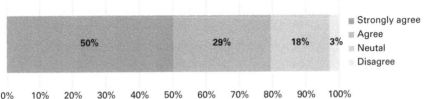

FIGURE 10.2 27% of sales professionals are not regularly taking part in personal branding

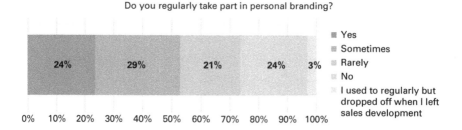

Do you regularly take part in personal branding?

| 24% | 29% | 21% | 24% | 3% |

0%   10% 20% 30% 40% 50% 60% 70% 80% 90% 100%

- Yes
- Sometimes
- Rarely
- No
- I used to regularly but dropped off when I left sales development

Research findings

The research highlighted three areas which, if addressed, could significantly improve the sales team's adoption of, and performance in, personal branding activities:

1 **Lack of confidence holds them back** – Although a large proportion of the team understand what personal branding is, there is some reluctance to get involved because of either the perceived complexity of the task or the public visibility of personal branding and the implications that might have.

   'If I think about my team, it really just comes down to fear, again, fear of people's opinions... of really putting yourself out there in terms of posting ... fear of opinions, fear of rejection. And how confident are you in your written communication? ... How critical is someone of themselves?' (Participant 1)

   The majority of the sales team are concerned about how they are perceived and whether they have enough experience or knowledge about their industry, and this nervousness is potentially increased in social media because of the public nature of the medium (Figure 10.3).

2 **A good reason to do it is essential** – Overwhelmingly, sales professionals want evidence that personal branding impacts results in their own organization (Figure 10.4). If they undertake personal branding activities, they want to be able to justify the time and effort with evidenced improvement in their personal sales performance. However, they are open to using personal branding and only 12 per cent are not doing it because it isn't in their performance objectives.

   'It's difficult to measure the return on investment of this kind of strategy ... and the team is quite busy at the moment. So it's difficult to just spend time on it.' (Participant 7)

FIGURE 10.3 Although reasonably well understood by sales professionals, a lack of confidence discourages more active participation in personal branding

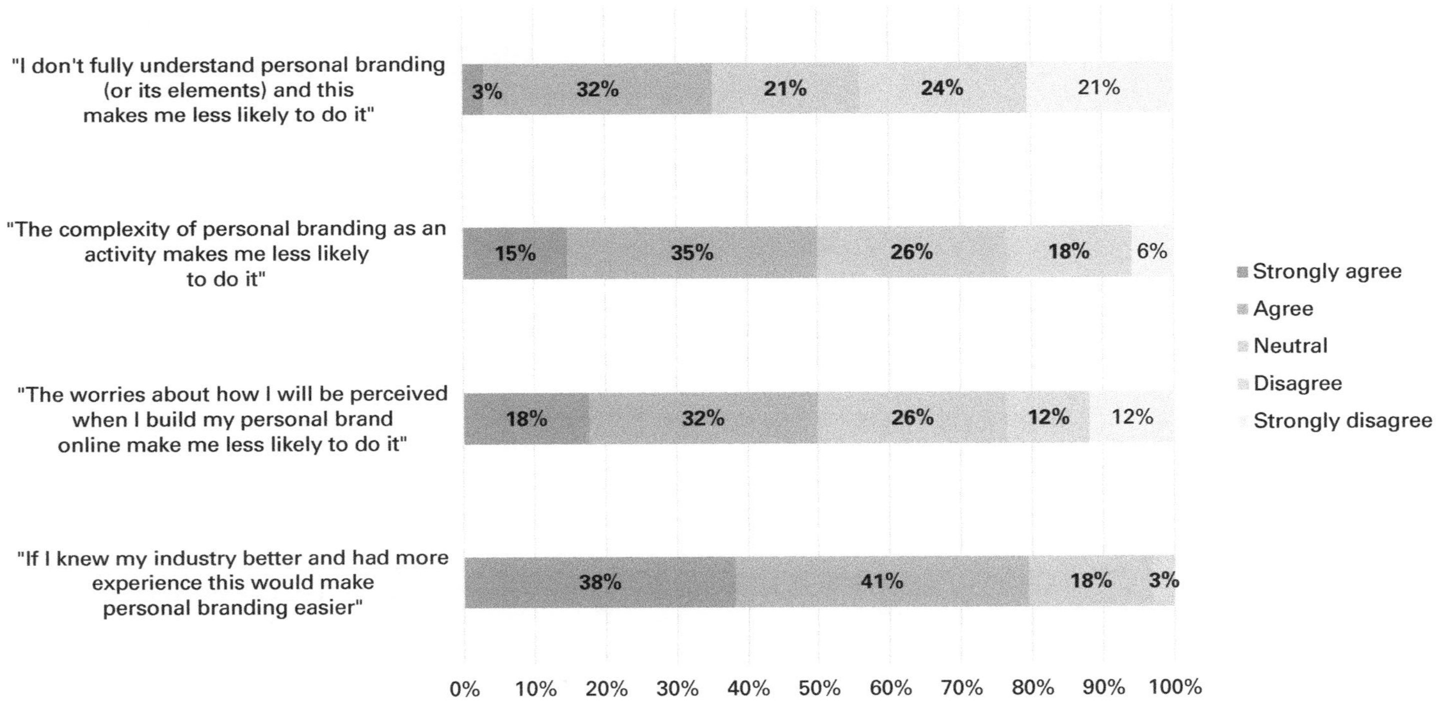

Legend:
- Strongly agree
- Agree
- Neutral
- Disagree
- Strongly disagree

"I don't fully understand personal branding (or its elements) and this makes me less likely to do it": 3%, 32%, 21%, 24%, 21%

"The complexity of personal branding as an activity makes me less likely to do it": 15%, 35%, 26%, 18%, 6%

"The worries about how I will be perceived when I build my personal brand online make me less likely to do it": 18%, 32%, 26%, 12%, 12%

"If I knew my industry better and had more experience this would make personal branding easier": 38%, 41%, 18%, 3%

X-axis: 0%, 10%, 20%, 30%, 40%, 50%, 60%, 70%, 80%, 90%, 100%

FIGURE 10.4 Sales professionals need a good reason to spend time on personal branding

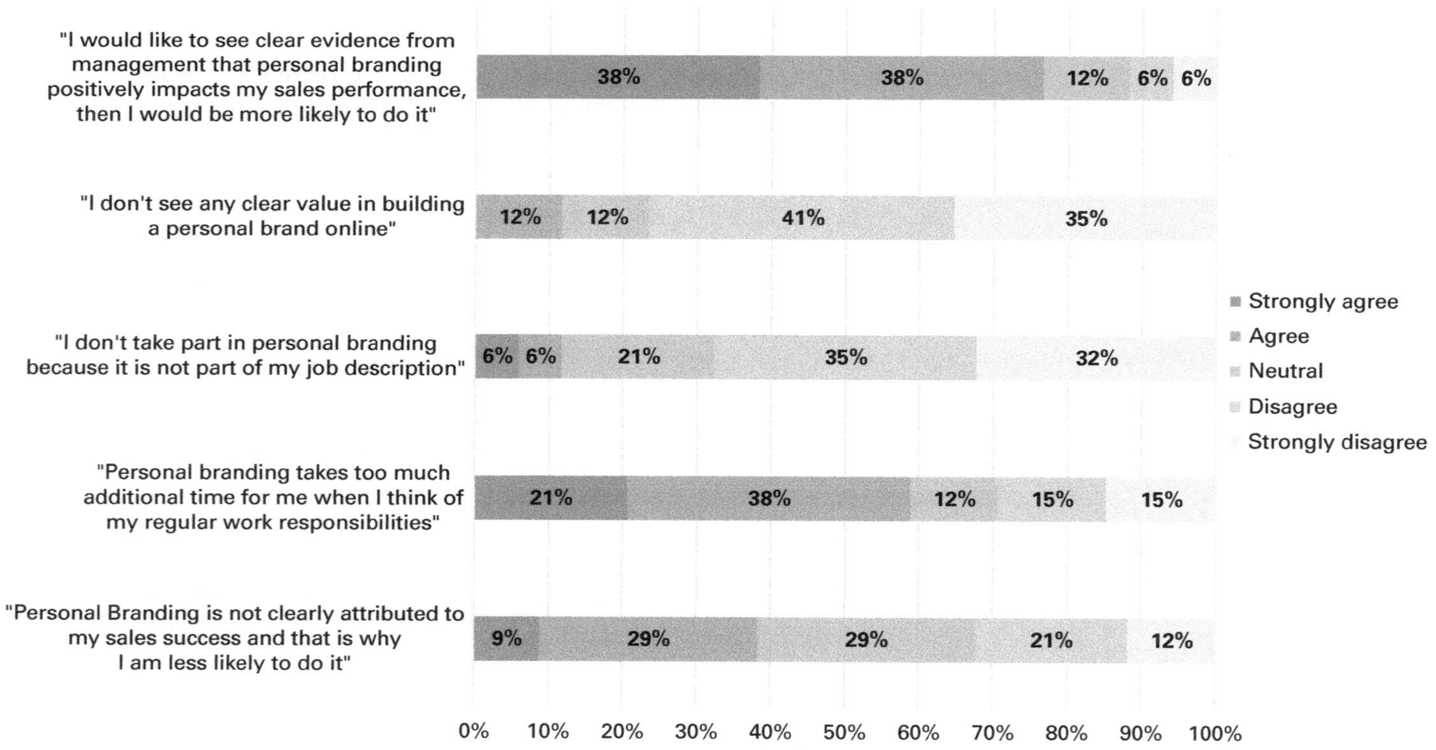

"I would like to see clear evidence from management that personal branding positively impacts my sales performance, then I would be more likely to do it"
38% | 38% | 12% | 6% | 6%

"I don't see any clear value in building a personal brand online"
12% | 12% | 41% | 35%

"I don't take part in personal branding because it is not part of my job description"
6% | 6% | 21% | 35% | 32%

"Personal branding takes too much additional time for me when I think of my regular work responsibilities"
21% | 38% | 12% | 15% | 15%

"Personal Branding is not clearly attributed to my sales success and that is why I am less likely to do it"
9% | 29% | 29% | 21% | 12%

0% | 10% | 20% | 30% | 40% | 50% | 60% | 70% | 80% | 90% | 100%

- Strongly agree
- Agree
- Neutral
- Disagree
- Strongly disagree

FIGURE 10.5 Support from employers and managers could significantly improve the participation and success of personal branding for sales professionals

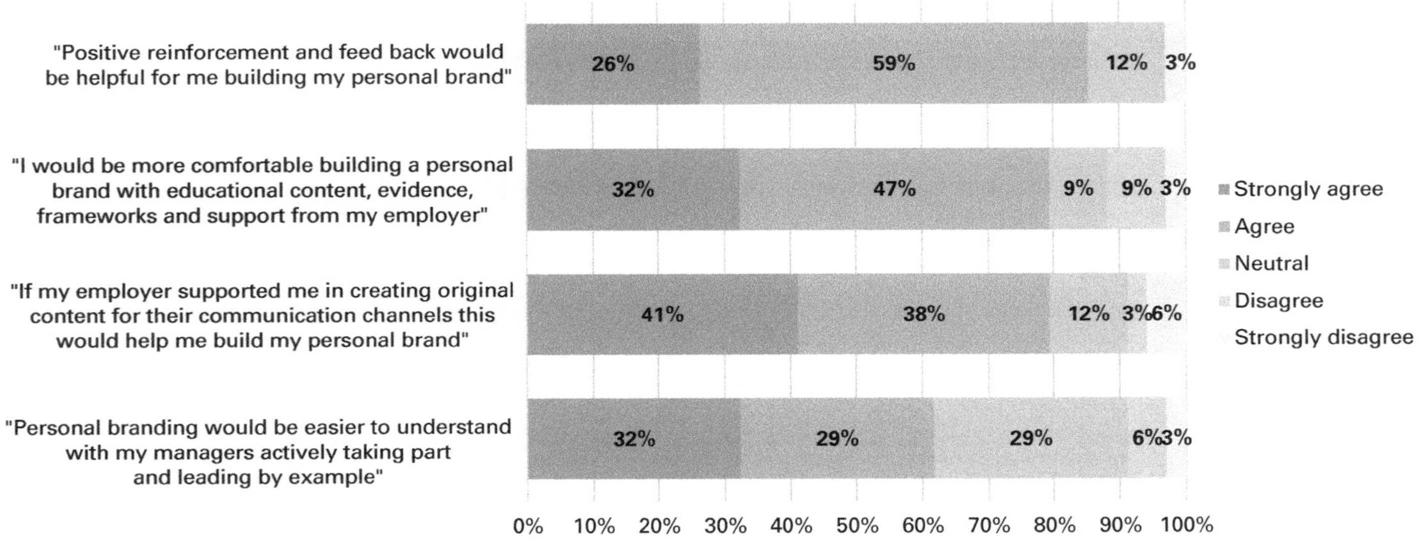

"Positive reinforcement and feed back would be helpful for me building my personal brand"

26% 59% 12% 3%

"I would be more comfortable building a personal brand with educational content, evidence, frameworks and support from my employer"

32% 47% 9% 9% 3%

"If my employer supported me in creating original content for their communication channels this would help me build my personal brand"

41% 38% 12% 3% 6%

"Personal branding would be easier to understand with my managers actively taking part and leading by example"

32% 29% 29% 6% 3%

0% 10% 20% 30% 40% 50% 60% 70% 80% 90% 100%

- Strongly agree
- Agree
- Neutral
- Disagree
- Strongly disagree

3 **A company-wide commitment is the game changer** – With a strong link to the lack of confidence mentioned earlier there is a real requirement for support and structure to enable personal branding activities to be embedded, with 85 per cent asking for positive support and feedback and 79 per cent for original content creation on corporate channels (Figure 10.5).

> 'I guess, just be more proactive and encourage it on a more regular basis. Providing some guidelines around what good looks like ... by providing a framework for what good looks like, where to find all the content and the right format to use, and also understanding how can we help them to ensure that they are getting traction on their posts and comments on LinkedIn and other channels.' (Participant 6)

Research conclusions

The sales professionals were keen to undertake personal branding as part of social selling but were looking for guidance, direction, content creation and training to enable them to have the confidence, abilities and assets to make it a success.

Gallagher's research provides some clear insights into how you can ensure social selling can work in your organization. Although the research focused on personal branding, the outputs are relevant to all four social selling activities of personal branding, information exchange, networking and social listening. Each needs support and direction, and arguably, personal branding and the behaviour associated with building your personal brand in themselves require you to effectively network, conduct social listening and exchange information.

Even if you cannot conduct a controlled test, as SAP did in the case study in Chapter 5, the results are clear: social selling works, but it can only be effective if you and your business provide a framework, invest in consistent and useful content, and support through encouragement and leading by example.

Six tips for creating a social selling culture in your business

To ensure you are able to successfully implement social selling into your business, consider the tips below:

1   **Audit where your social selling culture is today** – As part of your social media maturity assessment, consider your strengths and weaknesses in terms of the pre-conditions for social selling. Do you have a team with a good knowledge of technology and social media? Are they confident in social spaces and is activity there a regular part of their day? What industry are you in and how comfortable and active are your buyers in social media? The higher the score here, the quicker and easier it will be to embed social selling behaviour. One way to benchmark is to look at your team's social selling index. An index above 70 has a high correlation with improved sales performance as it indicates a consistent and strong level of interactivity with your social media network.

2   **Build a cultural transformation strategy** – Work out where you need to get to and by when. Be realistic about timings and what will happen at each stage. When embedding culture change, it is a good idea to put personal branding at the heart of your plan as this is ownable by individual team members, brings them personal and professional benefits, and is intrinsically linked to the other social selling activities of networking, information exchange and social listening.

3   **Set out a framework for delivery** – Recognize that there are different stages. Enablement might take longer if you are at an earlier point in the social media maturity journey. Identify who will be involved and put in place the content creation, tools, training and support to ensure the plan is achievable.

4   **Set realistic targets and expectations** – Don't expect too much straight away – you are trying to build confidence and change behaviour. Focus on quick wins where team members can start to see a real difference with a small amount of effort. For example, ensuring they have an optimized profile on LinkedIn and are starting to engage with insights can give a quick boost to their SSI and the visibility of their posts and comments.

5   **Be a champion and lead by example** – Identify who will lead the delivery. Who in the organization can be an ambassador and feed back and encourage the next stage of development? Make sure you have a mechanism for sharing best practice.

6   **Celebrate success** – Never lose sight of the fact that you are ultimately looking for sales even though this will be longer term. Set targets, measure effectiveness and celebrate the individuals and the new business wins.

YOUR SOCIAL SELLING INDEX EXPLAINED

Your SSI is a score allocated by LinkedIn. Everyone on LinkedIn has an SSI which is continually updated. The score is out of 100 and based on four components:

- **Your professional brand** – this looks at how complete your profile is in relation to its appeal to potential customers and whether you present as a thought leader by publishing relevant and meaningful posts.

- **Finding the right people** – this looks at how well you are using the search and research tools on LinkedIn to find the right people to connect and engage with.

- **Engaging with insights** – are you joining in and creating and sharing updates that generate conversations?

- **Strengthening relationships** – this looks at how effectively you are finding and engaging with decision makers to improve the strength of your network.

A score of 70 or above is considered to be reflective of an active social seller on LinkedIn and you can look at the breakdown of where you need to put more effort to help improve your score. In Figure 10.6, the individual has a score of 60, with their strongest area in personal branding and their weakest in finding the right people.

As well as a total score, the SSI gives you your score and ranking in relation to the industry you work in and across your network. In this example, the average score for sales professionals in their industry (sales and marketing) is 26 and they rank in the top 4 per cent for their industry. When compared to their network, the average score for their network is 47, which puts them in the top 23 per cent. You can also see whether their SSI has increased or decreased since the previous week.

If your organization has LinkedIn Sales Navigator you can look at the SSIs across the team.

Check out your own SSI at https://www.linkedin.com/sales/ssi

FIGURE 10.6 An example social selling index

How to create and implement your personal social selling plan

Whether you work in a large or a small organization, one way to help embed social selling behaviour and a focus on personal brand building is to create a personal action plan. Kathryn Strachan, MD and owner of the content marketing agency Copy House, is a notable thought leader in technology content and leadership. She regularly speaks at events and is a committed LinkedIn user. Her continuous, embedded social behaviour has really paid off:

> 'LinkedIn is not only a marketing tool, it's also a sales tool. I've built a personal brand through LinkedIn because I post four or five times a week and have almost 7,000 followers. I get a lot of engagement on my posts, which is really great, but it's also opened up a lot of opportunities for us. I use LinkedIn as part of my sales techniques. I love networking and I meet 50 new people every month, but after I meet that person, I always send them a LinkedIn connection request, so that they then follow me back. Then people start getting to know me and Copy House and this has been really successful. We have won some big clients and generated a lot of leads through LinkedIn. We also have a company page which we're active on, but my personal brand is a little bit different than the company page. I'm not just talking about company things, I'm also talking about things that I'm passionate about, am interested in, or thoughts that I have. This means people get to know me and my company' (Strachan, 2021.)

As this example highlights, it is the normalizing of social media activities, leadership and management support, and a commitment to developing your personal brand, that make the difference. As you start to embed these practices in your own behaviour and across your business you can download and use Template 10.1 to keep your own action plan on track.

Note: this checklist has been designed for LinkedIn, but similar activities can be used on other channels. The checklist has been built for use without Sales Navigator; if you do take this tool, additional insights and information will be available. Use this checklist to work through your own steps to building your personal brand to support enablement, embedded social behaviour and revenue generation:

1 Review your LinkedIn profile.
2 Update your LinkedIn profile.
3 Determine your core objective.
4 Identify your networked audience.
5 Match your content to your audience and objective.
6 Create a LinkedIn schedule.
7 Start optimizing content – posting, commenting and sharing.

TEMPLATE 10.1 Your personal LinkedIn action plan checklist

1. Review your LinkedIn profile	Complete Y/N
Check the key metrics and make a note of them: • Number of connections. • Number of followers. • SSI. • Number of times you appear in searches. • Number of profile views. • Number of search appearances.	
Check who you are connected to and make a note of them: • What are their job titles? • What industries do they work in? • What level of seniority do they have? • Are you connected to all the decision makers/ people you know? You can analyse your connections in a spreadsheet by downloading all your data from LinkedIn. Clicking on your profile image > data and privacy > get a copy of your data.	
Review your professional image and activity and make a note of what is a strength and where you need to develop: • Do you look professional? • Is your information up to date? • What do you talk about? • Who do you follow/engage with? • What content do you create? • What activity do you do the most of – liking, sharing, commenting, posting?	
Review your area of expertise and tone of voice and identify how to improve it: • Do you have a particular area of expertise and are you consistently active in this area? Does this fit with a content pillar your organization has? • If you don't already have an area of expertise identified, review your organization's content pillars and select one that fits well with your knowledge and interests. • Review how you write and the types of content you share. Can you improve in this area? You want to be professional but also show your personality and views.	

(continued)

TEMPLATE 10.1 (Continued)

Create an action plan: • Where are you in terms of social maturity? • What targets will you set yourself? Be realistic, take small steps initially with realistic goals. • Your 1st target might be to update your profile – even if you are a fantastic social seller, it is likely your profile needs a refresh.	
2. Update your LinkedIn profile	**Complete Y/N**
Make sure the 1st impression is professional: • Include a professional photo. • Include a branded background for your business. • Include your location and role title. • Include keywords that will help you be found. • Add 3 hashtags about your business/thought leadership area to help you be found – your content pillar will help you decide these.	
Make sure the 'About' section includes: • A customer relevant description of your role and personal achievements. • Details about your business and how you can help. Having a good understanding of your core buyer persona will help here.	
3. Determine your core objective Pick a primary objective – you can start with creating your personal brand and move onto lead and revenue generation later.	**Select objective**
Be found – Build your personal brand awareness.	
Find – Identify prospects and connect with them.	
Relate – Build a relationship based on social insights and engagement.	
Engage – Ensure lead conversion with relevant conversations and guidance.	
Support – Encourage recommendations and referrals.	
Set targets for each stage. For example: • Connect with 50 prospects per month. • Increase SSI by 10 points. • Increase search appearances by 100. • Drive 10 leads to the website. • Convert a sale from a LinkedIn initial connection.	

(continued)

TEMPLATE 10.1 (Continued)

4. Identify your networked audience	Completed Y/N
Each month or planning period, identify the networked audience(s) you want to engage with: • Are you targeting by sector/ company/ event attendees? • Do you need to join any groups/ follow new hashtags? Use advanced search, recommendations, and introductions to connect with each stakeholder. Refer to your core buyer persona.	

5. Match your content to your audience and objective	Complete Y/N
Plan to use a range of content across a defined period (1 month, 2months, a quarter?). Include a combination of: • Relevant corporate content with your own views /comments appended. • Trending and relevant topics for the sector/audience identified. Liaise with marketing and plan ahead to maximize the impact of strong content plans. Consider using a hero, hub, help approach.	
Make sure: • Your content meets the value criteria of education/ inspiration/ support/ information/ conviction/ entertainment. • Call to actions meet the needs of the customer journey for your overall objective. • Relevant hashtags are chosen for the sector and audience. • Experiment with different content types such as video clips, images, gifs, and blog posts. • Experiment with different messaging when you reach out to new connections or ask for referrals and recommendations. The hashtags you are following, the groups you are a member of, your notifications and your homepage feed will all be useful sources of external content you can use to stay visible and engage with your audience.	

(continued)

TEMPLATE 10.1 (Continued)

6. Create a LinkedIn schedule	Complete Y/N
Create a monthly plan for your objective with weekly milestones Depending on the objective, set personal monthly goals for: • Number of new contacts. • SSI increase. • Number of notification follow-ups. • Number of comments by you. • Number of views/shares/comments on your posts. • Number of leads generated.	
Review your social selling score each month. Review your dashboard and activity summary each month. Review what types of content, and connection and referral requests, work best. You might want to set a time each day/week to focus on LinkedIn.	

7. Start optimizing content – posting, commenting and sharing	Complete Y/N
Try out the following types of activity. Which seem to work best to generate engagement and/or leads? • Tagging individuals in a post. • Hashtags. • Joining in group conversations. • Asking for a recommendation. • Commenting on other people's activity. • Sharing other people's posts. • Commenting on your company's activity. • Sharing your company content. • Contacting new prospects. You might want to add to this list.	
Check for responses and continue the conversation – don't rush too quickly into a sales pitch/conversation. Make sure you ask permission to start a sales conversation.	

In conclusion

Social media has transformed the way we build and nurture relationships at home and at work. It enables us to network, collaborate, share and support each other publicly and privately, build reputations, meet new people, source ideas and create our own content. It is embedded in every part of our lives and an essential element in every business strategy. In B2B sales and marketing the importance of social media, and social selling in particular, continues to grow, and wherever your business is in its social maturity journey you can make a difference to your company's success and build your own reputation by adopting its practices. Businesses large and small are a testament to this and Strachan's impact on the exponential growth of Copy House is a great example.

INTERVIEW

Kathryn Strachan, MD and Owner, Copy House (Strachan, 2021)

Strachan is the founder of Copy House, a technology content marketing agency which has seen significant growth due to its consistent positioning and focus on social selling. She shares her single-minded approach here.

How important is social selling to Copy House's success?

It has been essential. You could say that Copy House is built almost entirely through LinkedIn because my first ever freelance client came from LinkedIn, it is where I have primarily built my personal brand and it is a cornerstone of our success.

How do you integrate your personal brand with other marketing and sales activity?

We have a marketing team that produces the content for the company's LinkedIn and Twitter pages and ensures we are regularly posting and commenting on our technology and content marketing pillars. In addition, I run my own LinkedIn page because it's important that my thoughts and my ideas are true to my personal brand. As well as talking about content and tech I focus on leadership and culture – it's more personal, important to me, and crucial to our success as a business.

Now that I have an established personal brand and the company visibility is high in the tech space, we are looking to increase the impact by investing time and training into building the personal brands of the wider leadership team and creating more thought leadership content in marketing.

How much effort does it take to build a strong personal brand?

I have only been active on LinkedIn since 2018 and started building my
personal brand in 2020. It takes time and dedication but has really been worth
it. I started by undertaking a personal branding exercise that helped me
brand my personal profile and gave me that foundation for creating content.

I make sure I remain present by focusing on networking and public speaking
and continuing that through LinkedIn. I do a lot of networking, I speak at one
event per week and meet 50 people a month, so I've met over 600 people this
year. I then connect with them and ensure I post on LinkedIn 4–5 times per week.

How important is your personal content to driving business growth?

Personal profiles are much more engaging than company pages on LinkedIn, so
my profile supports the visibility and impact of our other content. However,
because I talk a lot about our culture and values, my followers also get to see a
more human side and understand who we are, which has been important in
pitches.

For example, when we pitched for Meta, I connected with them at the
beginning of the process so they would see my LinkedIn content. The reasons
they chose to work with us were our specialist expertise and my leadership.
There's not much time to talk about leadership in a pitch but they would have
seen me on LinkedIn where I post about leadership multiple times a week.

When we talked about our company culture during the pitch presentation it
resonated with what they have seen on LinkedIn. This is the impact of social
selling – my personal profile on LinkedIn is part of the sales process, filling in
information to complement the sales calls and meetings. It's important because
in a sales call, you may only have half an hour to an hour of somebody's time
and it's impossible to tell them everything about who you are and who your
agency is in that time. But, if you're posting every single day on LinkedIn then
they will see that content, learn about you, learn about your agency and
then are far more likely to convert when you pitch.

How do you make sure your posts are relevant to your audience?

It's important to spend time observing, not just engaging, and posting on
LinkedIn to understand the kind of content that is working best for my
network, including what's performing well and the preferred styles and format.

How well do you know your audience?

We have a very clear idea of our ideal buyer and are very focused on what we do and don't do.

- We are – a content marketing agency specializing in technology and FinTech. This means we work with some big names like Meta as well as smaller specialists. But what makes our clients so unique is that all of them are super-niche and do something very specific and very technical. They come to us because they struggle to find somebody who can understand their technology that deeply.
- We are not – a generalist content marketing agency.

By knowing our audience well, we make sure our content is focused on their needs and can disqualify non-relevant leads early in the process. For example, we don't work with start-ups because you need a marketing manager in place to get the best value from our services, so we disqualify any company that is so early in the process that they don't have a marketing manager.

After we've sifted through any leads and disqualified anybody who either isn't a good fit, is looking for something that we don't do or is in an industry that we don't work in, or isn't quite set up internally yet to work with us, then we have a 70 per cent conversion rate from qualified lead to signing up a new client.

So, social selling is a gamechanger for individual and business success and will only become more important. We are social beings and social media enables us to engage, empathize, inspire and influence our networks beyond any other communication channel. With social selling, you have the opportunity to build an incredible reputation and support your business's growth, so grasp the challenge, live your personal brand and create competitive advantage. Go forth, create and deliver great strategies, and use the downloadable tools and templates to help structure your approach.

Bibliography

B P J C P N K Barney-McNamara (2020) A conceptual framework for understanding the antecedents and consequences of social selling: A theoretical perspective and research agenda, *Journal of Research in Interactive Marketing*, 15(1), pp 147–178.

S Gallagher (2021) *Social Selling: The supports and challenges to personal branding*, DMI, Dublin

LinkedIn (2022a) LinkedIn for business, business.linkedin.com (archived at https://perma.cc/34ZG-TUQF)

LinkedIn (2022b) Social selling index, www.linkedin.com/sales/ssi?src=or-search&veh=www.google.com%7Cdirect%2Fnone (archived at https://perma.cc/TTT8-MV8B)

C Oeullette (2022) Social selling statistics for 2022, optinmonster.com/social-selling-statistics/ (archived at https://perma.cc/Y4DL-T3YZ)

Reddit (2022) r/business, www.reddit.com/r/business/ (archived at https://perma.cc/7ATK-MLJU)

Slack (2022) Slack home page, slack.com/intl/en-gb/ (archived at https://perma.cc/KP5E-SPBW)

K Strachan (2021) Founder, Copy House [interview] (22 November 2021)

Twitter (2022) Business, business.twitter.com (archived at https://perma.cc/L5PN-E9ZY)

Veszeli (2022) Director, Social Media & Advocacy, Ericsson [interview] (18 February 2022)

APPENDIX

USEFUL TOOLS AND PARTNERS

The following companies have been included in the book and offer a range of services that can be useful for research, automation and implementation purposes.

Purpose	Business	Website	Description
Agency/ consultancy partners	Adroit Data and Insight	https://adroitinsight. com	An international data and insight agency that works with renowned brands such as Age UK, UNHCR, SSE, Plan International, PDSA, Baxi and the BMJ. They have a particular strength in social listening insight and analysis and use a variety of tools to help their clients differentiate themselves, identify new opportunities, and respond to changing customer needs.
	A.J. Wood Corporate Communi cations	https://www.linkedin. com/in/ajwcorporate communications/	A UK-based PR advisory delivering strategic internal and external comms and training. Specialisms include crisis communications management, social media, business transformation and change, employee engagement and corporate reputation.
	CaptainJV	https://www.linkedin. com/in/captainjv/	A UK-based consultancy that helps businesses to grow fast and develop long-term joint venture partnerships that generate leads, enquiries and sales.
	Copy House	https://copyhouse.io	A B2B content marketing agency specializing in the technology and FinTech sectors. Its clients include Meta, Klarna, Lendflo, Travelex and Money Dashboard.

(continued)

(Continued)

Purpose	Business	Website	Description
	Immediate Future	https://immediatefuture.co.uk	A UK-based independent social digital consultancy, building and delivering award-winning data-driven social media strategies for brands including IBM, Fujitsu and Motorola.
	Intermedia Global	https://www.intermedia-global.co.uk	A UK-based market-leading full-service provider of B2B data, digital, direct marketing and database solutions on a global scale.
	Jago	https://wearejago.com https://www.linkedin.com/in/ryan-okeeffe/	A certified B Corp guiding business leaders to develop their personal brand, enabling them to build their networks, deepen relationships and grow commercial opportunities.
	HERE/FORTH	https://www.hereforth.com	An independent, emerging technology advisory. Clients include 20th Century Fox, Meta, O2, Experian, WPP and Publicis.
	Leadfamly	https://leadfamly.com	A gamification platform used by B2C and B2B brands to increase engagement and drive leads. Clients include Carlsberg, Co-op, Legoland and the Data & Marketing Association (DMA).
	SEEN Connects	https://seenconnects.com	An innovative influencer marketing agency with offices in the UK and US. They work with influencers from celebrities to micro and their clients include eBay, Panasonic and LVMH.
	SAP	https://www.sap.com/	The market leader in ERP software, SAP enables businesses of all sizes to become more agile, improve operational efficiency, raise productivity, increase profits and enhance customer experiences.

Purpose	Business	Website	Description
	Small Wonder	https://www.small-wonder.co.uk https://www.linkedin.com/in/julieatherton/	The consultancy founded by the author. Small Wonder specializes in advising organizations (B2B, B2C and third sector) on embedding social media in their strategic development and growth.
	The Marketing Practice (TMP)	https://themarketingpractice.com/en-gb/	A global B2B marketing agency which specializes in creating growth for technology companies using social selling, ABM, demand generation, partner marketing and targeting as a service. Its clients include Salesforce, Citrix and Telefonica.
Content research	Answer the Public	https://answerthepublic.com	The site uses search data to provide insights into the most frequently asked questions on any topic area.
	BuzzSumo	https://buzzsumo.com	A powerful content insight tool used to generate ideas, create high-performing content, monitor performance and identify influencers.
	Google Analytics	https://analytics.google.com	If your company website has set up Google Analytics you will have access to important information on keywords, content consumption, customer journeys and other insights.
	Google Search Console	https://search.google.com/search-console/	A useful additional tool from Google to improve keyword and search strategies.
	SEMrush	https://www.semrush.com	A keyword research service useful for content creation, SEO, competitor research and hashtag prioritization.
CPQ	dealhub	https://dealhub.io	Configure, price, quote software to simplify and speed up the administration around deal closure.

(continued)

(Continued)

Purpose	Business	Website	Description
	Proposify	https://www.proposify.com	An all-in-one closing tool including tracking and monitoring on your mobile.
	Salesforce	https://www.salesforce.com	The world's number 1 CRM tool, Salesforce also offers CPQ software.
CRM	HubSpot	https://www.hubspot.com	An innovator, HubSpot offers sales, marketing, customer service and content management in an integrated CRM offering.
	Microsoft Dynamics 365	https://dynamics.microsoft.com	Comparable to Salesforce, Microsoft Dynamics is flexible and customizable to your business needs. It is more expensive than some other options but can be an attractive solution to businesses with the Microsoft 365 suite embedded across the organization.
	Pipedrive	https://www.pipedrive.com	A CRM system designed by salespeople and competitively priced. Pipedrive features a visual drag-and-drop interface and integrated automation tools that make it easy to use and highly sales focused.
	Salesforce	https://www.salesforce.com	The world's number 1 CRM tool, Salesforce sets the standard in creating an integrated sales and marketing ecosystem for your business. With multiple app options and integrations with other systems, it can cover every need, but can be expensive and take time to set up to be tailored to your business needs.
Customer success	ChurnZero	https://churnzero.net	Focused on maximizing LTV for SaaS companies, the platform supports client management and development from onboarding onwards.

Purpose	Business	Website	Description
	ClientSuccess	https://www.clientsuccess.com	The platform brings together your whole organization and ensures everyone is committed to and informed on how to maximize client success. Highly customer focused, it is visually appealing and easy to use.
	Planhat	https://www.planhat.com	Innovative and intuitive, this highly customer-focused platform offers multiple ways of considering customer happiness and highly visual actionable insights.
Digital transformation	Emerge Digital	https://emerge.digital	A Microsoft partner and award-winning technology provider, Emerge Digital supports businesses in IT and technology innovation as they move through digital transformation. Clients include Gloucestershire Rugby, Infosec and Cytoplan.
	Ericsson	https://www.ericsson.com	A Swedish multinational networking and communications business and 5G leader, creating groundbreaking technology solutions for businesses and consumers.
Marketing automation and ABM	Demandbase	https://www.demandbase.com	Rated as a leader in ABM technology by Gartner (Pun, 2022), Demand base is designed around accounts with data intelligence and insight, content and social media central to the delivery.
	Hootsuite	https://www.hootsuite.com	An innovative and widely used social media scheduling and automation tool with insights and collaboration opportunities to improve performance built in.
	HubSpot	https://www.hubspot.com	A CRM platform, HubSpot also offers automated marketing and ABM.

(continued)

(Continued)

Purpose	Business	Website	Description
	Salesforce	https://www.salesforce.com	The world's number 1 CRM tool, Salesforce offers automated marketing and ABM with Pardot.
	Sendible	https://www.sendible.com	Allows you to automate social media posting across multiple platforms and streamlines content creation with Canva.
Prospecting and sales intelligence	Cognism	https://info.cognism.com/	Provides access to globally compliant B2B data. Easy to integrate with LinkedIn Sales Navigator and CRM systems such as HubSpot and Salesforce, Cognism provides direct contact details on multiple channels for key decision makers.
	Dun & Bradstreet	https://www.dnb.co.uk/solutions/marketing-sales.html	With a global reputation for data and analytics, Dun & Bradstreet offer a 360-degree view of accounts using first- and third-party data, intent data and other sources. Their consultative data-driven approach guides business strategy.
	LinkedIn Sales Navigator	https://business.linkedin.com/	Designed to supercharge your visibility and utilization of LinkedIn as a sales tool for your business, it can be accessed by individuals or deployed at an organizational level.
	Pitch121	https://pitch121.com https://www.linkedin.com/in/laurahannan-sales/	A fully managed service which manages the LinkedIn profiles of key individuals in a business and uses their personal profiles for brand awareness and social selling.
	Vainu	https://www.vainu.com	Providing GDPR-compliant European business data and insights, Vainu connects with established CRM databases such as Pipedrive, Salesforce, Microsoft Dynamics and HubSpot.

Purpose	Business	Website	Description
	Zoominfo	https://www.zoominfo.com	Provides detailed data and insights using interviews in addition to other sources. It is especially useful for IT B2B sales.
Sales enablement and digital sales rooms	Get Accept	https://www.getaccept.com	Ranked as a leader in the digital sales room platform space by G2 (G2, 2022), Get Accept provides a customer-facing interface for salespeople and prospects to interact, share and sign documents and discuss the progress of a deal.
	groove	https://www.groove.co	The sales enablement platform available as an add-on to Salesforce users.
	Seismic	https://seismic.com	Supports sales teams, marketing teams and sales enablement teams with central content repositories, automation and personalization. Enables sellers to find, use and personalize the most effective marketing materials.
Sales productivity	Calendly	https://calendly.com	A low-cost way to allow your buyers to schedule meetings into your diary automatically and can be used on your website, in email and in social media.
	Chili Piper	https://www.chilipiper.com	More expensive than Calendly but with additional features including screening lead qualification prior to appointment booking.
	Trust Mary	https://trustmary.com	Automates and optimizes testimonial creation and usage, as well as video testimonials, lead-generation forms and chatbots.
	Turtl	https://turtl.co	Enables the creation of personalized on-brand digital proposals, reducing the time salespeople need to spend creating content.

(continued)

(Continued)

Purpose	Business	Website	Description
Thirst quenchers	Bradley's Juice	https://www. bradleysjuice.co.uk	A family-run business producing outstanding English juices and cider at Box Bush Farm in rural Somerset. Keep yourself refreshed and invigorated with hand-picked, small batch pressed apple concoctions.

GLOSSARY

ABC strategy approach – Standing for audience, brand and campaigns, this approach to social media and digital strategy was developed by Julie Atherton and introduced in her book *Social Media Strategy*. It prioritizes audience understanding, the importance and nature of their connection with the brand, and the combined influence of both on the development of a strategic plan. In this book the concept has been developed further to consider the importance of networked audiences, interdependent brands and continuous symbiotic campaigns.

Account-based marketing (ABM) – A strategic marketing approach utilized in B2B marketing which recognizes that multiple stakeholders are involved in B2B purchasing decisions. The approach identifies core decision makers and tailors content to suit the different stakeholder needs.

Account-based selling (ABS) – A multi-channel, multi-touchpoint, company-wide B2B sales approach focused on targeting high-value accounts. ABS focuses on delivering long-term value through acquisition, cross-selling and upselling.

B2B – Abbreviation for business to business which describes when one business sells products and services to another business.

B2C – Abbreviation for business to consumer which describes when a business sells products and services to individual consumers. Many B2B organizations use B2C tactics in B2B sales and marketing activities.

Brand – 'A brand is the sum of all expressions by which an entity (person, organization, company, business unit, city, nation, etc) intends to be recognized' (Interbrand Thinking, 2021).

Brand archetypes – Born from Jung's theories of collective unconsciousness, the 12 brand archetypes define deep unconscious human behaviour. When a brand is associated with an archetype it taps into the emotions that signal its culture and what it stands for. Each archetype's name signals those behaviours and beliefs. The archetypes are outlaw, magician, hero, lover, jester, everyman, caregiver, ruler, creator, innocent, sage, explorer.

Brand co-dependence – An idea developed from relationship theory, it describes an imbalanced consumer–brand relationship with little mutual trust, aversion to change and a desire to control communication and events.

Brand interdependence – An idea developed from relationship theory, it describes a balanced consumer–brand relationship with mutual trust, open communication, ready engagement and response, active listening and the confidence to stand up for core values central to their interaction.

Buyer – Your customer or prospect. Your buyer persona details your ideal and is a cornerstone of your social selling strategy.

CFO – Abbreviation for chief financial officer. Other titles for the individual with responsibility for a business's finances include finance director (FD) and business manager (BM).

Co-dependence (brand) – An idea developed from relationship theory, it describes an imbalanced consumer–brand relationship with little mutual trust, aversion to change and a desire to control communication and events.

Cold calling – Making unsolicited contact to sell goods or services. This could be either in person or by phone.

Content pillars – Thematic groupings that together articulate the differentiating position of your business. They can be created at an organizational/department level or at a personal brand level and provide a compelling reason as to why your buyer should choose you over your competitors.

COO – Abbreviation for chief operating officer. This individual has responsibility for the day-to-day operations of an organization. They are typically second in command.

CPQ – Abbreviation for configure, price, quote. Used to describes sales automation software that speeds up the sales cycle by automating these processes.

CRM – Customer relationship management systems are the backbone of sales and marketing deployment. They are typically the first and most important technology investment a sales and marketing team will make.

CSAT – Customer satisfaction score, a measure used to quantify the experience of being a customer of a particular organization in terms of their level of satisfaction. Several questions are usually asked around the full range of customer experience in order to calculate the overall score.

Customer success tools – Tools designed for beyond the sale to help preserve and extend revenues and deliver customer satisfaction. As social selling considers the post-sale relationship as equally important, these tools could be a useful option.

Demand generation – A term used to describe the B2B activity which creates brand awareness, generates interest and builds trust. This type of activity is often called brand building.

Demographics – Information which refers to a population's characteristics. Examples include age, race, gender, marital status, income, education, ethnicity. Used in marketing and sales to describe different customer segments, or groups, to enable specific targeting or messaging. All social media channels use demographic information, so it is easy to target different customer segments across both social media and other channels. Demographic information is usually used in combination with location, referred to as geodemographics.

Differentiation – A term often used in marketing and sales to describe how one business varies from another. Differentiation can occur by a variety of means, including product features, service performance, location, unique attributes.

Digital sales room – As more of the sales process moves online, the opportunity to engage directly with customers, reduce buyer friction, share content and meet virtually in a customer portal has become more important.

Discord server – Discord is a group-chat platform which allows users to both voice and video chat and livestream games and other programs. It is divided into servers which have their own members, rules, channels and topics.

Elevator pitch – The compelling, succinct description of why your proposition is important and relevant to your target audience or persona.

EMEA – Used to describe the region Europe, Middle East and Africa, which are often grouped together in the organizational structure of global businesses.

Emotional intelligence/emotional quotient (EQ) – A measure of an individual's ability to regulate and manage their emotions in a positive way and to recognize and effectively empathize with the emotions of others.

Engagement – A social media term used to describe the interaction with social posts and content. It can include both passive engagement (likes and shares) and active engagement (comments and conversations).

Engagement pods – Pods can occur on any platform when a group of users band together to help increase engagement on each other's social content.

Facebook – A social networking platform owned by Meta. Facebook Business is increasingly used by both B2B and B2C organizations to share content, build communities, create groups and advertise their products and services.

Firmographics – Information used to describe an organization's characteristics. Examples include company size, location, SIC code, turnover. Firmographics include demographic and geodemographic information.

Forum – A place where people meet to exchange ideas. In social media it can include blogs, messaging boards and communities.

Freemium – The freemium business model starts with a free tier and then upsells existing subscribers to premium (paid) subscriptions for additional functionality and service. Many SaaS businesses operate using this model.

Gatekeeper – Someone or something that controls access. Senior executives may ask a personal assistant (PA) or receptionist to screen their calls and emails and manage their diaries, which can significantly limit access. Because social media is a person-to-person connection, it can often be used to bypass these gatekeepers.

Gender pronouns – Rather than including a binary gender in your persona and when communicating with customers and prospects, capture and use their gender pronoun preferences or a gender-neutral pronoun such as they/them as a default.

Geodemographics – Demographic information described in relation to where someone lives or works.

Glassdoor – A website where current and previous employees can review companies and share insights on what it is like to work there. It provides a way to research company culture, but ensure you use additional sources to provide a more rounded view.

Hashtags – First used in 2007 on Twitter to group collections of tweets together, hashtags are now used by most social media platforms. Preceded by the # symbol they can be brand names, words or phrases and are used by individuals and algorithms to understand areas of interest. Hashtags are also closely linked to keywords.

HR – Human resources. In many organizations this term has been replaced and the chief human resources officer (CHRO) can have titles such as head of talent, talent director or chief people officer (CPO).

Influencers – In this book we consider influencers in their broadest sense as anyone outside of the decision-making group who has an important impact on the outcome of a B2B purchasing decision. They could be a colleague, contact, customer, KOL or industry expert and they may affect different stages of the buyer journey depending on who they are and their connection with the buyer.

Interdependence (brand) – An idea developed from relationship theory, it describes a balanced consumer–brand relationship with mutual trust, open communication, ready engagement and response, active listening and the confidence to stand up for core values central to their interaction.

Key performance indicators (KPIs) – The most important measurements in any campaign or project. These measurements will determine the success or failure of any social selling activity. KPIs can be set at a business, campaign or project level. Examples of social selling KPIs are sales, revenue, leads, net promoter score (NPS), customer satisfaction (CSAT) and lifetime value (LTV).

Keywords – The words and phrases used in search queries. Google looks for content on the web that matches the keywords to decide what to serve in response to the query. Organizations try to identify the top keywords their customers use to find out about their products and services and use these in their online and social media content.

KOL – An acronym for key opinion leader. In B2B KOLs are renowned thought leaders with large followings on social media, opinions on the future of your sector or specialism, and high recognition across the broad business community.

Lead generation – A term used to describe the B2B activity that captures contact information and nurtures qualified leads to a sale. This type of activity is often called sales activation.

LinkedIn – Owned by Microsoft, LinkedIn is the most widely used social selling platform and is the key channel for professional social media relationships.

LTV – An acronym for lifetime value, a term used to describe the value of a customer over their average time spent as a customer. LTV is a useful metric because often new customers may make a loss in the first year of a contract but a considerable profit over the lifetime of the contract or tenure.

Measurement – The quantitative assessment of data, determining whether you have met the objectives set. Measurements are taken at key points in a process when their validity is relevant and important.

Mentions – A measure of how many times you or your brand name have been mentioned on social channels. Including the @ symbol before a brand or person's name will alert them to the mention and is good way to increase visibility and engagement.

Monitoring – Describes the continuous close observation and analysis of information. It can include taking measurements, but it also involves qualitative information gleaned from listening, watching and noting behaviour or cultural changes.

Networked audience – An audience that is defined by its connections within multiple networks and the recognition that the businesses and individuals in these networks play a variety of different roles at different times in the sales cycle.

NPS – An acronym for net promoter score, a calculation used to ascertain customer loyalty and the likelihood of an individual to recommend a product or service.

Persona – A description of a typical buyer, not an actual customer. It represents an amalgamation of the insights and analysis you have conducted, but also should describe a pool of actual businesses and individuals who exist in your prospect pool. A persona should include four sections – the buyer, the business, the decision makers and the decision influencers.

Personal brand – The unique combination of skills and experience that enable you to demonstrate a consistent and differentiated presentation of yourself.

Positioning – A term used by marketing and sales to describe how a business positively promotes itself in comparison to its competitors. A differentiated positioning identifies the important promotional attributes inherent in a business and uses these to build a brand positioning, marketing and sales messaging, and to create content.

Procurement committee/practitioner – Usually employed by large organizations or when making purchases of significant value. Procurement practitioners ensure that the agreed processes and contracts are in place and applied consistently to all potential suppliers.

Proposition – A statement describing your core products and services. Often this will be a value proposition which explains what the value of your products and services is to your customers.

Purchasing committee – A group of relevant staff who have been designated to oversee and decide upon a specific purchasing decision. The committee may be facilitated by a procurement practitioner, but the ultimate decisions are made by the team/departments that require the products or services of the seller.

Quora – A social question and answer website where users share information and help solve problems.

Reddit – Often described as the front page of the internet, Reddit is a social news website and forum. Content is curated by members through voting and subreddits are used to focus on specific topics or interest areas.

RFP (request for proposal) – A document prepared for use with potential suppliers detailing the requirements an organization has for a new product or service.

ROI (return on investment) – A measure of the amount of revenue generated in relation to the amount of money spent to create that revenue.

SaaS (software as a service) – This term describes software that is accessed and managed on the internet. It is the modern way that many businesses manage these services. SaaS examples include Hubspot, Salesforce, DocuSign, MailChimp and Slack.

Sales cycle length – The time taken from first contact/discussion to finalizing the deal. The average sales cycle length for your B2B sales can be calculated by adding up the total number of days taken by each sale and then dividing that number by the number of sales. The cycle length is likely to be longer for larger and more complex sales and shorter for existing customers.

Sales enablement – A strategic, cross-functional approach to improving productivity and sales results. Underpinned by technology, it integrates content creation and management, training and coaching, and insights and analytics of the entire customer journey.

Sector – Businesses are classified into standard sectors such as energy, utilities, healthcare. These can be used to describe your customer and prospect industries.

Sentiment analysis – A measure of brand opinion on social media where a social listening tool analyses the comments about a brand and grades them as positive, negative or neutral.

SEO (search engine optimization) – The process by which visibility of your website is improved in search results. Keywords play a vital part in an SEO strategy and are closely linked to your hashtag strategy. Social media improves online visibility and drives web traffic which improves SEO.

Share of voice – A measure of how visible your brand is in comparison with your competitors.

SIC code – An acronym for standard industrial classification which is used by different countries to classify industrial activity. There are 21 high-level SIC codes in the UK (A–U), each with a number of subdivisions. In the UK you can find a SIC code list at the Office for National Statistics (Office for National Statistics, 2021). Each industrial region has its own list.

Slack – A messaging app for businesses, it provides a secure and structured way for teams to communicate.

SMART objectives – An acronym for the specific, measured, achievable, realistic and timebound goals that enable a business to measure its progress within a defined strategic cycle.

SMB – Abbreviation for small to medium businesses. Less well used than the SME classification, this demotes the smaller business with typically 0–100 employees. Turnover here is much lower than the bigger SMEs (Sangoma, 2021).

SME – Abbreviation for small to medium enterprises. Describes small businesses which make up the majority of all businesses. In the EU, SMEs have between 10 and 250 employees and make up 99 per cent of all businesses (European Commission, 2021).

Social listening – The process of monitoring and interpreting the conversations and behaviour of social media audiences.

Social selling – A highly personalized sales activity. Individual sales and business development professionals build relationships with customers, prospects and influencers in order to generate leads, build trust, nurture engagement and deliver sales.

Social transformation – Usually this term is used to describe the transformation of society due to globalization, technology, and societal and environmental factors. In this context it is used to describe the process whereby an organization starts to put social interactions and social media at the heart of its business strategy.

Sole trader – A term used to describe the way a business is structured. A sole trader is self-employed and is the sole owner of their business.

SOV (share of voice) – Used as a gauge of how visible your brand or business is in a certain market or to a specific audience. In social media, SOV is typically a percentage share of the conversation, measured by the share of brand mentions, in a specific industry or group of competitors.

SSI (social selling index) – A score created by LinkedIn which calculates your effectiveness on the platform. Scores of >70 are highly correlated with high-performing social selling revenues.

Thought leadership – Thought leaders are trusted opinion formers and experts in their field. Both individuals and businesses can demonstrate thought leadership.

Twitter – A micro-blogging social media platform, Twitter is great for in-the-moment conversations and can generate impact and visibility with topical and opinion-led conversations.

WeChat – The most popular social media channel in China and effectively the home screen for smartphones in China. It combines micro-messaging with integrated mini programs, WeChat Moments, WeChat Pay and WeCom.

WeCom – The enterprise, business arm of WeChat offering corporate and customer communications with the same experience as WeChat. The single ecosystem acts as a CRM platform for sales, including connecting and messaging customers and employees, video conferencing and appointment scheduling, posting promotional information and sharing thought leadership via WeChat Moments, in-platform payment via WeChat Pay and live streaming with WeChat Channels.

WeChat mini-programs – Small applications that are fully integrated within WeChat. They are essentially apps but Tencent, the holding company, had a dispute with Apple over the term. A WeChat account can be linked to multiple mini-programs.

WeChat Moments – The advertising part of WeChat with links to event pages, lead-generation forms, blogs and mini-programs. Moments appear in a similar way to Facebook posts in a newsfeed.

WeChat Pay – The encrypted payment system integrated into WeChat, having an 86 per cent penetration rate with China's online payment users (China Internet Watch (CIW), 2022).

INDEX

Bold page numbers indicate figures, *italic* numbers indicate tables.